now

i can

see

the

moon

now i can
see the moon

A Story of a
Social Panic,
False Memories,
and a Life
Cut Short

Alice Tallmadge

SHE WRITES PRESS

Published April 24, 2018
Printed in the United States of America
Print ISBN: 978-1-63152-330-4
E-ISBN: 978-1-63152-331-1
Library of Congress Control Number: 2017954198

For information, address:
She Writes Press
1563 Solano Ave #546
Berkeley, CA 94707

Interior design by Tabitha Lahr

She Writes Press is a division of SparkPoint Studio, LLC.

Names and identifying characteristics have been changed to protect the privacy of certain individuals.

For John, Mary, Wynlee, and Greg.

author's
note

Now I Can See the Moon grew out of the 1980s social panic over child sexual abuse and its impact on my life and the lives of people I love. The material the book covers is sensitive and certain issues remain controversial. For some readers, parts of the book may be difficult. It is not my intention or the focus of this book to judge or challenge anyone's experience of childhood sexual abuse, the effect it had on their lives, or the means they have chosen to heal from it. I wrote *Now I Can See the Moon* to get a fuller understanding of a fraught and disturbing time that had grievous consequences for my family, and for many other families as well. This book is a memoir, not a comprehensive or objective analysis. I chose to read researchers and journalists whose work and approach I felt to be most valuable and helpful—there are others who have written about this issue whose work I chose to bypass. The conclusions I've drawn and the opinions I've developed come from my experience, my reading, and my evolution. They are subjective, and not intended to be anything more than that.

Now I Can See the Moon is about a time in our shared history when rogue practitioners, as well as some who were likely well intentioned but misguided, ended up using approaches that created trauma, rather than healing it. I support all efforts that bring survivors of childhood abuse to a kinder, clearer acceptance of themselves, that make them feel connected to their community and families, that encourage them to live fully and joyfully, and that give them tools to recognize and reject anything that erodes that joy.

contents

author's note vii

prologue xi

chapter 1   pavane 1

chapter 2   ticker 11

chapter 3   secrets and faith 29

chapter 4   walks 48

chapter 5   rock hands 49

chapter 6   christmas in logan 69

chapter 7   wedding day 85

chapter 8   another michelle remembers 99

chapter 9   in the valley 119

chapter 10   memory 133

chapter 11   voices 147

chapter 12   provo 162

chapter 13   obituary 172

chapter 14   keening 173

chapter 15   marionette 184

chapter 16   good death/bad death 193

chapter 17   witness 200

chapter 18   backstory 211

chapter 19   unplugged 230

chapter 20   epilogue 240

chapter notes 243

acknowledgments 255

about the author 257

bibliography 258

prologue

The last time I saw my niece Michelle was at the Utah State Hospital in Provo in 1991, four months before she took her life. She was on suicide watch, but I had permission to meet with her for an hour. Our time was almost up. As our conversation wound down, she looked at me intently. "Aunt Alice, inside you, how do you feel yourself?" she asked, leaning in toward me, her blue eyes direct and pained. "I mean, do you feel like you are just one person? Or are there other voices, other people in there, saying things, speaking to you?"

I paused. I cherished my twenty-three-year-old niece, but she was deeply troubled. For the past two years she had been racked by "memories" of what she said was satanic torture during her childhood and adolescence. She believed her psyche was inhabited by a host of alternate personalities. She believed members of the satanic cult that had abused her in the past were tracking her every move, determined to punish her because she had spoken out against them. She trusted few people, and I was one of them. My answer had to be the right one.

"I feel like just one person," I said. "I mean, sure, there are different parts of me. But deep down, I'm always just me."

She slumped back in her chair. "I want so much to be a whole person again," she said, her voice wavering. "That's what I want, more than anything."

For almost a decade after her death, I had kept the questions surrounding the last years of Michelle's life muffled and stashed in a back corner of my brain. I had occasionally thought about trying to ferret out truth from delusion, fact from suspicion, in order to comprehend what curse of biology or belief had taken hold of my niece's insightful, curious mind and transformed it into a maze of self-torment. But each time I had backed away. And for good reason.

Michelle's last years were mired in a muck I didn't want anything to do with—not as her aunt, and certainly not as the journalist I was trying to become. She first disclosed her "memories" to me in 1989 when she was twenty-one and had already been hospitalized once for an emotional collapse. Her father, my brother John, was skeptical of Michelle's "memories." Her mother, my sister-in-law Mary, believed they were recollections of actual events. So did Michelle's last therapist, local leaders in the Mormon Church, and many of the caregivers at the hospitals where my frightened, confused niece had been admitted. At the time, I had no idea what to believe. I straddled two versions of reality—the rational world I inhabited in my home in Oregon, and, when visiting my brother's home in northern Utah, a world being undermined by an insidious cult creeping undetected through the country's underbelly.

I had tried to piece together events and conversations from Michelle's and my time together, but I hadn't kept notes or a journal, and I mistrusted my ability to remember details. There was so much I didn't know. Probing into Michelle's past would require having difficult discussions with my brother and his wife. My secular views clashed with their Mormon beliefs, and we shared no political common ground. Talking about their daughter would mean going deeper than either of those territories.

But then, one November afternoon, rummaging through a stack of old file folders, I found a trove of letters Michelle had sent to me, a slim pile I hadn't remembered saving. Some of the letters were tucked into their envelopes, some lay open and flat. Heat prickled through me as I recognized my niece's cramped, even script. I counted the envelopes. Four, five, six—all from before she began spiraling downward like a broken kite, unable to defy the insistent gravity that had sucked her into its suffocating embrace and refused to let her go.

I unfolded the pages one by one, smoothing their creases tentatively as if they might turn to confetti at my touch. A few were printed out on an old dot-matrix printer, the letters standing pale and gray in precise formation. On another, the scribbled words clung to the thin lines on the paper as if to keep her widening scrawl in check.

"This letter is going to get to you if I have to hitchhike to Oregon and hand it to you personally. Or tape it to my forehead until I chance on a mailbox. Or chain it to my wrist," she wrote in 1985 when she was seventeen.

And in another note: "When I am trying to work out a facet of my life, I work on that facet studiously, and disremember simple things, like hanging up my clothes, or getting good grades, or helping clean the house. I have told this to Mom, but she has a hard time believing I can walk through a foot-thick layer of clothes all over the bathroom floor without noticing. Amazingly enough, I do in fact have this talent. Therefore, my family finds it hard to believe I am real."

Her letters rang with the lilt of her smart, irreverent voice. Reading them, I saw her blue eyes roll in a show of frayed patience as she confronted yet another of life's unending absurdities. I saw her slouched shoulders and loping stroll. I saw again the shelf of blonde hair that hung over half her face, announcing to the world that we were only seeing part of who she was.

The letters were like a message calling me back, reminding me of what remained unfinished. I could no longer ignore the past, my memories, or the memories that had besieged her. Back then, I had no idea how central the very concept of *memory* would be to the memoir I had yet to write. Certainly I would be humbled by my own memory's gaps and inaccuracies. But I also was to learn how society's misunderstanding of memory contributed to a decade-long social panic over child sexual abuse during the 1980s. This nationwide panic ensnared my niece, her mother, and countless others into believing egregious claims of satanic sexual abuse in childcare centers, in families, and elsewhere across the country. The panic led to criminal charges that, despite a consistent lack of evidence, landed scores of innocent people in prison. The shared belief that recovered memories of sexual abuse were true without regard to how they were uncovered or their historical accuracy would shatter families and destroy lives. I would learn that all memories—not just the memories of those who write theirs down—are subjective and vulnerable to manipulation and reconstruction. And that the consequences of not understanding that were immense.

But all that was yet to come. That afternoon, it was Michelle's voice I heard and responded to. I felt her presence. I remembered the last words she had said to me. When it was time for me to leave the hospital ward, she had thrown her pale, stick-thin arms around me and drawn me close.

"Don't forget me," she had whispered. "Please, please don't forget me."

chapter 1

pavane

At the funeral home in Logan, Utah, Michelle's name was posted in plastic letters on a felt board hanging outside the spacious viewing room. A line of mourners snaked out the door and into the hallway. Earlier that afternoon I had met up with my eldest brother, Carl, and two of my sisters at the Salt Lake City airport. We drove north through the bleak, late-November landscape to the motel where our brother John had reserved rooms for us. John had deep roots in the town's widespread Mormon community—the motel host knew why we had come and was kind and attentive. I'm sure he was expecting a more somber group, but during the hour's drive from Salt Lake the four of us had grown punchy from the weight of the unfamiliar emotion we were carrying.

While checking in at the desk, one of us told a lame joke; the rest of us chuckled in response. The host looked up quickly, his eyes registering a shocked surprise.

We changed our clothes and drove to the funeral home. Once inside, we huddled together under the buzzing fluorescent lights, waiting for John to find us. Soon he came striding through the crowd, his clean-shaven face tight with the effort of composure. He gave each of us a hug and shepherded us to a private corner. There he choked out the story.

Michelle had been doing well at the Utah State Hospital in Provo where she had been a patient for eight months. Her doctors had given her permission to spend the weekend before Thanksgiving with him and Mary in Logan. It was a test, John told us, to see if she could handle being home for the holiday. The visit had gone smoothly. She helped Mary cook dinner and made John an apricot crepe for dessert. Afterward she massaged Mary's feet. She cleaned up the kitchen, then asked to borrow the car to visit a friend. "She really wanted to go," he said. "And she seemed to be doing really well. We said yes."

Tears welled in John's eyes as he paused. I had seen him dispirited and overwhelmed during the last few years, but I had never seen him this naked, or this raw. I caught a glimpse of Mary from across the room. She looked shell-shocked.

Michelle never showed up at her friend's house, John told us. She hadn't intended to. Instead, she drove to a grocery store, bought a large bottle of aspirin, and swallowed as many as she could keep down. She then drove several miles up Logan Canyon, toward Bear Lake on the Idaho border where the family had gone so often in the summertime to swim and camp.

She had planned it all out, he told us. She had tried taking aspirin before, but had taken so many she became sick. This time, she was more measured. She took enough, but not too much. "She knew by the time anyone found her it would be another hour before they could get her to the hospital," he said, his voice a hoarse whisper, his blue eyes bloodshot and hooded.

As he spoke, I thought of her pulling the fluffy cloud of cotton out of the bottle. The moist silence of swallowing. The white of each dusty pill.

2

A passing motorist noticed Michelle wandering along the side of the highway just past the crest of the pass, at an elevation of about six thousand feet. John didn't identify him that night, but years later I tracked him down. Eldon Robinson told me he and his wife, who are Mormon, had worked in the Logan Temple that evening and were returning to their home in Garden City, a few miles over the state line into Idaho. He noticed a car by the side of the road. It was odd, he remembered thinking, because the roads weren't that slick, but the car was stuck fast in a snowdrift. He checked inside and didn't see anyone. A mile later, he saw a figure stumbling along the side of the road. Michelle.

"I stopped and asked her if she needed a ride. She told me she was going to Garden City," he told me. "We got her in the car and drove a few more miles. I could tell she was confused. She couldn't tell me who she was visiting in Garden City. Then she quit breathing."

Robinson, who worked as a biologist with the state of Utah, pulled off the road and checked her pulse, which was weak. He gave her a few mouth-to-mouth breaths. She took in some air. He drove to a nearby friend's house and called 911.

If she had fallen into the drifts at the side of the road, she wouldn't have been found for days, Robinson told me. "She was only in the van five minutes before she stopped breathing. She wouldn't have made it." An ambulance crew from Rich County in Idaho drove Michelle back up the pass. At the state line they transferred her to an ambulance from Cache County. It sped down the mountain, back to Logan.

John and Mary raced to the hospital when they got the call. Doctors told them Michelle was alive, but barely.

John, a Mormon convert, prayed that she would let go, he told us, tears streaming down his face. He was afraid the doctors would bring her back, denying Michelle what she wanted most: release from the isolation, then terror, that had racked her for years.

At the hospital, the doctor suggested John give his daughter a blessing, a Mormon ritual used to ease mental anxiety or physical pain. In the last few years he had held his hands over his daughter's head countless times, praying for God's peace to ease her tormented spirit. But each time her fears had returned, relentless as greedy thieves. John agreed to try again.

"But I knew as soon as I started it was the end," he said, his voice by then a raspy whisper. Not a shred of propriety veiled his grief or his obvious relief as he spoke his next words. He knew what she had been through. He knew every attempt to help her had failed. "When they told me she was gone, I walked outside. I looked up at the sky and I said, 'Atta girl, Michelle. You did it. You finally did it.'"

People often say suicide is an act of anger, but hers wasn't, I thought then, and think now. Hers was utter surrender. She crossed over softly, the way snow falls.

I had received the call four days earlier. It was a typical blustery, rain-swept morning in Oregon's Willamette Valley. The night before I had begun spreading a new coat of paint on my kitchen walls. November is an uneasy month for me. I am wary of the fading light, the naked trees, the ominous pewter clouds that hang in the eastern sky. But that night I had felt unusually light-hearted while rolling fresh color over the dingy walls. Maybe it was because I was taking action to brighten up the space I lived in. Or maybe, I thought much later, I had felt Michelle's letting go. Time-wise, Logan is one hour ahead of Oregon. By the time I had finished painting one wall and pressed the top back on the paint can, Michelle had likely made it to the pass. By the time I rinsed out the roller and placed it into a tub of water to soak, she may have already been sinking into the arms of her last deep sleep. But those thoughts would come much later. That Friday night, I had told myself there was no need to clean everything up. That I had time. That I'd finish the job over the weekend.

I woke up the next morning, slipped into my red terry cloth bathrobe and heel-worn slippers, and scuffed to the kitchen to make tea. Catherine, the nineteen-year-old college student who rented a room in my house, was ensconced in her room with her dog. I could hear music playing from behind her door. While my tea steeped, I turned on the radio, sat in my favorite armchair, and surveyed my late-night paint job, pleased at how a few hours of effort had already made a difference.

When the phone rang, I grabbed my steaming mug and reached for the receiver. "Good morning," I half-sung into the mouthpiece.

"It's Caroline," said my younger sister, calling from her home in Ottawa. Her voice sounded somber and crisp. I started to answer back, but she cut in. "It's about Michelle," she said. "She's . . . There's been . . ." Her voice broke, then faded away. "Caroline?" I called into the phone. "Caroline? Are you there?"

I put down the mug, rose to my feet, and flipped off the radio. I stared out the large front window that looked onto the drizzling gray sky, my legs already beginning to tremble. News about my niece was rarely good. The slice of time was like that after touching a hot stove—you know pain is inevitable, but the synapses haven't yet transmitted the sensation.

The deep, efficient voice of my brother-in-law, Rod, came on the line. A surgeon, he was practiced at delivering difficult news.

"I'm afraid it's bad," he said, with excruciating tact. Bad wasn't the worst, I thought. Bad could be OK. An accident. More broken glass. Another cutting episode. "How bad?" I insisted.

"Very bad," he said.

I refused to make the leap. I made him say the words.

"She's dead."

I must have cried out. Catherine came running out of her room and hovered at my right side, her eyes wide and frightened. I turned my body away from her to face the wall. It was covered with cheap, fake wood paneling into which someone had, years before, willy-nilly pressed a staple gun to fasten it to the sheetrock underneath.

I fixated on the ugly paneling as Rod told me the little he knew. I took in bits and pieces, each a staple that nailed down a segment of the disconnected story: a visit home, a car, a mountain pass, aspirin.

I heard my sister weeping in the background. I stammered out a string of pointless questions: Wasn't Michelle a patient at the state hospital? Hadn't she been on suicide watch? How did she get a car? Rod told me what he could. I realize now that I didn't really want answers—I hoped that if I kept him on the line longer the news would change.

After we hung up, I slumped back into the chair. A draft of cold air slipped in from a crack under the front door and crept up my legs. I would be cold, it would seem, for months. A couple of years would pass before I finished the paint job.

Catherine plied me with questions. She was blonde-haired and blue-eyed like my niece, but young in a way I can't remember Michelle ever being.

"I'm so sorry," she said, stooping to be at my side. "Where was she? Was she depressed? Will you go to the funeral? Are you OK?"

Her questions hit like bullets, the words pushing the reality of Michelle's death in deeper and deeper, past my skin to tissue, bone, marrow, heart. I wanted to be alone, but I didn't know how to send Catherine away. She lived in a sugary, pastel world of big dogs, poster-sized superheroes, and college homework. She was young, open, malleable as fresh clay. She was new to death. She wanted to know why. The truth would have terrified her.

"Michelle had a difficult time the last few years," I said, deliberately sounding vague. "She was really sick. We knew this might happen."

As I spoke, the glut of words I couldn't say rose and locked in my jaw. I crossed my arms in front of my chest and, very slightly, began rocking back and forth. Outside, the leafless trees swayed in the wind. The bough had broken. This time, she had fallen.

The people at the viewing were gracious and caring. After we were introduced, one woman took me aside. She gestured toward the crowd of people waiting in line to say goodbye to my niece. "This is a testament to your brother and his wife," she told me. "They are very highly thought of. People are heartbroken this happened. To her. To them."

I thanked her for her kind words, but they couldn't dispel my grief, or the shadow that shrouded my niece's death. The specter of ritual abuse was like a mute, unwanted guest lurking in a corner of the viewing room whom no one wanted to acknowledge. Michelle had been emotionally unstable since her early teens. She suffered from severe bulimia, anxiety, and depression. When the flashbacks of abuse surfaced, nothing could quell them. One of her last diagnoses was multiple personality disorder, a condition that was believed to be linked to severe childhood sexual trauma. I noted a few visitors at the viewing had signed the guest book by adding "& Co." after their names, code for indicating that the signee, too, believed she or he had multiple personalities.

When my turn came to say goodbye to my niece, I looked down at the body lying in the casket. She was dressed in a simple navy blue dress. Her lush hair was combed away from her face. Her hands held a Book of Mormon over her heart. Mary would later tell me that the mortician had done a terrible job preparing the body, that he had used thick thread to sew her up after the autopsy, that Michelle barely looked like herself. I thought the same thing but for different reasons. The prim young woman in the casket looked nothing like the Michelle who lived in my heart—the profound, funny, insightful writer who could dance up a rock face and make a clarinet sing. She looked nothing like the young woman who had jogged with me in the rolling hills near her house, who had walked with me for hours at night under Logan's star-studded sky, discussing the mysteries and ironies of life. Nothing like her.

During the next day's funeral I sat next to Caroline. Our backs straightened when we saw our nephew, who was in the Air Force, stride down the aisle in full dress uniform after driving all night from his home in California to be one of the pallbearers. We nodded our heads as Michelle's friend Tammy reminded the mourners of her friend's brilliance, compassion, and courage. Midway through the ceremony, when two young people began playing a duet, Caroline nudged me. "That's really called the 'Pavane to a Dead Princess,'" she whispered, "but in the program they only call it 'Pavane.'" We grimaced as one speaker exhorted us to take up the cross against Satan. We didn't look at each other when John delivered his anguished eulogy.

Even though I was forty-one, I was new to grief. Or at least new to grief that carved so close to the bone. I wasn't familiar with its confounding paradoxes. I didn't know that, even in the midst of profound loss, the physical body hangs on to its appetite for food, sex, and sleep, even as the outer world feels tilted and surreal. When I sat down to eat in the church hall following the funeral, I was embarrassed by my voracious hunger. I shoveled down forkfuls of food I normally never ate—fruited Jell-O with marshmallows, cold pasta salads, a white flour roll. After we left the church, my sisters and I wandered into a thrift store downtown, an activity we usually enjoyed. I shuffled through the racks of hangers as if it were any Wednesday afternoon, as if everything around me didn't look like it was wrapped in gauze.

The next day at the airline desk in Salt Lake, the Delta agent demanded proof of Michelle's death in order to approve my bereavement fare. I pulled a folded copy of her obituary from my purse. It had appeared in the Logan paper and copies were available at the funeral. But opening it there, under the pitiless lights of the bustling airport, was like exposing the gaping, unfathomable questions that hung over her life, and her death, to the larger world. My shaking fingers fumbled as I tried to unfold the flimsy strip of newsprint.

From the time Michelle had first told me about her memories of being abused, I had fought against believing in the preposterous, gruesome scenarios she relayed with such assuredness. I maintained—but didn't express—my skepticism as Mary described the nationwide underground cult she believed was operating undetected at all levels of society. I held on to my doubt as newspapers published stories on the rise in occult crimes, and quoted young women who claimed to be victims of abuse that was eerily similar to that described by Michelle. I didn't admit it, but my doubt grew less assured as therapists in my community began including "SRA (satanic ritual abuse) survivors" in their lists of treatment specialties. Now Michelle was gone, her life summed up in a wrinkled, five-paragraph obituary. Whatever their veracity, her memories—or her delusions—had proved too strong for her to fight against. Somewhere deep inside me, a chorus of questions I wasn't ready to acknowledge simmered. What had really happened to my niece? Had my reluctance to join with Mary and others in believing in her memories blinded me to something I should have seen coming? Or had I, in some way I hadn't been able to see, become caught up in the same sticky web of paranoia that had ensnared Michelle, Mary, and so many others? I wasn't aware of those questions that morning. I was years away from even being able to formulate them.

I tried to smooth the edges of the obituary. The agent drummed her painted fingernails on the counter. My sister Anne reached over, grabbed the paper from my hands, and thrust it at the agent. "Is this good enough for you?" she said, her voice sharp and commanding. I often bristled at my eldest sister's authoritative tone, but at that moment I was grateful for it. The agent took the obit from her, glanced at it, and nodded. At the gate Anne and I hugged tightly, wordlessly, before I boarded the plane back to Oregon.

chapter 2
ticker

Her nickname as a child was Ticker. When I asked John and Mary where the name had come from, they said they couldn't remember. But her sister, Wynlee, just fifteen months older than Michelle, told me it was because of the noise Michelle made as an infant when she sucked on her bottle. I preferred her given name. I liked the way it started with a hum and remained quiet through the *sh* and *elle*. But throughout her childhood, the name Ticker stuck. It brings to mind a wind-up clock's steady, rhythmic beat. Later I would realize it's also the sound of a time bomb: something about to go off.

Certainly that was the tenor of the time she was born into. Her arrival on July 7, 1968, followed two assassinations—Robert F. Kennedy two weeks earlier, and the Rev. Martin Luther King Jr. two months before that. The gentle "free love" mantra of the early 1960s had turned sour. The incomprehensible Vietnam War had confused and polarized the country. A sizeable chunk of the baby-boomer generation had come to view authority with suspicion and hostility. Angry young men spat on the flag, yelled obscenities at politicians, and burned their draft cards. Destabilized by riots and looting and years of neglect, ghetto neighborhoods across the country teetered toward anarchy.

But the country's clashing political views were the least of my brother John and his wife's worries that summer. A few weeks after Michelle, not yet Ticker, was born, Mary was blind-sided by a crippling postpartum depression. "An absolute black hole," she called it, one that robbed her of her ability to cope and sent her to the hospital for several days. When she returned home, she couldn't meet the challenge of caring for Michelle and her toddler sister. The family lived in Minneapolis, hundreds of miles from Mary's Utah roots. John's job as a salesman for Dow Chemical Company frequently took him away from home. My sister Caroline flew west from upstate New York to help out.

"I remember when Wynlee was a baby, how delighted they were," Caroline remarked to me, years later. "But there just wasn't the same sense of delight around Michelle when she was born."

From the beginning, it seemed, she was born under a difficult star.

A year earlier, in the summer of 1967, my father had hitched a tent-trailer to our car. With my mom, three sisters, and me in tow, he drove from our home in upstate New York to the state of Washington to meet up with John, Mary, and our newest niece, Wynlee, then four months old. I was a restless and peevish sixteen-year-old, and the trip tried my patience. I spent hours in the back seat counting telephone poles and thinking about my boyfriend back home. At night when we stopped at a campground and set up our camper trailer, I shut myself into a pay phone booth and shoved quarters into the coin slot to try and reach him at his favorite bar.

When we finally hit mountain country, I woke up from my backseat torpor. Those mountains. The emptiness. The sharp, high-elevation air stung my throat and jolted my lungs, awakening me to a heightened experience of breath. I forgave everyone everything.

We met up with John and Mary at a campground on the Strait of Juan de Fuca, a watery boundary between the United States and Canada at the northwest tip of Washington. Wynlee had a partially collapsed trachea that made her breath rumble and wheeze, but doctors had assured John and Mary it would heal on its own. I watched, fascinated, as my new niece lay on the bed in our camper, her wide eyes gaping at the leaf shadows on the canvas roof. As she watched their quiet dance, her tiny hands waved in the air and choked-up awe gurgled in her palm-sized chest.

But there was no cross-country family jaunt to meet Michelle after she was born. In fact, I didn't set eyes on her until she was far older. Was the first time when she was five? When she was seven? In my life, those years were tempestuous, confusing and blurred even while I was living them.

Two weeks before Michelle was born I had graduated from my all-girls' Catholic high school, wearing a hand-sewn black-and-white dress with a flashy red lining underneath my black robe. During the ceremony I focused much more on the night's coming parties than on my future. The political storm churning through the country hadn't yet broken through the insulated, apolitical cocoon I lived in. That summer my focus was on preparing my college wardrobe—making sure the plaids of my jumpers met at the seams, that my hemming stitch left a smooth, unpuckered line, that I chose a wool check for a skirt that matched the plum hue of my new cable-knit sweater.

I was also fighting back intuitions about the future of my relationship with my boyfriend—a funny, charming college sophomore whom I was very attached to, but who had a dependency on alcohol no one spoke of. I didn't know what words to use, but I knew something was amiss with my first love. Our dates increasingly involved him downing large quantities of alcohol, staggering out of the car, and heaving onto roadside bushes while I looked the other way. I was becoming uncomfortably aware of how he never said no when his friends urged him to slug back "one more" for the road. I had begun noticing how rooted he was to our hometown, how his future plans were as safe and prescribed as the golf courses he loved to play on. Even though the private college I was headed for—Hobart and William Smith Colleges in upstate New York—was just an hour's drive away, I had a premonition that, once I moved there, my life would change drastically.

"But why do you think that?" he pressed during one of our late-night talks. We were lying on the living room couch in my parents' house, our legs wound together in a comforting, yet chaste, braid of familiarity. His large green eyes—sober at the moment—were pained. "How can you know things will be different?"

"I don't know," I said. I didn't know how to tell him that, when I envisioned the future, it looked like a stormy sky on the brink of breaking open. "I just do."

By the time Michelle was a year old, he and I had split up. I had traded my matched plaids for paisley, my tailored jumpers for bell-bottomed blue jeans, and my Catholicism for a leftist philosophy I didn't quite understand. By the time Michelle was two, I had marched against the Vietnam War in Washington, DC, and sucked down the requisite amount of marijuana smoke. I had also adopted my rebellious peers' self-righteous arrogance. At one of my parents' parties, I informed a couple whose son was killed in the Vietnam War that he had wasted his life—a cruel proclamation I still wince to remember. By the time Michelle was three, she had a new brother, Greg. I was struggling to reconcile my student and protester selves and was scrambling through the underbrush of romantic relationships. In June of 1972, a month before her fourth birthday, I dropped my first dose of LSD, earned a Phi Beta Kappa key, and graduated with a bachelor's degree in English literature and no idea what to do with the rest of my life.

I moved to Boston with a friend to try my hand at adulthood and living in a big city. Both demanded every shred of attention I could give them. My friend and I rented a fourth-floor walk-up apartment on the shabby side of the Beacon Hill neighborhood. I was still passionate about my anti-capitalist, pro-worker politics. During the day I scuttled around at a grungy cafeteria job—Vera, the fat, steely-haired manager, barked orders; Stan, her gaunt, wheezing husband, smoked and swore under his breath—and read philosophical treatises at night. I got acquainted with the nighttime scrabbling of cockroaches and dodged piles of dog poop on my way to and from work.

I tracked my brother's growing family sporadically my first few years in Boston, gleaning information about them from the family grapevine or through photographs my parents snapped when they drove out to Logan. My brother's family wasn't on my radar. I'm sure I wasn't on theirs.

Since Michelle's death, I've asked her siblings and her parents about her childhood, but their recall of the "good times" was scant. I look through family photos to help fill in what they couldn't remember and I hadn't been around to witness. I know the lens through which I peer at the photos is filtered by all that transpired after the camera solidified the images. Viewing the photos, I am alert for any clues hinting at Michelle's later vulnerability and psychological collapse—an unmasked sadness, a vacancy in her facial expression, a reluctance to face the camera. But I don't see any of that. The photos are precious but unremarkable. In frame after frame I see a little girl with bright, shining eyes, pudgy arms, and a delighted smile. In one she and her sister are sitting under a Christmas tree, dressed in look-alike red-and-green outfits; a white beret is perched on Michelle's head, accentuating her glowing face. In another she is nestled next to John on the couch, her hair pulled back into pigtails, giggling into the camera. All the summertime photos are outside shots. She is bent over some black rocks looking for bugs or snakes; sitting in the back of John's rusty blue Chevy pickup; wading in a mountain lake; leaning over a tin tub helping scrub a soapy dog. A wintertime shot shows her stuffed into a blue parka, standing next to a snowman that towers over her. She faces the camera square on, grinning. Her smile is open, sweet, unafraid.

As Michelle grows older, she becomes lean and leggy. She wears her light brown hair in a short bob with a line of bangs covering her forehead. Her mouth and teeth are too large for her narrow face. She is playful. She crouches in the fork of a gnarled tree, vamps for the camera at a highway rest stop, strikes a fashion model pose on the edge of the family's vegetable garden. She wears lots of stripes, lots of red. But it is a cheerful red, not a flag of warning. I see no foreshadowing of the chaos to come.

My first recollection of Michelle should be from the summer of 1975, when she was seven and I was twenty-four. A pitiless, moist heat had settled on Boston like a suffocating fog. I was newly unemployed and entangled with a wild nighthawk of a man who drove a taxi, painted murals on his bathroom walls, and drank a six-pack of beer just to warm up for the coming evening. My evolving feminist/socialist/anti-establishment philosophy provided plenty of ammunition for bashing the status

16

quo, but it was far less helpful when it came to providing guidance in navigating the world of jobs, bills, and an incomprehensible attraction to someone with values so utterly different from mine. Later I would identify this as my "bad-boy phase," but I didn't have a name for it then. I read philosophy; he read comic books. My life was defined by other people's rules; he was a law unto himself. He had begun working with a friend of mine who loved her wine as much as he loved his beer. I quickly became a third wheel, sober and ignored, in their boozy shenanigans. I couldn't escape them, or the heat.

Jealous and desperate, I called Caroline. She reminded me that John and Mary had moved back to Mary's hometown of Logan, and were living in the house she had grown up in. They had an open-door policy for folks who were down on their luck or just passing through, Caroline said, and for family members. I paid attention. Even though I hadn't seen my brother for years, and there was a two-thousand-mile gap between us, a trek to Utah sounded like a plausible solution to a swarm of troubles I didn't know how to sort out.

I answered an ad looking for someone to share expenses for a trip West. During my previous cross-country trips, my father did all the driving, and we traveled only in daylight, stopping at as many tourist attractions as he would tolerate. But the trip out of Boston was all business. My partner and I drove straight through, not stopping to sleep, barely to eat. At night, when it was my turn to drive, he dozed. As we drove further into the country's heartland, the massive blackness that soaked up the land and sky intimidated me. I hallucinated towering bridges spanning the highway and hulking creatures staring out from a landscape that had no shape I could discern.

Several bleary days and nights later, we arrived at my brother's house on Center Street in Logan. I unloaded my backpack, waved goodbye to my driving partner, and turned to greet a world where everything appeared scrubbed in light. To the west were the immaculate, manicured grounds of a yellow-brick Mormon church. To the east lay the mounded foothills of the Wasatch Range. My brother's cottage of a house looked as if it were lifted from a storybook—the home of the crone witch or the hermit woodcutter, but with children added in. The backyard was strewn with a domestic jumble of bikes, balls, sticks, tools, and toys. A yellow Lab pulled at his tether underneath a sprawling tree.

I squinted in the bright sunlight. Before I left Boston I had stopped by my boyfriend's house to say goodbye. I had met him in a martial arts class. He was biracial, agile as a cat, and when he worked out, sweat beaded on his swarthy forehead. The morning I left he had stumbled out of his house in the Mission Hill neighborhood, hungover but eager to show me a *Playboy* spread featuring the round, bare haunches of a woman bent over in a teasing come-on. I recalled how his teeth glowed in his dusky face like pearls, how the sun glinted off the glossy pages like a lewd wink, how his fingers had caressed the woman's unavailable body. I had felt like a fat, pimply teenager who showed up at the wrong house, who was living the wrong life. By escaping to Utah, I wasn't just fleeing Boston's heat, but the whole mess of my life there. My leftist philosophy encouraged aligning with the working class, but the low-paying jobs I took were boring and repetitive, and I never came across the blue-collar heroes celebrated in political theory and classic folk ballads. I chose to live on the gritty edge of life. I thought it would be cool to hang with the rebels and social misfits that hung out on the seedy side of the hill, an area where the charred hulks of cars that had been torched in efforts to scam money from insurance companies remained for months like burnt-out hopes. But instead of gaining street smarts, I had lost the contours of my original self. I didn't know how to get her back.

18

I shook my head to disperse the image and followed the walkway to the back porch, where hammers, saws, and bags of fertilizer kept company with flowerpots, bags of dog food, hard-used sneakers, and a leaning stack of bushel baskets.

"A bed and three squares," John proclaimed a few minutes later when I was seated in his kitchen, wolfing down the simple, delicious lunch Mary had set in front of me. His eyes were the same brilliant blue I remembered. He exuded the same self-confidence that made me think he could do anything. Eleven years my senior, he had always struck me as half-human, half-myth. When he lived at home, my parents would alternately shake their heads or chuckle at his exploits: Boy Scout camping trips gone amok, wayward canoes, weekend revels, once a "borrowed" car and a late-night call from the local police. He had fished for salmon in Alaska, rounded up cattle in the Rockies, fought wildfires in Arizona, choked down dust on a cattle drive in Wyoming. Seeing him in his home, wearing his trademark faded Levi's, his torso taut, his forearms thick from his job milking cows at a nearby dairy farm, made me feel safe.

He eyed the scarf tied around my forehead, my paisley shirt, and ragged, cutoff jeans. "So what do you do there back in Boston?" he asked as I savored the freshest food I had eaten in days. I mumbled something evasive about being between jobs. I left out everything else—the alcoholic boyfriend, my lack of career direction, my castigating self-doubt. I figured the omissions were safe. I knew he wasn't a guy who probed for hidden secrets. He liked his world clear and out in the open, where he could see, touch, change, or charm it.

"We're not fancy, but you're welcome to stay," he said again. "See ya at supper," he called as he banged out the back porch door on his way to the afternoon milking.

Michelle had just turned seven the summer of my first Utah visit. Wynlee was eight, and their plump, amiable brother Greg was three. To me, they comprised a blur of blond hair, blue eyes, pumping limbs, and chirpy voices. I had a hard time following their staccato conversation, which ranged from giggles to arguments to tears in a matter of seconds. In the mornings, after a late rising, I would make a breakfast of toast and tea and bury myself in the town's thin newspaper. John and Mary would have been up for hours—John for the morning milking, Mary to tend to laundry, shopping, the garden, canning, dishes, phone calls, or church responsibilities. By midmorning, a bunch of neighborhood kids swelled my brother's brood to what sounded to me like a mini-army. The multi-limbed gang whirled through the backyard in a kaleidoscope of color and motion. They rode their bikes up and down the gravel driveway, chucked green apples at each other, and bickered over the rules of their intricate games. They gobbled mountains of tuna fish sandwiches at lunchtime and gulped down endless glasses of Kool-Aid throughout the afternoon. At night after dinner my nieces and nephew collapsed on their upstairs bedroom floor like played-out puppies. In the morning, they woke bright-eyed, cheerful, and ready to do it all over again.

I was awkward around little kids. I didn't know how to think up fun projects, settle spats, or fix broken bicycles. In my teens I babysat for the money, not because I was good at it. I rarely warmed to my charges, and they didn't particularly like me. That first trip to Logan I considered my adult-sized problems of far more import than my nieces' and nephew's waist-high lives. But even in my distracted, child-numb state, I couldn't help but notice how each day was shiny new for them, not stalled as I felt about my own life. One morning, while walking through the garden, I spotted a stunned sparrow lying in the dirt. I called out for Wynlee, who even then was devoted

20

to anything with feathers, to come and check it out. I watched in quiet amazement as she picked up the tiny, quivering creature and stroked its brown feathers with small, assured fingers. "Don't worry. It just got knocked out. It'll be fine," she told me as she gently placed it deep in the branches of a nearby bush.

I may not have been comfortable interacting with them, but my brother's brood knew what to do with me. In the late afternoons when the backyard gang thinned out, they took me with them to play fetch with the dog in the nearby Logan River, or on forays to the corner market where the penny candy was, indeed, a penny. I was an extra hand or a long reach when they needed one. At night I was a willing audience. I hooted as Greg stomped around in his dad's shoes, and at Michelle when she donned one of her funny hats and struck exaggerated poses, her head thrown back, splayed hands on her bony hips.

During that first trip, I needed to believe my brother's world was as idyllic as it appeared. But just because I didn't pick up on any tension in the family's dynamics didn't mean it wasn't there. Even by then, I would learn much later, Michelle had surfaced as the family's sour note, the piece that didn't quite fit, the family's temperamental wild card.

Later Mary would explain that she knew what to expect from Wynlee and Greg—what would make them angry or tearful, how they would respond to different situations, what their final straw was likely to be. "But Michelle was always askew, always way outside the realm of predictability," she told me. "You never knew which fastball would come. You didn't know if you were going to get beaned in the head."

Mary partially blamed herself for Michelle's volatility. She described herself as "a yeller" when it came to raising her kids. Michelle, she feared, got the brunt of it. "I don't think she had the wherewithal to cope with it," she said. "The other kids had their skins, but she didn't have hers."

John was more succinct. "She always kept us off balance. She was hard for everybody," he told me. "And we never really got along."

Over the years, stories of Michelle's hair-trigger temper became part of family lore. If there was friction among the kids who congregated in the family's backyard to play, more often than not it involved Michelle. Once she deliberately ran over a neighbor boy's foot with her bicycle, causing him considerable pain. When Mary told me the story, I could imagine the scene. Michelle is astride her bike, facing the taunting boy. Her bony elbows protrude from her short-sleeved shirt. Her fingers grip the handlebars, her eyes blazing. He is standing close by, hands on his hips, maybe a smirk on his face. He baits her. Maybe he even likes her. She doesn't know how to trump him. Wynlee is cool and reserved, and knows how to not take the bait. Not Michelle. She yells back, chews on her lip, shoves her bike forward.

Her volatility didn't abate as she grew older. In third grade she fought with her teacher over a book report. The teacher claimed Michelle had made a mistake; Michelle knew she hadn't. She was whip-smart, but she hadn't learned to back down, particularly when she thought she was right. She argued back. The teacher's hand swiped across her face. "She could get real mouthy. She had difficulties in school," Mary told me. But that time the teacher had gone too far, even given Michelle's stubbornness. "That time I went to the principal."

Greg remembers Michelle as being short-fused from the get-go. When they were kids, "she was the one you had to watch out for," he told me. "Wynlee might get mad, but she'd walk away. Michelle would come after you. She would provoke some sort of crisis. And if you got into a fight, you knew there was going to be fingernails involved."

Of the photos of her childhood I studied, one stands out. The family is sitting around the kitchen table, John at the head. Michelle is looking at him from a few seats away. She looks wary, watchful. Her fingers are bunched in front of her mouth—maybe covering her slightly buck teeth. Someone else might see her as simply listening, but I know the look: Defiant. Stubborn. Not going along.

"Even when we were kids there was something different about her," Wynlee told me. "She was never at ease. She just didn't fit in. She didn't identify with anyone."

In the ensuing years I left Boston and started another life in Oregon's Willamette Valley. Now that I lived in the Pacific Northwest, in my mind the Logan family and I had become practically neighbors. Instead of taking four days, I could cover the distance between us in eighteen hours, not including a night's sleepover in a campground. Logan became my summer lodestone, my place of refuge and unconditional belonging. Little by little, thanks to shared genetics and a penchant for feeling we were swimming upstream in our respective worlds, Michelle and I began to discover each other.

During my visits, usually not longer than a week, I spent most of my time with Mary. John would be off working his various jobs, Wynlee was absorbed in her world of birds and projects, and Greg spent his days playing with the neighborhood kids. I hung out with Mary in the kitchen, trying to stem some of its persistent chaos while she told stories, often about individuals who had endured harrowing circumstances and emerged stronger and wiser because of them. Michelle, who had difficulty making friends, often joined us. I listened while she and Mary chatted about the foibles of various neighbors, friends, and relatives. Precocious and observant, Michelle wasn't shy about sharing her observations. "Oh, he is so obtuse," she would say about someone, her slight lisp tripping over each *s*.

All three of us were readers, and our midday chats invariably turned to books. We read for many reasons, but mostly because each of us loved to catapult ourselves away from the present into other realms. Mary favored books whose characters got themselves into ridiculous or awkward social entanglements. She had great recall, and when she recounted memorable anecdotes, she laughed so hard tears rolled down the sides of her face. Michelle would chime in with her own favorites. She liked mysteries and anything by James Herriot, the rural British veterinarian-turned-writer. I never wrote down most of the titles that so captivated her. I didn't think there'd be a time when I'd wish I had.

Every room of the Logan household was awash with books. They were piled in sloping stacks in the living room, on the kitchen bookshelf, and on the dining room table. I found them mixed in with junk mail, lying underneath mounds of air-dried sheets, or facedown on the back of the toilet. They made it out onto the porch and into the family car. Some, particularly library books, seemed to migrate of their own accord, disappearing for weeks at a time. "Oh we've gone and lost another one," Mary would lament after receiving yet another late notice.

I read mostly at night, but Mary and Michelle went by other rules. While cooking, Mary often held a book in one hand while stirring a pot with the other. In the middle of vacuuming or straightening up the living room, it wasn't unusual for her to stop, pick up a book, sit down on the couch, and disappear into the pages. Michelle, too, could read anywhere. I often found her draped over the couch or sitting amidst a heap of dry, wrinkled laundry, her head bent to the fold of a book. Or she might perch in a tree in the backyard orchard, her hands cradling a book and her teeth picking at the yellow skin of an early apple. One afternoon I saw her stalking around the yard, a book in one hand, her eyes scrutinizing the ground before her. "What are you doing?" I asked. She was ten years old that year, all eyes and angles. She looked up at me as if I were impenetrably thick. "Sleuthing," she said, the word slightly mauled by her lisp. "Nancy Drew." She waved the book at me and, without further explanation, continued on her mission.

When she was in the fifth grade, Michelle hit a rough patch. Pre-adolescence is a tricky time for most kids, but hers seemed particularly trying. For a reason no one could explain, her hair turned ragged and brittle and wouldn't grow beyond her chin. Big teeth crowded her tiny mouth. She hunched her shoulders and seemed barely able to corral the arms and legs that sprouted from her torso like pale, gangly roots. The art of friendship continued to elude her. During my visit that summer, Mary told me that, earlier that year, a teacher at Michelle's school had mistaken her for a boy, and ordered her to use the wrong bathroom. Michelle was mortified, and the incident dogged her for weeks. "I call that kind of thing a social accident," Mary told me, later. "But there were a lot of social accidents in her life that didn't happen with the other kids. It was as if people could spot her vulnerability."

I couldn't. Or, if I did, I didn't call it that. Michelle's position as a social outsider increased her sensitivity to other outliers, and that would have been me in those early visits to Logan, dog (first one, then two) in tow, my backpack bulging with yet more unsolved dilemmas. Living in my adopted state felt right, but the move wasn't a panacea. When I arrived in Logan for my summer visits, I was usually between jobs, short of cash, or smarting from yet another torpedoed relationship. But I must have made a very different impression on my sharp-eyed niece, who rarely encountered a rebel she didn't admire. I embodied a feminist philosophy completely at odds with the Mormon teachings she was brought up to believe were sacrosanct. Instead of tending to a family, I worked in a Volkswagen repair collective. Instead of a husband, I had my dogs, a twenty-five-year-old VW Bug, and my freedom. Michelle invariably built me up, burnishing everything I did to a flattering sheen. "You make the best dinners," she'd say after I had stir-fried a bunch of vegetables and squirted them with soy sauce. Or, not realizing that I had no natural mechanical skills, would declare, "It's so cool that you know how to fix your car." Thin-skinned, wound tight, volatile as a summer storm? Not the Michelle I knew. I thought her quirky, thoughtful, and deliciously ironic.

On the surface our time together was unremarkable. We walked to the corner store, visited the library, hung out in the shade of the backyard trees. Sometimes Michelle and I cooked dinner, chopping up vegetables and experimenting with herbs and spices. At night we tucked ourselves into the couch or nestled in upholstered rockers and watched family-friendly videos—episodes of *Anne of Green Gables* or John's favorite westerns. Sometimes we'd pass each other in the house without a word; sometimes we'd fall to talking or giggling. Thread by thread, we wove a bond.

Michelle turned twelve the summer of 1980. A botched permanent had turned her hair into a tangle of dry, unwieldy frizz, and she refused to leave the house without wearing a straw hat to cover it up. I took a picture of her during that year's visit. In the photo, she is staring out from underneath the brim of her hat, smiling slightly, her face dappled by shadows and sunlight. She is cradling a gray kitten. She holds her lips closed over her teeth, which are fitted with braces. She looks shy and guarded. She looks as if she is holding something back. Later I learned she had already weathered her first bout with anorexia and had begun the cycle of bingeing and purging that became her refuge and jailer for the next decade. "You know the people of Ammon? How they had committed such wickedness they were afraid if they even killed to defend themselves they would not be forgiven? That is how I feel," she would write in her journal. "I wonder which binge will be the one that goes beyond repenting."

Besides her struggles with food, her social isolation, and her frequent fits of temper, Michelle developed an odd gait, holding her left arm across her waist and her right arm swinging straight from her side. "I remember watching her walk and feeling such a pain in my heart because I knew something was not right," Mary wrote me once. "We knew she was askew. Everybody knew she was askew—her peer group, us. Everybody knew that she wasn't on center."

Everyone, but not me. I remained oblivious to the extent of her inner angst. Yes, she talked to me about her trouble making friends, about feeling overlooked and misunderstood by her parents and siblings. But she was a smart, sensitive preadolescent struggling to find herself, as all girls do at that age, I thought. I didn't suspect anything more serious was weighing on her. I had no clue she had begun trying to control her life through food. To me, I was the one coping with big issues—spiritually adrift, in constant indecision about my life path, and frustrated about the string of relationships that entered and exited my life like characters from a collection of short stories. Perhaps my vision was so myopic at the time I couldn't see what was in front of me. Maybe I refused to see that the niece I so enjoyed was struggling with issues as monumental to her as mine were to me. Or, as I've since learned, often you have to know what you are looking for in order to recognize it, even when it is staring you in the face.

That same year, in a universe as far from Logan as I could have imagined at the time, two unrelated events set off a chain reaction that would alter the lives of countless individuals throughout the next decade, including Michelle's. In January, an emotionally unbalanced woman from Bakersfield, California, MaryAnn Barbour, became obsessed over what she believed was the sexual abuse of her two step-granddaughters by their step-grandfather (not Barbour's then-husband). As Barbour's paranoia increased, the severity of her abuse accusations intensified—the girls, she would later insist, had been tied up, chained, beaten, taken to motels, and sold for sex—and the number of perpetrators she accused increased. Despite her history of mental imbalance, Barbour's claims found traction among child protectionists who had found fertile ground in southern California. Barbour and her supporters helped pave the way for the McMartin Preschool case—a multi-year sex abuse drama involving hundreds of supposed child victims, dozens of alleged perpetrators, and sexual abuse charges that ranged from torture to satanic ritual abuse. (1)

Several hundred miles to the north, a British Columbia psychiatrist, Lawrence Pazder, and his client, Michelle Smith, published the book *Michelle Remembers*, a chronicle of Smith's supposed memories of horrific childhood abuse she claimed to have suffered at the hands of a satanic cult. (2) At another time, these two events would likely have caused a minor ripple in the culture before vanishing into legal and publishing archives. But, for reasons that social science researchers would later debate and analyze, they helped ignite a modern-day social panic over child sex abuse, including satanic ritual abuse, that spread to communities across the country throughout the 1980s. It would take until the middle of the decade for the panic to gain full momentum, and few more years for the flame to reach my already struggling niece. When it did, it hit like a lightning strike in dry timber—fast, hot, and unstoppable.

28

chapter 3
secrets and faith

On a hot August afternoon in 1981, I pulled into my brother's gravel driveway, drove to an open spot near the garage, shut off my rattling VW engine, and let out a long sigh. No one was waiting to greet me, but I wasn't surprised. I had been vague about my arrival time and the reasons for my sudden visit. A few days earlier I had called Mary from a phone booth in a small vacation town in the mountains of northern California. "I was thinking of dropping by for a visit," I had said, trying to make my voice sound casual. "Is that OK?" I knew she wouldn't think of saying no.

I pushed open my car door, unfolded myself from the driver's seat, and let out the dogs. I arched my back and pressed my right fist into my lower right back. A deep ache often developed there during road trips, probably from my foot pressing on the accelerator hour after hour and throwing my hip out of whack. But that summer, the throbbing pain felt like a fault in my interior structure, a misalignment of bone and muscle that signaled a hidden truth about the person I thought I was.

I gazed at the familiar domestic disorder. John had established his own tree service business by then, and his stained and reeking spray truck sat in the far corner of the lot. The family's off-white and turquoise 1970s-era camper rested next to it on blocks, tilting to one side. A banged-up pickup truck was parked next to a long, haphazard woodpile. During the sweltering two-day trip to Logan from northern California, I had conjured several explanations for why my plan of spending the summer with two friends in the foothills of the Trinity Alps had fallen through. "Something came up they needed to take care of," was one. "I couldn't get enough work," was another. Or, "I only intended to stay for a little while." The truth was, my friends and I had had a major falling out. An objective outsider might have seen fault shared amongst the three of us, but I shouldered all of the blame and felt the loss keenly. Not only had my summer plans fallen through, I believed I had lost two friends I cared for deeply. I was bereft at yet another relationship failure.

I followed the dogs to the back porch, sidestepping a couple of bicycles that lay in my path. The porch was its usual jumble of hammers, ropes, saws, bags of fertilizer, flowerpots, pet food, birdcages, sacks of wheat berries, and piles of hard-used sneakers. I managed a smile. Some things had changed since I had begun my yearly trips to Logan, but not the friendly disarray that peppered the yard, the garage, and the inside of their modest home.

Mary stepped out to greet me. "You made it!" she said, spreading her arms in a welcoming hug. "How are you? How was the trip?"

She, too, seemed unchanged. A cap of short, tawny curls fit close to her head. Laugh lines spread outward from her deep-set blue eyes. She wore oversized jeans and a loose cotton shirt. Her voice, tinged with a Western drawl, was warm and melodic.

"Are you hungry? How about some lunch?" she asked. She called out to John as she ushered me inside. She was unruffled by the clutter of pots, pans, dishes, books, mail, papers, and napkins that overflowed from every nook in the kitchen. She rifled through the refrigerator and pulled out two fat red tomatoes and a hunk of cheese. She sawed two slices of bread from a homemade loaf on the kitchen counter, plunked it all on a plate, and handed it to me.

My brother strode into the kitchen. His frame was still slight, but his hands, thick and scarred from physical work, hung from his sinewy arms like leather mitts. He gave me a nod. His eyes reflected the bright Utah sky.

"So, what brings you to these parts?" he asked.

I took a breath, then let it out. "I was going to spend the summer with some friends, but something came up," I said. "There aren't any jobs in Eugene, so I decided to visit." I didn't tell him my friends were a gay couple or that I had inadvertently created a wedge in their relationship. I didn't tell him I was at yet another crossroads, trying to figure out my identity, my path, my home.

John nodded. "Well, you know the deal. Three squares and a bed," he said. "You can stay in the rental. It's small, nothing fancy, but it's got a roof." It was daylight, and as usual he had somewhere to go. "See ya later," he called on his way out.

After I finished lunch, I picked up my pack, called the dogs, and walked through the back garden to the tiny brown house where John stowed visiting relatives when it wasn't rented out. I stood in the doorway of the cramped, stuffy bedroom and sighed. Moving to Oregon was a needed respite from Boston's suffocating racism and urban blight. I loved the size of my new town, its safe streets, and its welcoming atmosphere. I allied myself with the alternative business sector and its vibrant women's community, but with that came a new set of problems.

The VW repair cooperative I joined was replete with fighting, accusations, and power struggles. We argued incessantly about money and commitment. Finally I had quit. After I visited my friends' rural home in northern California, and experienced their back-to-the-earth lifestyle, I thought staying with them would provide a supportive, nurturing environment where I could live my beliefs. That dream had collapsed, too.

The old order had its downside but so, I had discovered, did the new. Once again I was without an anchor. And where was I seeking refuge? With a family rooted in Mormon ideology—the kind of rigid, patriarchal, homophobic religion that my California friends and I had railed against again and again. But the truth was, my brother's path was taking him somewhere. He and Mary were a team. They had a home and a community. They paid their bills. Their kids, as far as I knew then, were thriving. They had enough to share with others. Clearly, their way was working; mine was not. I wasn't a prodigal sister, but close. And a grieving one, at that.

I dumped my pack in the corner of the airless bedroom and unrolled my pad and sleeping bag on the floor. Photographs of top Mormon elders—every one of them male, tight-lipped, and gray-haired—hung on the wall. Their eyes felt piercing and judgmental. I put my pillow at one end of my sleeping bag, shoved my journal underneath it, and walked back through the fledgling tomato and bean plants to the house on Center Street.

As I had before, I slipped into the family's daily swirl as if into a pool of warm water. John had become a jack-of-many-trades. Besides running his tree-service business, he oversaw a storage unit outfit and managed two large apple orchards on the outskirts of town. I pitched in whenever he asked. I drove the spray truck when he needed me to, even though I was opposed to agricultural chemicals and the smell nauseated me. I helped him pile brush in the back of his pickup after tree trimming jobs. In the evenings I accompanied him to the orchards to lug irrigation pipe or scythe grass between the rows of trees. I sometimes cooked dinner, often washed dishes, and in general tried to bring order to the kitchen. On Family Home Evenings—a weekly Mormon tradition designed to bring the family together—I sat at the kitchen table with the kids, making craft projects and slurping sticky-sweet ice cream sodas. When I returned to my tiny house at night, I was met with the stern eyes of the Mormon elders. It was as if they saw through the face I wore throughout the day straight into my less obvious Oregon self, and didn't approve of what they saw.

One morning several days into my visit, I sat down on the back porch step next to Mary. She was watching a bedraggled hen whose backside was swollen and featherless.

"What's wrong with that poor chicken?" I asked.

"Oh, she's got an egg stuck inside her ovoid tube," Mary said. "The other chickens are pecking her all to heck. If somebody doesn't do something, she'll probably die."

"Shouldn't you call a vet or something?" I asked, settling down beside her. Mary let my comment slide down onto the grass, unanswered. That summer the family's backyard menagerie included twenty chickens, a dozen caged pigeons, two rabbits, a castrated lamb, two parakeets, and two large dogs, with mine bringing the number to four. Later I figured it out—seeking out a vet each time one of the menagerie wobbled, drooled, or fell ill would have been financially untenable. Vets were for true crises, not a stuck egg.

Mary, I knew by then, had a mild demeanor on the surface, but underneath she was pure pioneer grit. She fussed, but she didn't shirk from rolling up her sleeves and dealing with whatever task was at hand, whether it was a basket of beans that needed canning, a climb up an impossibly steep ridge, a whining child or, that morning, a chicken in pain. She reached for the miserable bird and wedged it between her knees, its bobbing head facing away from her.

"Well, here goes nothing," she muttered. I watched from my perch next to her, half-amazed and half-horrified, as she picked up a long-handled spoon that lay by her side. She hit the chicken's taut, reddened backside bulge with a timid strike. The chicken struggled. She hit it again, harder. The swollen mound didn't budge. "Dang it," she whispered under her breath. She set her lips, tightened her hold on the captive chicken, and brought the spoon down again. This time the shell gave way and a stream of liquid mixed with bits of white chips dribbled out of the bird's hind end. She released it and it lurched away, squawking its disapproval. I finally let myself breathe.

"Well, it'll either live or it won't," Mary said, shrugging her shoulders and wiping her hands on her jeans. I was in awe of her offhand bravery. She possessed courage I suspected I didn't have—and wouldn't ever have.

Mary and I spent a lot of time together that summer. Bit by bit, while we were doing dishes or driving to pick up one of the kids, I learned more about her life and her Mormon beliefs. She had grown up in the LDS church. Her religion was her touchstone. She had strayed once, but it was years ago, she told me, and she was back for good. The LDS church is built on the family unit, which it elevates to sacred status. A husband is the economic and spiritual head of the family; he provides for his spouse and their children and is responsible for the family's spiritual well-being. A wife's primary duty is to her husband, then to their children; any other aspirations are secondary. Abortion is, no exceptions, murder. Sexual purity before marriage is a must, and lust is to be quelled whenever it stirs outside of wedlock. Questioning the church's tenets is frowned upon; obeying them is essential. Marriage is a sacrament. "When a couple marries in the Temple, they are united for eternity," she told me. "Families stay together forever."

She and John met while both were attending Utah State University in Logan. They courted for a while, but he graduated and moved back East, eventually getting his masters in forestry from Yale University. He and Mary continued to correspond, and he became more interested in the LDS faith. Eventually, he decided to convert. My Irish Catholic mother had written him long letters to persuade him his new religion wasn't legit, but it didn't take. His decision to convert shook her very roots.

John, I, and our five siblings had been raised in our mother's strict faith. For me, the church calendar anchored each week and wheeled us through the seasons. I knew the rituals before I learned the alphabet. Fall ushered in Thanksgiving, then Advent and the build-up to Christmas. The end of winter brought six interminable weeks of Lent, then the bloody, solemn pageantry of Palm Sunday, Holy Week, and, finally, the deliverance of Easter. We attended Sunday High Mass with regimented regularity, fasting from the time we woke up so we could take communion. In the summer the air inside the church grew stuffy. As the priest's sermon droned on, the elastic band from my straw hat cut into the underside of my jaw. In winter, frigid drafts seeped underneath my coat and up my legs. But I feasted on the wafting incense, the light filtering through the stained glass windows, and the haunting harmonies floating down from the choir loft. I was awed by the majesty of the priest and his solemn Latin intonations. It gave me a quiet thrill to murmur responses whose words I barely understood: *Deo gracias. Ora pro nobis. Et cum spiritu tuo. Mea culpa. Mea maxima culpa.*

When I was a girl, the apostate power the Church warned

against—Satan, or Lucifer, and his detestable spawn of sin—fascinated me as much as the splendor of the mass. Back then, the Church required kids attending public school to attend weekly religious instruction classes. Every Saturday morning during the school year, I sat with the other "publics" at ancient wooden desks in the parish elementary school. I ran my fingers along the inked grooves left by my forebears and listened rapt as nuns in gauzy veils and stiff white wimples told stories of martyrs who refused to give up their faith, even when their feet were seared by red-hot coals or their backs ran with blood from vicious whippings. Sin left black marks on your soul, the nuns told us. If you died with minor sins on your soul, you would be sent to purgatory, which meant you could be delivered from eternal punishment—but only if you had stored up enough prayers or if people prayed for you after your death. But if you died with mortal sins on your soul, you were doomed to burn in Hell forever. The fires of Hell were horribly hot, hotter than the hottest fire, the nuns said. The damned burned and burned, but never died.

I believed all of it. I pined for Heaven and I was terribly afraid of Hell. Not of Satan, but of the fires of eternal damnation. Nonetheless, I sinned. I fought with my sisters, I yelled back at my mother, I didn't keep my room picked up. I wasn't sure what impure thoughts were, but I figured I probably had them. Every other Saturday afternoon our mother drove us to church for confession. When it was my turn, I entered the austere, musty-smelling wooden box with my memorized list of child-sins. When the priest slid back the screen that separated his face from mine, I recited them, murmured a sincere act of contrition, and listened to my penance. Back in the pew, I whispered the requisite number of Our Fathers and Hail Marys. When I walked out of the church into daylight, I felt buoyant, radiant as a tiny sun.

I was a preteen when John sent my mother his letter telling her he was leaving the church. My mother read it while sitting in the dim light of the kitchen corner after the supper dishes were done. As a boy, John had shown a spiritual inclination that my mother had nurtured. Family photos show him dressed in the loose white tunic of an altar boy, his blond hair slicked back, his face composed and serious. But despite her efforts he had slipped away. When she told me about his decision, I was shaken, too. Teenage rebellion hadn't begun to course through my blood. I felt as if our family unit was a fragile bowl that had cracked. I feared something essential would leak out the gap. I thought my brother incredibly brave but mistaken. Maybe even lost.

As it turned out, I needn't have worried. John converted to Mormonism soon after he married Mary. He and the LDS church were a good match from the start. He tended to see the world in black and white terms and Mormonism, with its strict dictates about God, family, and morality, also doesn't tolerate much gray. The church eschewed creative interpretations or deviation from its rules. His new religion fit my brother like a pair of his well-worn jeans.

John's initial embrace of Mormonism was guarded. He was a tepid convert, more of an onlooker than a belonger. But a persistent back injury changed all that, Mary told me in one of our conversations. The pain had kept him in bed for days. For an active guy, the confinement was devastating. He tried rest. He tried drugs. He tried to tough it out. Nothing worked.

"I begged and begged him to let elders from the church give him a blessing," she told me. "Finally, he said yes."

The elders came and prayed over him. Soon after, he was able to get out of bed. Then he was walking. Within days he was back at work. "They cured him," Mary said, her voice, even years later, hushing in reverence.

The experience opened him up, John told me, and he got

serious about his new religion. By the time I began my summer trips to Logan, Mormon teachings were cemented into the family's daily life. Copies of the Book of Mormon were scattered around the house along with magazines providing tips for preserving food, creating holiday crafts, and keeping a marriage solid. John took Boy Scouts from the church on weekend camping trips. He rose early Sunday mornings to tend to church-related business. At night, during my visits, he challenged me with made-up quandaries to illustrate to me his faith's commitment to a higher moral ground.

Like many Mormon wives, Mary belonged to the Relief Society, the church's group for women. She taught Sunday classes at the church or accepted whatever task the church hierarchy assigned her. As per Mormon custom, she kept the house stocked with a year's worth of food in case of a major disaster, and the family pantry overflowed with sacks of grain, five-gallon jugs of oil, and tubs of lard. Cases of canned goods were tucked underneath beds and on hallway shelves. Jars of home-canned tomatoes, beans, and peaches lined their root cellar. "Visiting teachers" dropped by periodically to check on the family's welfare, and John and Mary were themselves "visiting teachers" to other families. It was impossible to separate John's family and their Mormon lifestyle. As much as I disagreed with some of their church's doctrines, I could see how the church community provided my brother and his family strength and a sense of belonging. Sometimes it tugged at me, in spite of myself.

I had been the next to break away from our childhood faith. Unlike John's careful, well-considered departure, mine was hot and sudden.

It was 1969. Michelle would have been one year old; I was a freshman in college. Throughout my first winter away from home, I had trudged across campus every Sunday in the thin, flat morning light to attend Mass in the school's Catholic chapel. But I had begun to be influenced by the cresting wave of concern for human rights, disdain for institutional authority, and right to self-expression sweeping through college campuses. As my politics took shape, my religious devotion waned. I muttered my responses to the priest in a bored drone. I fidgeted throughout the readings, thinking instead about the lanky, loose-limbed boy I was trying to get to notice me. Catholicism seemed increasingly irrelevant in light of the political and social issues I was becoming aware of—poverty, racism, deceitful politicians, the carnage of the Vietnam War, women's second-class social status. The Vatican's stance against birth control, and its refusal to allow women the spiritual clout of priests, galled me. The wonder I once felt when the priest held up the host at the climax of the Mass evaporated. The world is falling apart and still all the hubbub about Christ's body and blood? Please, I thought to myself, not yet daring to admit my feelings aloud.

That spring I went home for a weekend visit. I had been out late on Saturday night, and the next morning my mother bustled into my bedroom to wake me for church. I was bleary, hungover and grumpy.

"Why aren't you ready?" she demanded. "It's eight thirty. Time for church. Get up."

John had been able to debate with my mom, but her power cowed me. I never learned how to fight with her. Like my father, when I was angry with her, I retreated inward, and sulked. If I wanted to defy her, I did it in secret. But seven months in college had changed me. I had watched my fellow students challenge our professors. I had learned from them how to be rude, arrogant, and self-righteous. It was the dawn of a new order, and a whole crowd of anonymous peers had my back.

From my bed I mumbled something peevish. She repeated her order to get up.

"I'm not going," I announced. "I don't believe in it. Going to church doesn't mean anything to me anymore." I did not acknowledge my younger sister staring at me, wide-eyed, from her bed across the room. She knew this was a new script, a new me. "I refuse to be a hypocrite and go to church just because you want me to."

I was standing at the edge of an abyss. Heat, excitement, and fear flooded me. I didn't realize it then, but deep in my psyche, God, the Church, and my mother had formed a triumvirate of almost unassailable power, their identities so intertwined I could not separate one from the other. Nor, I believed, could I get rid of one without jettisoning the others. As I watched my mother stalk out of my room, I jumped into the unknown. I chucked all of the guides that for years had molded my values and anchored my being. I turned my back—or thought I did—on the all-seeing eyes that damned and honored, demanded and pardoned.

I may have sounded brave that morning, but the truth was I wasn't prepared for my spiritual system to collapse. No one had told me that my once-fervent faith might be temporary, that what seemed inviolable at age twelve and fifteen could, by age nineteen, seem trivial, even childish. I felt freed, but also unmasked and oddly betrayed by the change that had come over me.

I fell, it would seem, for years.

Outwardly I proclaimed my antireligious fervor with missionary zeal. I lambasted Catholic dogma whenever the subject came up. My disdain grew to include all Western religions. I revered my churchless status. But inside, I felt hollow and adrift. I ached for a closer relationship with my mom, but my decision had created a major rift between us. I tried for years to find something to fill the space once occupied by my childhood faith. Feminism worked to a point, but its politics collided with the spirituality I yearned for. I practiced Zen meditation and yogic breathing. I devoured books on palmistry, astrology, the mystical Kabbalah, and Jungian psychology. I tried chanting and martial arts. I consulted the *I Ching*, an ancient Chinese text and oracle. All of it helped; nothing was enough to fill the hole.

Sundays were the hardest. Growing up, the first day of the week had been special. My father, a staunch Presbyterian, stayed home while the rest of us went to church. In the peace of an empty house, he cooked his one meal of the week, an elaborate breakfast of scrambled eggs and bacon, French toast, or pancakes. We returned home, famished, to a kitchen table set with half grapefruits at each seat, a half maraschino cherry at the hub of each tart, pink wheel. He'd pull a pan of French toast or a pile of pancakes out of the oven. We ate and talked, argued and laughed. Sunday afternoons meant short jaunts to the country. In the summer we headed to the beach or to one of the nearby rocky gorges in the Finger Lakes region for a hike, swimming, and a picnic. In the early fall we picked prunes, grapes, and apples at nearby orchards. Later in the season we drove to an old cement-block cider mill with a sticky floor, a sweet aroma, and an overflowing bin of culled apples. "Take one. They're free," the sign said.

On Sundays, the Logan family's bustling rhythm shifted, too. Wynlee and Michelle traded their shorts and T-shirts for dresses with round collars and delicate flower prints. Greg washed his face, combed his hair, and emerged looking like he had just slid down to Earth from Heaven. Mary put on a dress that lightened her face. John shaved, donned a navy blue suit, and morphed from grizzled cowboy to polished church elder. By 9:00 a.m., the family had taken their place at the yellow brick church next door.

Mary unfailingly invited me to join them. "You know we'd love to have you come with us," she'd say. "No thanks," I'd respond. "I've had enough of church to last a lifetime." I did go, once, early on in my string of visits. I sat in the austere church among the primly dressed congregation, the men in suits, the women in long sleeves and muted colors. I listened to what sounded to me like singsong, vapid hymns. The Bible readings and the sermon were delivered by men. I was restless and itchy. I felt like an imposter or a prisoner. It took all my restraint not to leave before the service was over.

During my long summer stay in 1981, I never joined my brother's family at church. After they left, I wandered through the eerily quiet house. I flipped through the Sunday paper, read the comics, and brewed a second cup of tea. I dried dishes and folded laundry. I went outside, threw sticks for the dogs, and waited for the family and its lovely noise to come back home.

I arrived in Logan for that visit in early August, expecting to stay a couple of weeks; I ended up staying three months. As my visit stretched on, Michelle and I spent more and more time together. She was thirteen that summer and still wrestling with the curse of few friends, bad hair, and the bulimia I was unaware of and she couldn't speak of. I was thirty, unemployed, and harboring my own stash of secret failings. I wasn't practiced at hiding things, but by then Michelle was. She was good at picking up subtleties—maybe she suspected I wasn't telling my entire story. Maybe that made her feel safe.

The two of us bypassed each other during the day as errands and tasks took us in different directions. But often we met up in the late afternoon, once the air began to cool and the sun's rays slanted low and golden through the trees. "Going running?" one of us would ask the other.

We both had taken up jogging, but both of us eschewed typical running gear. She favored sweatpants and loose white T-shirts. I was partial to cutoffs and my favorite forest-green T-shirt. As we ran, I was aware of how her light, quick bounds contrasted with my heavier, plodding gait. The egret and the cow, I thought to myself as I pushed myself to keep up with her. Ever since college my weight had been a perennial preoccupation. Being busy helped keep it steady, but when I wasn't, it crept up. I ate to tamp down my anxiety and restlessness. I ate when I didn't know what to do with myself. I ate when I was lonely and when I wasn't. Self-criticism about what I ate, and how much, buzzed in my brain daily. In my journals I excoriated myself for taking extra helpings I didn't need, for the second slice of bread, for not saying no to late-night ice cream.

Of course, I thought later, Michelle had noticed my tug-of-war with food. How could she not? Maybe that was another reason she felt a kinship.

Often we ran along the whispery, dry fields outside of town, not saying a word until our legs were spent and we were headed back toward home in the twilight. Other nights we walked, rambling through the streets in the cool night air. I listened to her frustrations with friends, boys, self-image, her siblings, and parents. One night, after describing yet another confrontation at home, she said, "Aunt Alice, they just don't get me. I try, but I just don't fit in."

I tried to keep to the role of listener and counselor. But the longer I stayed, the more I shared about myself. I lamented my endless interior wrangling over deciding on a career. I told her that I, too, often felt like an outsider in my social circle back home. I agreed with her that males operated with different rules, and I shared sanitized versions of my paltry string of failed relationships and friendships.

Michelle listened closely to my tales of woe, nodding her

head and inserting supportive nods or comments at the right time. "I hate it when people do that," she'd assert on my behalf. Or, "I know just how you feel."

Part adolescent, part peer, she hooked into my heart, deeply. Whether from her eccentric nature, her social isolation, or her love of reading, a premature wisdom had taken root in my niece's gawky, budding body. Her perceptive, pungent insights made it difficult for me to keep up the guise of the worldly-wise aunt who had cracked some of life's confounding riddles. She would flip from pouting adolescent to sage observer of human frailty with startling ease.

One night in the living room, John was explaining to me where some pipe needed to be moved in one of the orchards, saying something along the lines of, "You need to move the pipe between the rows of Macintosh in the northwest corner."

John often used compass directions when he explained where something was located. I found the practice confounding. I wasn't used to orienting myself to the sun, and I hadn't bothered to figure out the directional lay of the land once I got to Logan. As he went on, I bluffed as long as I could, but he caught on, and launched into a condescending explanation of directions.

"Now, where is south? You don't know, do you?" he said. "Well, in the morning, the south is to your left when the sun is at your back. And in the evening, it's on your right." I knew the tone. As much as I loved my brother, I wasn't blind to his shortcomings. He could be self-righteous, patronizing, judgmental. Unfortunately, that night he was right. I didn't know southeast from northwest. My face flamed redder and redder as he chastised me for my ignorance. I was aware that Michelle was sitting in a corner chair, witnessing my comeuppance, and that embarrassed me even more. When John finished his lecture, he got up and strode out of the room.

Michelle and I sat in silence. Then she spoke up. "Don't mind Dad," she said to me, gently. "He can be like that sometimes. You just have to forget it."

Surprised by her comment, I nodded my head. "I know," I said. "He's my brother, but sometimes . . ." She smiled. I got up to go back to the rental. "Thanks," I said. She nodded. I knew she had been subject to her dad's withering disapproval, warranted or not. She knew what I was feeling. We were kin.

I don't know if people who harbor secrets sense one another, as addicts vibe each other out in a crowd. Something subterranean drew Michelle and me together that summer—maybe we read between each other's lines, or filled in the missing blanks with what we wanted to believe about the other. We came to trust each other without knowing our respective secrets. When I went back to my tiny bedroom each night, it wasn't Michelle's problems that paraded through my head as I lay down to sleep, but my own. In the mental movie I was starring in, I was the outsider, the one with the flailing ego, the wanderer without a map.

It never occurred to me that, while lying in her own bed at night, Michelle grappled with troubles far more tangled than my own. I didn't know, then, that her suffering went far beyond nightly remonstrances in her journal, but frequently up her throat and into the toilet. I didn't know she was already resorting to purging as a way to feel in control of at least one part of her thirteen-year-old world. Or that bulimia would be just the beginning of her long descent into isolation so profound no one could penetrate it.

"I am meeting with [a counselor] again," she wrote in one of her journals I read later. "Not because of the bulimia. I have that in control, pretty much, but because of a terrible depression. We think it is a space left where bulimia used to occupy.

I don't know. I can function o.k. It's not paralyzing. The bad thing is the loneliness."

If I had known more of what Michelle was going through, maybe I could have told her I knew what it felt like to feel alien inside your own skin, to feel that your inner voice does not match with the words you hear yourself say. I want to think I could have been a wiser listener, a more helpful presence. But I didn't know her secrets, not the bingeing, not the purging or the despair that dogged her days and nights. And when I found out about all of it, it was too late. It was only years after she died that I began asking about what I didn't know back then, about what I hadn't been able to see—the hardening of John's jaw during exchanges with Michelle, the set of Mary's mouth when her daughter exploded into a hurricane of accusations. I hadn't even grasped her own words.

"I have figured out a lot of things," she wrote in one letter. "Like not to drown loneliness in words, talking, writing it away. It doesn't work. And not to search for someone to take it away. Not to sink in it. Not to pull it all out and wear it like a shroud, peering through it at the far away outside world."

At night, as the end of apple season approached, I tossed in my sleeping bag under the eyes of the Mormon elders. I felt safe living with my brother's family, but I also knew that, living in Logan, I had left a part of myself behind—in Oregon, on the road. Somewhere. John and Mary had introduced me to an unmarried, non-Mormon woman whom they had befriended. She was a divorced mom with a bitter edge who had named her dog Lobo because, she told me, living in Logan made her feel like a lone wolf. Was that my fate if I stayed here? Eugene was still mired in an economic recession. I wasn't sure where I would live or how I would support myself when I got back. But it was time to go home.

46

Over the next few days I gathered my gear and packed my VW with parting gifts from the family: a tape recorder from Mary, two cardboard boxes of apples from John. Mary had decided she and Michelle would sew me a quilt, two sheets with batting in the middle secured by knots of yarn. Mary had started to work on it once I fixed my departure date, but Michelle had put off doing her part. The night before I left I could hear her puttering around upstairs. Finally she came down and presented me with the quilt. It was made from a white, gray, and orange flowered sheet on one side, and a solid orange sheet on the other. Later, when I examined the quilt closely, I found Michelle's true parting gift. Instead of the unobtrusive white thread Mary had used to sew her seams, Michelle had sewn hers using bright turquoise thread.

chapter 4
walks

I guess bulimia is a deadening agent. It fogs pain up nicely. Unfortunately, it fogs everything else up, too. Sometimes it is almost worth it, it seems, just to have the pain fogged up.

When I am restless and feel this anger or discomfort inside me, my physical self cries out for activity. Usually I deny it and this is because when I walk, at night, I walk the same cold footsteps of many times before, when everything was different. And memories of thoughts slip out behind the trees and follow me silently, expectantly. Some from months, some from years past. Thoughts I scattered as I walked those footsteps before. Some caught in trees, some slipped down underneath the grass and lay dormant until my footsteps, familiar, echoed into their sleep and beckoned them. And now they rise and follow me, a forlorn funeral procession silently plodding into the night.

If that's what happened to you, would you want to go on walks?

—An excerpt from one of Michelle's journals,
"Michelle the Scrupulous, 1985–1986"

chapter 5
rock hands

I don't remember when or from whom I learned of Michelle's bulimia. But at some point, both Michelle and Mary assumed I knew about it, and each of them made subtle references to it in their letters. Initially, I wasn't that concerned. I considered Michelle's battles with food a temporary release for her internal angst, and figured the bulimia would dissipate once she got past this difficult adolescent "phase." I wasn't acquainted with the bulimic Michelle, and it was easy to push her to the side of my consciousness. I couldn't—or wouldn't—imagine the Michelle I knew bent over a toilet, two fingers stuck down her throat, retching up food she had binged on just minutes before. The Michelle I cherished was a blossoming teenager who sporadically wrote me smart and funny letters.

"I got for Christmas a lovely darling little rabbit that was white and had floppy ears," she wrote in the summer of 1982, when she was fourteen. "It had the cutest personality. It would growl and attack you if you teased it, but it was really friendly if you didn't. It loved to be petted. It would close its eyes and lean on you. Anne [my sister and Michelle's aunt] came down to stay with her dog, Tinker, who is an obese, ugly, senile garbage dog. And her dog killed my rabbit. I hate Tinker."

A few months later: "It is raining down here, and the [next-door neighbors] graveled the road so all the water runs right down our sidewalk. It is a total mud hole. We will never know how many visitors have come to see us, because they have sunk out of sight, never to be seen again . . . Pogie [the family dog], flourishing from the devoted slavishness of our neighbors, is now so fat that he cannot sit properly. He sits in this weird way that looks like a king, lolling on his side, calling for wine. One of these days he is going to have a massive coronary attack."

And a year later: "I decided I'd drop you 63 lines and 265 words. I have worked up to five miles, six times a week with my stubby legs. The first mile up Cliffside Hill I curse myself soundly and practically crawl. After that, I enjoy myself. However, running in the cold is a different thing. First two miles, three snowballs thrown by lovely little children playing in the snow. The next three miles my lungs frosted over and my nose threatened to turn me in for cruel and unusual punishment."

I loved the keen eye my niece cast on her life and the world around her, and her ability to express it. We shared a need to chronicle the way we experienced our respective worlds. Maybe that's the way I wanted to see her—as a confrere, not as someone who was wrestling with far more sinister angels than my own.

I chide myself, too, for not understanding the intensity of her social struggles. It took me too long to understand how, living in her dominant Mormon culture at school as well as at home, her failure to cultivate friendships must have affected her. I don't know if the same holds true today, but back then the pressure for Mormon girls to groom themselves to please future spouses was relentless. From childhood, girls were urged to learn to cook, sew, tend children, and make themselves attractive to boys. Church-sponsored magazines instructed young women on remaining pure and how to cultivate personality traits that would make them a pleasing mate. The concept of exploring the self—a writer's job and Michelle's singular quest from early on—wasn't encouraged or valued. I doubt that kids like Michelle who didn't fit the mold were considered "cool" by their peers. Whether it was her innate difference or her temperament, Michelle's inability to build friendships with girls her age, much less handle the far more dicey social arena of boys and dating, continued into high school. Even though she tried to make light of it, the pain must have been piercing, like air on a newly drilled tooth.

"School is not too great," she wrote in one note, her penciled handwriting round and slanting downward like that of a younger girl. "I watch Wynlee blithely work her way through numerous boys, while I sit on the sidelines careful not to take my foot out of my mouth. I think it is permanently attached. I think I'll bury myself until I'm 20."

Over time I came to understand the code Michelle used to refer to her bulimia. The phrase "doing better" meant she was bingeing less; "not doing so good" meant she was back in the grip of it. But early on, I didn't read between the lines. I didn't realize the degree to which bulimia ruled her life.

"This year in school has been incredibly better than last year, but these past few weeks have not been so good," she wrote when she was a junior in high school. "I don't know why, but I can't figure out what is myself and what is a feeble wimp-me groveling to be accepted, and what is a lack of confidence. All in all, I would have to tell you it is quite a disturbing experience to be caught in the throes of adolescence, but there is not too much I can do about it. And so we conclude this session of 'Michelle's Search for Tranquility.' (P.S. Do not think I am an airhead. I am just trying to arrange a juxtaposition of my self and myself.)"

At the same time Michelle was making her way through the brambles of high school, I was back hitting the books as well. Fed up with working at low-paid, labor-intensive jobs, I was ready to reclaim the intellectual self I had abandoned after college. In the fall of 1984 I enrolled in the University of Oregon as a post-baccalaureate student, and that winter I was accepted into the university's School of Journalism. It was a leap of faith. My writing at the time consisted of personal, ruminative essays that I typed out in fits of late-night inspiration. I didn't see how I could exchange that intermittent outpouring for hard-edged daily news—I felt so out of the mainstream I wasn't sure if I could ever fit back in. But I was thirsty for a world larger than the one I had been living in, and my journalism courses stimulated my thinking. Some also challenged me. I was used to writing alone, in silence and usually at night. But in my reporting class that spring I had to write on deadline in a roomful of other students, typewriters clattering like miniature jackhammers. For the three agonizing hours my head buzzed as I tried to order lists of facts and numbers into a logical story. At the end of each session, I limped out of the classroom utterly spent.

I stuck it out and by the close of spring term I felt close to triumphant. Back in Logan, Michelle was feeling better, too. She had finished her junior year and had snagged her first part-time job—a counter girl at Sizzler, a regional steakhouse chain. One of her duties, she wrote me, was to keep the salad bar area clean and stocked.

"My puny little arm muscles are sore from carrying crocks back and forth and back and forth and back and forth. And inevitably I end up spattered with bleu cheese from my eyebrows to my toes," she wrote me in July 1985. "Not thousand island, not ranch, but bleu cheese. Our chemistries must match or something."

I could imagine her dressed in the plain brown uniform,

her now thick and lustrous blonde hair (I never asked, but by then she likely lightened it with help from a box) tucked into a matronly hairnet, deftly dodging cooks and waitresses as she moved through the crowded kitchen. No longer the gangly girl of middle school, by then she carried her lithe body with a beguiling nonchalance. Her braces were off and her mouth now fit the rest of her thin, expressive face. But the old, barnacled doubts about her self-image remained. The popularity she longed for continued to elude her. But that summer, she wrote, not only had she met a guy she found interesting ("I hadn't known you could have intelligent conversation on dates. Alice, why didn't you tell me?") but she had formed a group of friends with whom she felt she could be herself.

"We get along famously and on our common ground find endless things to talk about . . . They are the only ones I can tell I shave my legs only once a month. And that sometimes I don't wash my hair until 3 in the afternoon. And that once I walked down the street with a paper bag over my head at 11 p.m. just because I wanted the people driving by to have the experience of seeing someone walking down the street at 11 p.m. with a paper bag over their head."

She had been seeing a counselor during the school year but had stopped, she said, partly because of the expense but also because she was feeling better. "I am happier now than I have ever been. I feel comfortable when I am by myself, just thinking. Now I hope when school starts I don't fall to pieces all over again. I don't think I will."

These notes are among the last upbeat letters I would receive from her. I assumed she had successfully made it through the whitewater of adolescence. I didn't look for problems in the scattering of letters she wrote in the ensuing months. But when I read Michelle's later letters now, in the sepia light of hindsight, I see tiny warning flags I hadn't previously noticed waving from the pages. I see her minimizing her bingeing and how it isolated her from her peers and eroded her relationship with her parents. I see a hairline fracture forming between the person she described on the page and the one who lived in the world. I see an adolescent whose concept of self was growing slippery and loose, like an egg without a shell.

Her journals show she felt those things, too, even though she didn't communicate them to me. They were where she expressed the other side of her life—the frustration and hopelessness she felt as she struggled daily against an undertow she could not name or resist, and that would eventually draw her into the troubling epidemic that even then was seeping into communities across the country.

From the journal "Michelle the Scrupulous," October 1985–1986

Oct. 23

I found a list of things to do today. It listed practice, homework, etc. and at the very end, smally scribbled, it said Please please Michelle do not binge. Save me please. And this is how I feel late at night sometimes when I am alone and in the middle of the day as I sit in school wondering how lost I really am. Today when I got off work I blithely binged. I got off early, drove to Sconemaker and bought onion rings. Then I drove to Pete's and ordered onion rings there. And I went and bought a shake and 6 doughnuts, that was my binge. Now I wish for hundreds of hot onion rings and gallons of ice cream, boxes of donuts to bury myself unhesitatingly in. But what I need I cannot get from that. Because of my doubt in myself ever being capable and worthy of getting what I need, I settle for cheap thrills. I don't have faith I can get what I need.

This is bad. I need to have faith, which is not there. I see the world thru an iron cage. Everything is out of reach. Sometimes I can touch with my fingers, but that is all. I must keep people away. I must have them near. I am a big mess.

Oct. 24

I went to the garage and retrieved a beautiful golden delicious apple with red tinted sides. I ate it. It was sweet and juicy and comforting. I hastily grabbed another one and went inside. I ate both of them and my hunger still was in me, uncomfortable and restless. I thought of getting another one, and another, and a sandwich and milk. I felt anticipation and the familiar need rise in me. Then, for a flickering moment, I felt capable of stopping right then and not doing it. I snatched at that moment desperately, ravenously. I held on to it, I held it in my hands and in myself I said, "God, I cannot find faith in me. I need You so badly. What can I offer to You, out of this snarled mess I have created. I have nothing right now except this moment, when I almost felt I could." And I did. I walked away.

Oct. 26

I am finding out about myself. I don't think I like her. I know I don't . . . I know no knight in shining armor is coming to take me away from her. It is only she and I. I hate this being alone with her. She has me cornered. I despise her. She is the reason no one can like me, except Tammy. Tammy sees her completely and accepts her. She is the only one in all the world.

Tammy had first noticed Michelle in the seventh grade, when she witnessed Michelle lambasting a group of her classmates for teasing another student. "She told off the most popular kids in the group," Tammy told me, years later. "She verbally laid into them, calling them to accountability for their behavior. I remember thinking, 'Wow, she has a lot of courage.' Her level of intensity and confidence in what she was doing in seeking justice was a pretty powerful force."

In high school, Tammy became one of Michelle's few friends, drawn together by their shared love of observation and philosophical musing. Both of them believed that analyzing their worlds from as many perspectives as possible was a fascinating, not a time-wasting, pastime. They, too, would go for rambling walks around Logan or on hikes up the canyon, hopping over rocks while mulling their social and personal conundrums.

"She was a hundred percent the real deal. That's what kept us connected. She was completely sincere," Tammy said. "There was nothing superficial about her, the way she talked, dressed, her values. She was not materialistic at all. With her, I always felt in the presence of someone who was an anomaly. She had a very philosophical mind, a great deal of love in her heart for people and for nature. She intensely valued justice."

Long before Michelle confided in Tammy about her bulimia, her friend suspected something was amiss. But Tammy didn't pry. When Michelle finally shared her secret, Tammy surprised her by not recoiling. "She expected that when she told me, I would no longer want to be her friend, that I would think she was disgusting. She expected I would reject her, but she took the risk. And I didn't."

Oct. 29
I am going crazy. I have been doing worse on throwing up. Dad is getting uptight about it again. I cannot

56

stand it if he openly rejects me again. He does not trust me, he thinks I will fail. Why can't he accept me? He has no respect for my words. Or me.

Oct. 31

In a way, writing in here is a form of praying. Of letting God see myself and my feelings. Which are in turmoil at this minute. I went to the school dance where B danced exclusively with a thin, striking girl. And then I went to the college dance where B was with V. And now I am going to sleep and unless it's a whole lot better when I wake up, I'm going to kill myself. I'm sorry, I just can't handle this. I don't want to be at the mercy of a guy because I need him, ever again. And I don't want to be alone. So I will simply never wake up.

Nov. 1

Unfortunately, I did not inform Mom of my intentions and at 6:10 a.m. she cheerfully dragged me out of bed. Things can't get worse. That's one consolation.

Nov. 12

I feel better tonight. Almost as if I can cope. I finished my essay paper early on AP English, and slipped out to walk home. As I walked the roads were a muddy brown with the new fallen snow and bits of gravel flecked the muddy brown. It was very bleak, the road. I put each foot down in the snow, it was soft and fluffy, but very cold as it melted in my shoes. I thought, "My life is like this road. It is foreign to me, as if I had been thrown in arbitrarily. It feels like this, unnatural.

Nov. 13

I did nothing but binge today. 4X, still not out of control. I was ravenous, terribly ravenous, all day long. I don't know why. It felt good to retreat back into warm comfortable bulimia. It felt so secure. And it breeds such the opposite. I have not slept well for a long time. I read my scriptures, pray and turn off the light and close my eyes, but my mind prods me until I get up. It prods me with odd thoughts, foggy ones and dark ones, ones that become a dim ache until I get up to get away from them.

Nov. 27

Today being Thanksgiving, I naturally did badly. I got off work and came home and binged. Mom came home and came to me and was about to give me a hug. "Control thyself," she said. I walked away. I was so angry. After nights like this I want to shake Mom and Dad awake and say Please. Please tell me you love me. Tell me I'm OK. Forgive me, and tell me I'm OK. Don't give me up to this.

It is a golden cage I built around myself. It's got to stop. Here in my murky room, my soft darkness. Take me out in the glare and starkness of day and I would shrivel and collapse. I know binging isn't the only alternative. I feel it is the only one that will turn pain into hazy discomfort. Now I have to live with cragged edges, fragmented realities, foggy distortions. All of these and I eat together, sleep together, throw up together.

Dec. 14

Night strips away pretense. It parasitically sucks all life from it and leaves behind a hollow, translucent shell holding fear itself. Fear and pain, frustration and despair, like a kaleidoscope they turn and form intricate webs, to entangle me.

Dec. 31
Even if I was not bulimic, there are so many other holes in my life it looks like fishnet. There. That's what I am. Fishnet. Thin strands tying me together between the gaping holes.

Jan. 24, 1986
I went to a New Beginnings program tonight. I had to introduce the speaker. I wore a black dress, black nylons, black shoes. Someone leaned over to my Mom and said, "Your daughter is gorgeous. Is she a model?" I wanted to cry. I have no excuse for failing. Why do I?

I am playing a concertino with orchestral accompaniment for our next concert. I am competing in poetry for our next debate meet. I am doing fairly well in all my classes. I'm terrified. If I fail, if I succeed? People walk by me in the halls. What will I do? I have thrown myself off a cliff.

Feb. 2
Today was the orchestra concert where I played my concertino solo. Before the concert I practiced a little and went in my bedroom and prayed. I prayed that I would do OK. So long have people looked down on me, I wanted a chance to be respected for my ability. I slithered into my black dress and got ready to go. I was not nervous. I stood up there, alone, with my stand, and, at a nod from the conductor, started.

I played with ease. I hit all the little fingerings and swept through my runs beautifully. When I sat down I was so impressed with myself I screamed silently with glee. Everyone, everyone was stunned. Including myself. I never thought I could do so well. So this is what it feels like. My first public success. Followed by a wave of loneliness that nearly drowned me. But it receded and now I am . . . fine?

Feb. 10
I haven't thrown up at all today. My clarinet teacher told me I had enough talent to be professional if I wanted. Who says I am not worth anything? Who says I cannot succeed in something?

March 15
It is too bad that I fear God so much. This puts a barrier up. It is not respect fear, but fear fear. That is not how it should be. If God and I could work together, we could get more done. We could be partners. I would feel better about it. I'm sure he doesn't want me to be like this. It's not a very pleasant thing.

. . . A boy I know, very exuberant, easy-going, was walking down the hall. He saw me. "Michelle!" he said and was about to throw his arms around me. I evaded him teasingly and continued my trodden path. How shocked he would have been, to touch me and find out. I don't know, I can't discuss it with anyone, I can't write it here, I feel discomfort when I do. Should I bury it? Will it only fester and spread? But what if I am crazy, really. What then? If there is really something wrong with me, what could I do?

March 22
Michelle plans thru her regulated and well modulated, precisely calculated day, so if she falls into the pit of despair, she will have knotted all the ropes to climb up.

April 15
Here I am lying in bed, listening to the wind, at night. As it blows through my open windows in and out of the room. If I wasn't so tired I would go out there & wander around in that lovely, lovely wind. In that wonderful calm dark.

Today after I got home from work my body said We're hungry (my body is plural). We want dinner. So I said OK body. You're a good body. What would you like. Well there was some muffins sitting there. We want a muffin. OK. And we want those potatoes intermixed with peas in some kind of casserole in the 'fridge. OK body. I will give you enough to make you happy, but not to make you binge. OK. And off we went to bed.

April 19
I feel I am caught between Scylla and Charybdis. There is nowhere I can go. No one to really confide in, because I don't think anyone can help me. How can they help me if I don't know what's wrong? If I unloaded what is in my soul on someone they would turn around and never come back. I wouldn't blame them.

May 8
I binged yesterday. It was wrong. If I had been reading my Scriptures for 50 minutes a day it wouldn't have happened. If I let slip these things, my backbone will not support me when I need it to.

May 17

*I am developing the most pristine & religious reputation.
It is unwanted but comes as a result of the way I
dance (arm's length) and my distancing methods in
conversation, plus my general niceness. In other words,
I am thought of as a prude. . . . Please don't stop at my
walls. They're glass. See through to me.*

May 30

*How do other people live? What does it feel like to
be them? Is it peaceful, calm, relaxed? Envy creeps
into my pen. I, though, I have the night, the wind,
the stars. My legs stretched and limply twitching. I
have aloneness that no one can touch. I have late
hours studying and concentrating, using my brain
cells fiercely. All this I have, hands that move up and
down the clarinet with pleasure. I am rich in me.*

As I neared the end of my spring term in 1986, Michelle was
finishing high school and preparing for college. She had been
offered a music scholarship at Ricks College, a two-year Mormon school in Rexburg, Idaho. (Ricks is now Brigham Young
University/Idaho.) Neither the campus nor its students attracted
her, she wrote me, but she was ready to leave her hometown. "I
feel an oppressiveness here that I want to escape from. I want to
leave everyone I know, even those whose ties will hurt terribly
to break. Because, I think, I feel so alone inside."

I wasn't aware of how difficult her last weeks of high
school were until I read Mary's journal from that time. The
weeks surrounding Michelle's graduation were ones of "acute
discomfort and palpable loneliness," Mary wrote. "The entire
experience was obviously pure misery to her and consequently
to us."

This is what Michelle wrote me about the event: "I graduated, the prominent memory on that occasion being the 42 bobby pins to hold my two-sizes-too-large hat on."

The day after the ceremony, she and two friends took off on a weeklong camping trip to Yellowstone National Park. The same letter that was short on describing the graduation was effusive about their adventure.

Food: "Cooking was interesting. We cooked out of two pans the whole time, a saucepan and a frying pan. Not having soap to wash them out, they retained the flavor of everything we ever cooked in them, including chicken, potatoes, hamburger gravy, orange juice, hot chocolate, spaghetti, ravioli, pancake batter. Have I said enough? With, of course, a fine sprinkling of camper spice (soot, ashes and twigs) over everything. It was great."

Weather: "On the fourth day I felt a wet spot seeping through my sleeping bag. It usually only dribbled rain at night, so we were damp, but it had been raining steadily. I tried to balance on one of my hipbones to keep the rest of me from getting wet, but it didn't work. So we woke up and fled to the camp bathroom, warming ourselves on the hot air hand dryer. We hastily concluded to move to the Tetons, so at 5 a.m., we packed up. But it was snowing at the Tetons so we drove home. Picture three clods of dirt uprooted and sitting in the front seat of a tiny car packed with loads of dirty, wet, unrecognizable things, and you will have our exit. I would have liked to have stayed longer, but when you get sogged out, you get sogged out."

She ended the letter saying that, despite her earlier misgivings, she was looking forward to going to Ricks, and intended to arrive there with her frying pan and popcorn popper "and live among the natives of Idaho doing studies on their rural behavior for psychology background. And I will be OK."

I was looking toward the future as well. I had signed up to take a three-week trip to the Soviet Union with a group that wanted to promote peace between our countries. President Reagan had dubbed the Soviet Union the "Evil Empire" and the leaders of both nations were engaged in verbal saber rattling, backing up their threats by stockpiling nuclear arsenals. That April, an explosion at the Chernobyl nuclear power plant in the Ukraine had released a massive cloud of radioactive fallout. The disaster made it clear that some things were more important—and more deadly—than political differences.

Our group wanted to spread the message to Soviet citizens that a majority of Americans didn't consider them or their country to be "evil." Our itinerary would take us to five different cities in five different regions. My plan was to create a slide show focusing on women in the Soviet Union and use it as part of my master's thesis. My parents helped me with expenses, and I received a small grant to help me produce the slide/tape presentation.

That summer while I was busy with preparations, Michelle continued to wrestle with her bulimia.

June 23

I threw up today. I threw up and couldn't stop until I threw up a piece of me. I screamed inside and ran away to hide in the darkest corner but the holes in me kept screaming. What can I do? Only I can know how it feels to throw up now. I fight and fight against it.

I don't feel condemned anymore. I fight too hard to be condemned.

July 9

I passed my AP English test with a 5. Perfect score, one of the two highest in the school. I was sure I had flunked. When Mrs. S called, I was elated. I must be intelligent.

July 10

I have started to throw up again. I have no excuse. I walked over to the corner of my room and picked up a picture of me. I looked at it. It was a good picture. I knew, though, what is beyond the paper face. I knew she could not afford to stumble. But she was stumbling.

July 27

Something I have to get over is my family. I don't matter to them anymore. I should not blame them for this. I originated it by pushing them away because they could not help me, and now I cannot stop it. Sometimes I almost hate them for it.

Aug. 3

S and I went out last night and shot bottle rockets. Then we went for a walk in the cemetery. He held my hand and, at long last, while we were sitting underneath a tree, he even put his arm around me. Was I pleased? What do you think? It was nice and warm, like I remembered.

Aug. 15

Incidents came back to mind all day, on wings of pain, what it had been like. I tried to let the pain slip through my hands, but when I looked down at them they were stained with blood. . . I don't know why the pain. All I know is that, inside, I die some nights.

Michelle left for Ricks in late August. At first, things went well, she wrote. Her classes were stimulating and she enjoyed exploring the unfamiliar landscape of potato fields and winding dirt roads that led to unknown places. "I met someone late at night also plodding through the fields, without a Walkman. I offered him a few songs on mine. In turn, he directed me back to campus, for I was mildly lost. Mildly, mind you." Her fears about fading into a culture she didn't feel part of abated. "They are great, nice people. But how could I ever want to fit in when I never did before? So I can be myself and all my experiences are not in vain, but serve as pins in my framework, my perspectives. I will be myself, no matter."

But, again, her journal fills in what she left out of her letters. She was protecting me from the truth of her divided psyche. It turned out that, despite a temporary reprieve, bulimia remained her closest companion. She kept her bingeing self secret, and the split between that self and the one that wrote papers, studied in the library, and created joyful music on the clarinet fueled her deepening sense of isolation. She walked a taut rope between determination and despair.

Sept. 3
The cafeteria presents a bit of a problem, as selecting a healthy meal is next to impossible most of the time. I blew it today, panicking. I went running at the outdoor track to make up for it. I practiced the clarinet and could have stayed for hours. It was wonderful. The hint of insecurity is only manifest on the insides of my heels, where I scuff them as I walk, when I am uncomfortable. Sores were there all thru high school, they faded for the 1st time during the summer and now they are back. I will be fine, though, because I can do anything. Anything at all.

Sept. 24
I walked over to the Snow building to practice my clarinet, thinking the last thing I wanted to do was

practice, I wanted to crawl under a bush and die. I
practiced and felt better. I will take off my lonely skin
and go to bed.

Oct. 1
How can I ever go back to people when my aches are
eased, and I am more warmed by the night and the
lack of people and houses than I am by people?

Michelle did not occupy much of my mind that fall. After returning from my trip to the Soviet Union, I was immersed in sorting images, writing a script, and working on a final paper. Boxes of slides, file folders, and reference books were scattered all over the floor of the dilapidated studio apartment I rented in an industrial flatland across the river from Eugene. Other people thought the unlit, rundown neighborhood risky, but it suited me. At night, stiff from sitting, I took my dogs for walks in the drizzling rain. I had made friends with an elderly neighbor named Zilpha who had twinkling blue eyes and a gritty sense of humor. She, too, was a Mormon, but unlike the early risers I had met in Utah, she was a confirmed night owl. The rainy October night I finished my project, I sat in mute, pleased excitement, not knowing what to do. It was nearly 10:00 p.m. I put on my coat, leashed up the dogs, and walked a few blocks toward the yellow bulb that glowed in front of Zilpha's shoebox of a house. I knocked, knowing that despite the hour she would answer, and grin at the sight of the motley trio dripping on her doorstep.

In Rexburg, Michelle turned elsewhere for friendship.

This night I went running where my feet led me until
I was running through mud-packed farmer fields
and climbing through fences. Until the wind blew
dry the sweat on my face, and I watched the thunder

glowing in the distance, as I heard the sound of my feet through the fields. I was alone. Not to share with anyone. The night by me, the wind, the dampness of after-rain, the scorched sky blackness, all this to be me. That I could pick it up, as the rocks I find on my walks when I am lonely, and rub them against my cheek, smell their coolness. Hold them in my hands. More than human hands, I would have them be. Sacred rock hands, made by God, which will never lose their smoothness, but lie in my hand to comfort my loneliness. Rock hands, softer than human hands.

chapter 6

christmas in logan

In mid-December 1987, I sank into a plush leather seat close behind the cockpit of a large jet, buckled my seatbelt, and accepted a glass of red wine from the flight attendant. I was flying from Portland, Oregon, to Salt Lake City, where I would meet up with John for a holiday visit in Logan. I felt rich and expectant. For the first time in years I was self-supporting and secure in my world. I wasn't running away from anything. I had a job in my field—putting together a trade magazine for the state's grocery industry. I earned a decent monthly paycheck, and I felt like I had a future. I wasn't obsessed with what to do with my life or how I would pay my bills. Finally, at age thirty-seven, I was stroking, not treading water.

Apparently life thought so, too. "The plane is full," the gate attendant had told me when I checked in. "We're putting you in first class."

The plane taxied to the runway and took off, hurtling through the gray mass of clouds that presses on western Oregon throughout the fall and winter. Once we had leveled off, the flight attendant served me a warm breakfast of eggs and ham. I savored every bite as I looked forward to seeing the Logan crew.

A few weeks earlier, when John had invited me to visit, he had enticed me by describing the mountain yurt he had rented in the Wasatch Mountains. "We'll ski in and carry all our gear on our backs," he said. "It's not that far. And it's got a wood stove." I still didn't commit. I had heard from my siblings about some of my brother's wintertime "adventures." They didn't always live up to his four-star billing.

"Michelle's home, too," he added. "She'd love to see you."

He knew there was no way I would have turned him down after hearing that last bit of news. Since going off to Ricks, Michelle, then nineteen, had sent me only a few letters describing her experience of campus life. Sadness wafted from the pages like a plaintive melody, but I had hoped it would pass. I hadn't heard from her in a while. It was time to catch up.

"Sure, I'll come," I had told him. "I'd love to see everybody."

Later, I would go over my brother's invitation in my mind to see if I had missed anything—a tone, an inflection, a give-away word—that I could have picked up on. But nothing stood out. His focus, as usual, was on the adventure he had concocted. When he mentioned Michelle, his voice had been offhand and casual. Likely by then he had become a master of not exactly deception, but of skirting around the smoldering volcano living inside his home.

I was happily unaware of his disrupted family life as I sipped my wine and looked out the window. The plane broke through to a shimmering blue sky. Thoughts bounced lightly through my mind. I had been at my new job for four months, and I was starting to feel comfortable with its demands. My office was in Salem, which meant an hour's commute each way on Interstate 5. I had traded in my six-volt 1959 Bug for a 1980 Toyota sedan with a twelve-volt battery, ten-inch-long windshield wipers, a working radio, and a heater that, unlike my stingy Bug, exuded warmth. To me the compact sedan might as well have been a pricey luxury vehicle. When I drove on the highway, my Tercel accelerated to sixty-five miles per hour as if it were built for speed. At night, the dash glowed with lights.

"More wine?" the flight attendant asked.

I nodded. I knew there would be no alcohol or caffeine at my brother's house. The taboo was the least of my objections to the family's religion, but I had decided long ago I wouldn't let their beliefs become a barrier between us. I had learned to pack my own tea bags and forgo thoughts of the evening cocktail hour that I enjoyed with the rest of my family when we were together.

We flew south and east, I looked down on the terrain from this new vantage point. Snow glistened on a line of jagged mountain peaks. The light shining through my oval window was so bright I had to squint. I had brought with me a hand-made lampshade decorated with garlands of pressed flower petals as a gift for John and Mary. When I first saw it, I envisioned how it would cast a warm, pastel glow in a corner of their worn living room where I had spent so many hours wrestling with my various dilemmas and watching G-rated movies with the family. I decided I wanted it even before asking the price, an unheard-of act in my typically cash-strapped life.

The plane touched down in Salt Lake, smooth and steady. Back then, family and friends were allowed to meet arriving passengers at the gate. I scanned the crowd until I spotted my brother—a tractor cap atop his head, a restrained welcome in his half-smile. I retrieved my suitcase and we walked to the parking lot. When we got to his dented and scraped pickup truck—no matter the year or model, all of his trucks ended up looking the same: hard-used and weary—he threw my suitcase into the back and I hopped into the passenger seat. I cradled the bag with the lampshade in my lap as we headed north. We made small talk—weather, flight, job, car. Then we hit the highway.

"Things aren't going well with Michelle," John said, shaking his head slightly. "It's a really bad deal."

I snapped to attention. It wasn't like him to confide anything personal about his family, especially a problem he had yet to lick. And particularly when it came to Michelle. I sat up straighter but kept my eyes on the road.

Earlier that fall, Michelle had dropped out of Ricks and taken a job as a nanny in New York. She shared an apartment with Tammy, her one constant friend from high school. "But bulimia is all she did over there," he told me. Michelle had told him and her mom that she spent almost all the money she made in two months—$1,700—on food. "After work, she'd go to the store and buy cookies, ice cream, donuts—stuff like that," he said. "Then she'd go home, scarf it all down, and throw it back up. The next day, she'd do the same thing all over again." Finally, her obsession got the better of her. She quit her job and came back home.

"I don't see how she can do that to herself," he said, his thick, work-scarred fingers clutching the steering wheel. "Or why."

I shifted in my seat and tried not to buzz him with too many questions. I didn't want to scare him quiet.

"Is she getting any help, seeing a counselor or something?" I asked. I considered Mormons woefully behind the times when it came to mental health issues. Too often, I thought then, they ascribed a person's emotional imbalance to moral failings, not to a real illness or a chemical imbalance in their brain. Counselors had helped me in my struggles to find my place in the world, and I was a champion of the therapeutic process. But I doubted that Logan had very many good ones.

"Yeah. Mary took her to someone who put her on antidepressants," John said. "But I don't think they're doing any good."

It pained me to see my brother's face so drawn, his eyes uncharacteristically clouded and lost. When he was a student at Utah State University, he would come home just once during the school year, at Christmastime. He arrived long after I was in bed, but early the next morning I would creep downstairs and peer around the corner into the living room to glimpse his hunched form asleep on the couch. I inhaled the musty odor that rose from his canvas duffel bag slouched in the front hall. It hinted of adventure and faraway places.

Even before he became a Mormon, John's worldview was spread over a simple grid of black and white. The way he saw it, the only choice a person ever had was to do the right thing or the wrong thing. His bite-the-bullet approach to life went like this: when things got tough, you coped, you hung on, you rode the horse you had. That's how he made it through graduate school at Yale. That's how he became a successful salesman for Dow. That's how he ran his tree business. He was the kind of guy who would climb a tree in the middle of a windstorm to cable its forked trunks together so they wouldn't split. Who thought nothing of shepherding a gaggle of Boy Scouts through the wilderness to test their mettle, or taking on wayward kids who needed a mentor, or a roof.

But that winter his own daughter had him stymied. His experience didn't extend to murky scenarios without a clear moral signpost, such as the compulsion to gobble down copious amounts of food and then throw it all back up. I had much more tolerance for moral ambiguity than he did, but when it came to Michelle's bulimia, I felt as helpless as he seemed.

"I'll try and talk with her," I told him.

He nodded his head. "That'd be good," he said. "Maybe you'll get somewhere. We can't."

That visit was the first time I had been to their house in winter. Snow blanketed the lawn except near the woodpile, where it was stomped flat and littered with chips of bark and chunks of wood. Inside, the cast-iron stove that served as a shelf and catchall in the summer radiated warmth. The familiar jumble of papers, bills, magazines, plastic bags, books, and scattered groceries covered the kitchen table. Mary gave me a cautious hug. I felt her tensed shoulders through the weave of her sweater, and I noted the tiny lines around her mouth had deepened. She knew John had briefed me. We'd talk more later.

After several minutes, Michelle appeared in the living room from her upstairs bedroom. She had the sliver-thin body she had craved throughout high school. Her thick blonde hair veiled one side of her face. Her uncovered eye peered outward, warily, from her pinched, blank face. When we hugged, I felt like I was encircling a shadow. She made polite conversation for a few minutes, but she couldn't maintain a focus. She retreated back upstairs. Mary and I sat down in the kitchen.

"I'm at my wit's end," she said. "I don't know what else I can do." Compassion didn't work, she said. Neither did anger or dire warnings about bulimia's health effects—ruined teeth, a weakened esophagus, bad skin.

"We tried to talk to her, but she got furious and threw a bowl of oatmeal at the wall," she said, her lips compressed into a tight, quivering line. I listened, but as with John, I had nothing helpful to say. The need to prepare dinner was a welcome diversion.

Six of us sat around the table that night. Greg was in his senior year of high school and Wynlee was home from college for her Christmas break. John said grace, his arms folded across his chest in the usual Mormon prayer posture. He gave thanks for me being there. We passed around the plates of food.

Michelle was contained, polite, simmering.

"So, Aunt Alice, how do you like your new job with the magazine?" she asked. The family was aware of the patchwork of jobs—school bus driver, VW car mechanic, yard worker, secretary—I had tried over the years, and my attempts to find something for which I was better suited.

"It's great," I said. "Everything I wanted, and more." I told her about learning how to use desktop publishing software and how my palms sweated when I first set up columns and attempted to flow text.

"Cool," she said, as she picked at her food.

It was my turn to ask her a question, but I didn't dare. All the portals of communication were blocked. I couldn't ask how she liked New York City. I couldn't ask about her job as a nanny. I couldn't ask about her plans now that she was back in Logan.

Around the table forks scraped across plates. Someone asked for salt. I took a second helping.

Michelle asked to be excused as soon as she was finished and went back upstairs. Mary and I cleared the table. Greg and Wynlee left to visit friends. Once the dishes were washed, the counters wiped, the lids snapped tight on the tubs containing the leftovers, John, Mary, and I talked in the living room, trying to fill the air with something besides the silent tension that rippled through the house. After a while we heard a creak as Michelle crept downstairs and into the kitchen, just around the corner from where we were sitting. Our conversation faltered like a sputtering wick. The sound of rustling paper and the crinkling of thin, brittle plastic snaked into the living room. Earlier, Mary had explained the ritual. Michelle would ingest whatever sugary food was available—cookies, cake, ice cream. She'd finish her binge by downing a bowl of watery oatmeal and a glass of tepid water. To make the purging easier, Mary said.

After a short while we heard Michelle step toward the bathroom, just a short distance from where we were sitting.

"Oh, Michelle, please don't," Mary pleaded. The door clicked shut. John clasped his hands and stared at the floor. Mary's eyes watered. They had heard that dismal click many times before.

In my job I was used to dealing with words as symbols. I rearranged them at will, cutting and pasting them where it suited. I could say the terms bulimia, frustration, despair. But witnessing the bleak reality played out in my brother's home was another matter. I couldn't use an X-Acto knife to trim out John and Mary's pain—or Michelle's. I couldn't delete words I didn't like, or chop off what I had witnessed to make the story fit an allotted space.

Outside, the sparkling snow I had so much looked forward to lay in fluffy, white mounds. Stars I rarely saw during the Oregon winter months studded the black sky. But inside my brother's house, the season's beauty was turned inside out. During the day, John intercepted the holiday goodies dropped off by well-meaning neighbors and church members. He smiled his thanks, shut the door, then heaved the red-and-green-wrapped sweets into the trash so they couldn't feed his daughter's sickness. Mary tried gentle persuasion and exhorted Michelle to lean on her faith. "You don't have to do this," I heard her tell Michelle one morning. "Pray for the strength to control yourself." Michelle was apologetic but unmovable. "I know, Mom. I'm sorry," she answered, her voice thin and trembling. "But I have to do this. I just do. Please, please, just leave me alone."

When reason and authority didn't work, John tried force. One day he blocked Michelle's way into the kitchen. "Get out of my way. You have no right to stop me," she screamed at him, her eyes hard and angry in her white, splotched face. "You can't tell me what to do. You have no right."

Mary filled in what Michelle hadn't made clear in the letters she wrote me during her first year at Ricks. Michelle had been alienated from the college community the entire year,

Mary said. Despite southern Idaho's sharp winter wind and freezing temperatures, Michelle had insisted on wearing only a cloth coat and thin canvas shoes. By spring, she had developed panic attacks so severe that she couldn't get out of bed. Her grades plummeted. When she came home for the summer break, she spent most of her time in her room, reading scripture.

"She circled all the passages with the word 'affliction,'" Mary said. "She couldn't sleep and would go walking in the middle of the night. If I knew she was going to go out, I tried to go with her, but I didn't always know."

Six years earlier, during my extended Logan stay in 1981, I'd spent hours with John and Mary in the apple orchards he managed outside of town. After the September frosts had "set the sugar," making the apples ready for harvest, he, Mary, and I drove to the orchards in the early mornings to pick. We climbed tall, three-legged fruit ladders and reached into the branches to grab the frosty, glistening fruit—Red Delicious, Yellow Delicious, red-and-green striped Macintosh, and ruby-red Jonathans. We dropped the apples into the canvas pouches that hung from our necks like giant external stomachs. When they were full, we climbed down, waddled to the truck, positioned our swollen sacks over a box, and released the apples in a loud, luscious tumble of red and yellow.

I came to know the trees intimately that fall, grasping my hands around their rough, gray bark, balancing my weight in the fork of their branches, and breathing in the scent of their dry, powdery leaves. My spine grew stronger and more supple as I stretched to grasp one perfect apple after another. I used my legs until they shook with fatigue and I had worked up an honest hunger. Back at Center Street, we sorted the apples and packed them into boxes. On Fridays we stacked the boxes in the bed of the pickup truck. Saturday mornings I drove the truck to a busy corner in downtown Logan, parked, and set up my sign. People crowded around and I raked in the dollars. At the end of each Saturday I proudly handed John a thick pile of bills.

By the time the harvest was done that fall, I was patched up and ready to face my life back in Oregon. I knew whatever happened there, the Logan crew had my back. I had been grateful to John and Mary ever since. On that Christmas trip in 1987, feeling strong and centered, I wanted to repay their kindness. But once I arrived, I, too, was stymied. John and Mary didn't say so outright, but I knew they thought Michelle and I had a special bond. I felt they hoped I might extract some nugget of information from her they couldn't access, some explanation for the obsession that now ruled her life. I was cowed by the responsibility. I had seen the determination in Michelle's jaw, heard the ragged desperation in her voice. She showed little inclination to talk with me. This wasn't the witty, wry Michelle I had come to cherish, whose writing I admired, whose insights impressed me. I didn't know this rude, angry, self-destructive Michelle. I didn't know how to talk with her. I didn't know if she would tolerate me trying.

On the morning of the planned trip to the mountain yurt, we piled cross-country skis, supplies, and backpacks into the pickup. Michelle stayed behind at Center Street. Wynlee and Greg, a sunny guy who tended not to get caught up in family drama, followed us in a second car as we drove up the canyon. At the trailhead we buckled into our skis and hefted the packs onto our backs. Greg and Wynlee sprinted ahead. John, Mary, and I pushed on. We made a bedraggled trio. I wasn't used to the five-thousand-foot elevation, and my breath soon turned short and ragged. John was getting over the flu, and he, too, stopped often to lean on his poles and gasp. Mary shuffled through the ski ruts. Her joints bore the burden of her emotional stress, and her shoulders, knees, and ankles protested the unaccustomed effort. We arrived at the yurt as the last of the day's light slipped from the sky. Greg and Wynlee had lit the stove and some lamps, and the yurt was a beacon of welcome in the midst of the blackening forest. We fixed dinner and ate quickly. No one mentioned Michelle, but she was on our minds. We turned in early.

I woke the next morning surrounded by an immense silence. Outside, newly fallen snow lay knee-deep in the woods under a crystalline blue sky. After breakfast, Mary and Greg skied back to the car. Wynlee, John, and I took off for the promised cross-country ski tour. We cut through the drifts, arcing between the sparse trees and down the mounded slopes. Wynlee leaned into her telemark turns with grace and confidence. John, less graceful but managing to stay upright, followed in her tracks. I tried my best to keep up. I was finally on the trip I had expected, but by then sliding through the dry, powdery snow seemed like a surreal blip, as if someone had inserted the wrong reel into a movie I was watching. The visuals didn't sync up with the plot. The story line had forked and twisted.

The last night of my visit I went upstairs and knocked on Michelle's bedroom door. "Do you have a minute to talk?" I asked.

She invited me in. She was lying in her bed in the dimly lit room, her body barely making a bulge beneath the covers. I sat near the foot of the bed, being careful not to touch her—since I had arrived, everything that emanated from her signaled "stay away." I didn't bother with ice-breaking patter—she knew what I was after and took the lead.

"I know it looks bad, but I do it because I have to," she said, her voice unapologetic. "It's what gets me through the day.

I don't know what I would do without it." As she spoke, she ran her hands through the lining of a pair of gloves I had brought to show her. Her fingers gently probed and stroked the thick, furry pile. I remembered she had once loved rabbits.

She was running from something, she admitted. It had surfaced a few years back. "I had this nightmare. It was in the middle of the night. I woke up. A face was staring at me from the window," she said. "It was white and huge and terrifying. It meant something horrible, but I didn't know what." She looked beyond me when she spoke, as if trying to find on the wall behind me the words that would convey the enormity of her fear.

"It feels like the face is a part of me. Or knows something terrible about me. Something secret and bad," she said. "Throwing up helps keep it away."

I scrutinized her face. A blotch of red bloomed high on each of her pale cheeks. Her blue eyes stared past me at something only she could see. For years I had believed I could relate to the inner disquiet she had talked about when we were together. But I could not follow her down this path. I couldn't relate to the fear she had expressed. Or to what she did to control it.

The distance between us on that bed was whisper-thin and a chasm wide. I shifted my weight and tried to reach across it.

"So, does talking with your counselor help at all?" I asked. She shook her head. "He's OK," she said. "But he doesn't really get it."

I tried another tack, one that had brought us together in the past: a story.

"Have you ever read *The Little Unicorn*?" I asked her. She stared down at the gloves in her hand and barely shook her head. "This young, beautiful unicorn is being stalked by a fierce, red-eyed demon," I told her. "She's terrified. She runs from him for days, but he pursues her. She runs and runs until she's exhausted, but the monster won't give up." I couldn't tell if I sounded ridiculous or preachy. She looked up at me a few times. I felt like I was offering a Band-Aid to a person with blood spurting from an arterial wound, but it was all I had. "After days of running, when she is close to death, she finally turns around and stares the demon in the face. And that's what broke its power over her," I told Michelle. "She faced him. That's what the unicorn had to do to set herself free."

Michelle stared into her lap. "That's what she had to do," I repeated. "Face it."

Michelle was quiet for a bit, then spoke to me like an elderly person does to a young child who tries to be helpful, but cannot fathom the depth of the elder's discomfort or isolation.

"Being able to throw up is the one thing I've got," she repeated, her voice quiet but firm. "It's my best friend. I don't want to stop."

Years later I spoke with a friend who had been bulimic for decades and was trying to stop. "I'm in mourning," she told me. "It's always been there for me. It's been my best friend." But back then, I saw only the repulsive, obsessive side of bulimia. I didn't know purging relieved stress and produced a brief, but intoxicating, endorphin high. The idea of it being Michelle's "best friend" made no sense to me.

"OK," I said, quietly. "OK." I didn't push. I didn't want to turn parental. I wanted to maintain our connection, no matter how tenuous. "But keep talking to your counselor, please? He might turn out to be helpful." She nodded and handed the gloves back to me.

"Thanks, Aunt Alice," she said, as I turned to leave her room. "Thanks for coming."

Years later I spoke at length with Tammy, the friend Michelle had lived with in New York. The two of them had shared a one-bedroom apartment. Tammy explained that she had slept in the bedroom and Michelle had slept in the living room on a trundle bed. "There wasn't a sound she made that I didn't hear," Tammy said, answering the question I hadn't yet posed.

At first, the two often stayed up late talking, as they had in high school. Like me, Tammy appreciated Michelle's acute observations of the world, her philosophical bent, and her keen wit. But by then there were two Michelles, and Tammy couldn't reach the second one. "We talked about the usual things—friendship, our opinions and philosophies," she told me. "But then, an hour later, she'd go into the bathroom and turn herself inside out. She would cry and retch and sob. And there was nothing I could do."

One night early that December, Michelle's retching sounded deeper and more desperate than Tammy had heard before. She pleaded with Michelle to let her in the bathroom. Michelle was adamant she be left alone. Tammy insisted.

"Finally Michelle screamed, 'Help me, God. Help me, God. Someone help me,'" Tammy told me. "She opened the door and fell into my arms."

Tammy wrapped Michelle in a thick red quilt and held her. For hours. "She was so emaciated that, when I hugged her, the only thing I could feel was bone and skin. Every time a cry came out of her mouth, it was the cry of a wounded mother animal that had lost her children. There was nothing that could comfort her." The next day, Tammy convinced Michelle she had to go back home.

The morning after my talk with Michelle I said a wrenching goodbye to Mary, begging her to keep in touch. John drove me to the Salt Lake airport. Our parting hug was silent and brief. On Christmas I had given them the lampshade I had been so enamored with, and they had expressed genuine appreciation. But by then the cheerful garlands of pressed pink and lavender petals seemed sadly naïve and beside the point.

I flew home in coach, jammed in a planeload of holiday-sated travelers. Portland greeted me with clouds, rain, and a sky the shade of faded metal. The encroaching nightfall made for a grueling two-hour drive south. A major trucking route, Interstate 5 was usually crowded with a stream of massive semis, day and night. I was familiar with the traffic from my weekday commutes. When I started at my job, the days were long and I enjoyed driving through the acres of farmlands and pastures on my way to and from work. But once the days shortened and the fall rains began, I came to detest the hour-long drive back home. Over and over I would find myself behind a churning semi whose spinning tires kicked up water from the road and splattered it onto the windshield of my low-slung compact. The spray of dirty water made it difficult for me to see, even with my wipers on high. I could stay behind the truck and endure the spray or try to get ahead of it. But each time I approached a semi's cab to pass, there were several seconds when the backwash of dirt, rain, and water obliterated my view. I felt unmoored in those few seconds, as if I were plunging full-speed into a territory without knowing its borders or the lay of the land. My gut inclination was to brake and pull back, but in order to get to a place where I could see clearly, I had to will myself through that blurred patch of nothingness. No way to go but forward. No matter how many trucks I passed, I never got used to the sensation of being momentarily ungrounded and at the mercy of blind trust.

On the drive back to Eugene after that trip to Logan, the sense of skidding across the road each time I passed one of the massive trucks was even more pronounced. I turned my windshield wipers to high. Every time I pulled up alongside a churning, splashing semi to pass, I clutched the steering wheel in a death grip. I muttered a short, demanding prayer that something would get me safely to the other side of the blur and blackness I was about to pass through.

chapter 7
wedding day

One morning in early January 1988, a few weeks after I returned from my Christmas trip to Logan, Michelle drove to her psychiatrist's office in Logan and told him she was moving to Salt Lake City. She drove back home, walked into the kitchen, dug through John's tool drawer, and grabbed a hammer. Two days earlier, she had broken all the glasses in the kitchen. This time she strode into the living room, pulled back her pale, bony arm, and swung the hammer into the television set. She brought the hammer down again. And again. When the television screen was in pieces, she turned her sights on a mirror, then to the framed pictures on the wall. She smashed anything that could reflect her face.

John and Mary came home to a living room littered with shards of glass. When they tried to talk with Michelle, she picked up a knife, waved it at them, then pointed it at herself. Her parents called the police. Michelle collapsed in a fit of weeping. She agreed to be admitted to the Behavioral Health Unit at Logan Regional Hospital.

It was weeks before I heard about Michelle's hospitalization. In the beginning of her deterioration, John and Mary kept details about her situation private. Not to be secretive, I think, but because they were so confounded by Michelle's psychological state. It was a pale sort of blessing that they delayed telling me. I would have felt even more at a loss for how to help than I already did.

The admitting psychiatrist at the Behavioral Health Unit was the same one Michelle had fired the previous day. He knew her history. "The client feels hateful towards her parents because they tell her what to do. She felt a need to destroy property to assert her will with her parents and to show them the hate she has for them, and towards herself, " he wrote on the admission report. He described her as "very verbal, perceptive, filled with anger . . . She states that her problem is, 'I need people, but I don't trust them.'"

He described John as analytical and intellectual, and Mary as overprotective and over-reactive. "Both parents are very controlling and advice-giving with the daughter, feeling that she is never able to measure up or have control of her own life," he wrote.

Years later when I read his report, I felt a prickly indignation. Of course John and Mary were controlling and advice-giving. They had been dealing with Michelle's volatility for years. Now her mental health was disintegrating for reasons no one could explain. None of the professionals they had turned to, or the drugs they had prescribed, had helped her. Instead, she had turned destructive. What were their options?

Although the behavioral unit strictly regimented her food intake, Michelle made a point to inform her caregivers that, once back out on her own, she had no intention of giving up her daily binges and purges. "My bulimia produces a level of satisfaction rather than [me] being miserable and helpless," she told an occupational therapist. "It is a matter of expression to me."

She remained on the unit for three weeks. In her discharge interview she told her psychiatrist what he wanted to hear: she would move home until she could find an apartment; she would volunteer at a community agency and work toward returning to school. Instead, she moved back home and continued to roil the Center Street household with her demands and emotional outbursts. She made no attempt to corral her bingeing.

The two letters I received from her that spring were from the "other" Michelle, the one I had first glimpsed at Christmas. Her tone rang with defiance and rancor. Before her hospitalization I had seen my niece as a victim of unnamed fears and an obsession she couldn't shake. But the letters she wrote after her breakdown showed me another side of her—a self-righteous child rebelling against parental authority and seemingly proud of it. She was beginning to make me angry.

"We're stuck with a $10,000 hospital bill—$500 a day for a chance to analyze the workings of a mental health care unit," she wrote. "It was strictly behavioristic. I was not impressed. I don't like being treated like an organism who hasn't learned to press the right levers or hit the right buttons. When actually I am this living human being who has a glorious time throwing up and making her family miserable and chaotic, and unbalancing people right and left. For deep, psychological reasons that are unfathomable."

Later I discovered from reading Michelle's medical records that one of Michelle's many diagnoses was borderline personality disorder, a psychological condition with a host of symptoms that include unpredictable mood swings, impulsive behavior, instability in relationships, and feelings of emptiness. People with this disorder are experts at provoking others, experts say, and tend to have extreme reactions to seemingly trivial comments or external events. "The attacks can be brutal, pushing away those they care most about," wrote one author.

I didn't know about that diagnosis, but I knew Michelle was severely bulimic. Throughout the long Oregon winter I tried to find out everything I could about it. At the time, I thought bulimia was Michelle's biggest problem, and I wanted to learn about it and share what I learned with her. I perused library shelves and magazine indexes for information. I called sorority housemothers and local therapists for interviews, telling them I was doing research for an article, even though I wasn't. The issues underlying bulimia, I learned, had to do with self-image and control. The eating disorder was usually temporary, but sometimes it became a fixation. Treatment approaches varied and no one method had emerged as key to breaking the bulimia cycle.

Questions reeled through my mind as I navigated up and down I-5 through the winter's unceasing mist and rain, pulling abreast of unending semis, accelerating into the watery night. The dots didn't match up. Nothing I read explained Michelle's panicked obsession with being able to binge and purge as a way of life. Nothing spoke about a young woman using bulimia to control a nameless terror. Nothing about it becoming her "best friend."

After Michelle had spent a few months at home, John and Mary agreed to pay her portion of the rent on an apartment she moved into with two other young women. As she had in Idaho, she refused to wear warm clothes, despite the cold northern Utah winter. "It was so painful to see her walking around town in that pitifully thin jacket and those canvas shoes, her shoulders hunched up against the cold," Mary wrote me. "She was like the walking dead." Michelle landed a babysitting job that paid for her binge stash. She wrote me saying she had developed enough control that she didn't have to worry about eating her employers' or her roommates' food. "Slowly, in all this pathologicalness, a conscience is forming, or maybe values or a moral or two."

I sent Michelle a book on bulimia, *The Hungry Self*, that I thought offered some good insights. She wrote a letter thanking me. "I think it has valid points," she wrote, but it was clear from her tone she was keeping both me and the book at arm's length. She didn't want to ditch her "best friend." She was seeing a therapist at a mental health clinic in Logan who wasn't a specialist in eating disorders but whom she trusted, she told me. She added that her social life had perked up. By the spring, a young man was taking her on hikes and motorcycle rides. She told him she had gone through a nervous breakdown and that she didn't like being touched. He was OK with it, she wrote. "He has a high opinion of me; you have no idea how wonderful it is to be treated so well—for just being myself!"

That was the Michelle I was familiar with, but a few sentences later the other Michelle surfaced, arch and haughty. "I have a picture, really clear, of what this family would be like if I was not a member," she wrote. "A lot smoother, calm, a peaceful coexistence among strangers. But here I am and I intend to shake everyone up and make them think instead of just live."

I suspect now that, underneath her defensiveness, Michelle felt cornered. She was nineteen, an age when many teenagers are growing into their identity and breaking away from their parents and family. Her family—and the Mormon Church—set high standards of achievement for young adults. Wynlee had for years planned to become a veterinarian, and had the grades and drive to achieve her goal. Greg was popular, did well in school, and planned to embark on the two-year mission that young Mormon men make in their late teens and early twenties. But

Michelle was hobbled by her emotional instability, the amount of time and money her bulimia demanded, and her inability to manage her life. As smart as she was, she undoubtedly felt like a failure. She used what she had—words, drama, purging—to grab whatever power she could.

"My eating is the same as always: terrible," she wrote. "I'm keeping Greg and Wynlee shook up and on their toes with my efforts to control my eating (there aren't any). They're around more than Mom and Dad so they know how bad I'm doing. I'm careful not to enlighten them—they wouldn't be so complacent as they are. I'm working things out. Ha ha."

Maybe it was the "Ha ha" that pushed me to act. I remembered the cords of tension that wound around the Logan household during my December visit. I recalled her illogical rants about why she should be able to eat and throw up as much as she pleased. I saw again the furrows in John's and Mary's pained faces. I had witnessed Michelle's refusal or inability to acknowledge the effect she was having on them. Maybe she was sick, but she was also acting like a jerk.

I wrote her back, challenging her. It was such unfamiliar territory for me that I kept a copy of the letter. Maybe I had an intuition that I would want to remember the words I had written. In the letter, I told her I loved her and that her bulimia didn't—and wouldn't—change that. But I insisted she take responsibility for it.

"I am upset, not because of the bulimia, but because you are not dealing with it," I wrote. "You say people's lack of respect hurts you, but we always respond most violently when we suspect a core of truth in someone else's words. Are you respecting the way you are treating yourself? Or are you letting it make you a victim so you 'can't deal with it'?

"I do not for one minute believe you are crazy or insane. I have a reliable sense of what crazy is. You are unique but not crazy. 'Crazy' is just a word to hide behind. It says, 'If I am crazy, I don't have to take responsibility for abdicating my life to bulimia.'

"You have to look at yourself square in the mirror, face whatever it is that keeps you hooked into behavior that is inhibiting your development as a person. You cannot be doing OK in your life if you are still throwing up. No one can live a lie to themselves or others without paying the psychic price, especially someone as fundamentally honest as yourself."

Now, reading my words, I wince at my arrogant certainty. Back then, I had a deep need to be right, possibly because the universe of things I actually knew something about was so limited. I tried to rein in the tendency, but when it came to mental illness, I thought I had a certain depth of experience. In college I had read books by trendy radical therapists who explored the condition of schizophrenia from a cultural and family perspective. I was fascinated with the idea that some people with schizophrenia or other mental illnesses might be attuned to a higher level of consciousness, and that was why they couldn't handle the complexities of everyday life. After graduating I had spent a year as an aide at a community mental health unit in Boston, where the patients I worked with suffered from mental illnesses including schizophrenia and what then was termed manic-depressive disease. I had witnessed irrational frenzies and delusional thinking. I thought I knew something about psychological states, about what was and wasn't "crazy."

Maybe I knew something, but it wasn't nearly enough.

I sent the letter. As I feared, she didn't respond. It chafed that she wouldn't accept my insights. She shunted them aside just as she did her parents' attempts to help her. Each of us used what we had to try and reach her. Each of us fell far short.

Mary wrote me that Michelle had moved back home for a few months, left again, returned. That fall she was admitted to the hospital after threatening to commit suicide. Mary had finally accepted that her daughter was very ill; she groped for the reason why.

"Michelle is in bad shape. I doubt anything will budge her from home. She is still deeply angry and resentful but needs the support we offer," Mary wrote in her journal a few weeks before Michelle's suicide threat. "She earns between $150 and $200 a month babysitting and spends it all on food. I no longer react with such physical pain to her problem, but when I hear the water running in the middle of the night my whole body flushes with emotion. . . . She no longer attends church. She is angry at God and everybody else."

And a few paragraphs later: "I have felt, and still feel, that she is possessed," Mary wrote, "but I am alone with that opinion and not strong enough to do anything about it."

I am sure she never shared this fear with Michelle. She wrote this entry several months before Michelle began experiencing her "memories," before the hysteria over satanic abuse would erupt into their lives. Perhaps Mary was prescient. Or perhaps the social panic I had yet to learn about had already begun to creep into her consciousness. Or perhaps her faith gave her no other alternative for the source of her daughter's obsession.

In April 1989 I received a letter from Michelle, the first she had sent in several months. I tore it open eagerly, hoping she had made some sort of breakthrough.

She had, but it wasn't the one I had hoped for.

"A few weeks ago some things happened that enabled me to tell Greg something that I have never told a soul, and for seven years had not even admitted happened to myself," her letter began.

Her tiny, cramped writing slid down the page as if pulled by a heavy weight.

"When I was thirteen, I was walking home from the roller-skating rink at night and I was raped by four boys in Central Park. One of them I knew, and he knew me," she wrote. "They told me I was only good for fucking, that I wanted it, that I started it—all these vile things they said to me. The whole thing was so utterly shocking and horrifying to me that I decided it didn't happen." She also decided to never tell her parents.

Even though she had buried the memory, she took on as truth the words the boys had flung at her. "I believed every single thing they said," she wrote. "I knew I could never tell anyone, that I would be silent forever on this, and because of that, I would always be alone. No one would know who I really was except for those four boys."

To keep from facing her soiled identity, she immersed herself in Mormonism, she wrote. (And bulimia, I thought to myself.) The dodge allowed her to function until she fell apart in New York City. "A tremendous deal of pain was always with me, and I never knew why," she wrote. "I never knew why I could be so alone and unable to be reached or helped, or why everything was so hard."

After I finished reading the letter, I turned it over and read it again. Outside, spring was displaying its fullness. Lilac buds swelled on the backyard bush. The cedar tree in my patch of front yard sported vibrant green shoots. But by the time I had reread every word of Michelle's sloping script, the fresh, eager spring had turned cold and brittle. It didn't matter that the violation had occurred years earlier. It didn't matter that now there was a likely explanation for her bulimia and why she had clung to it for so many years. I wanted to scream or rip something apart, but there was no one around to hear and nothing to shred.

It would be years before I would think to question the

veracity of Michelle's story, to wonder whether it was yet another ratcheting up of her personal drama, another desperate grasp for attention and control, or maybe to explain the self-hate she had wrestled with for years. Back then I accepted her story as true, as did her parents and the therapist she was seeing. I don't remember if I called John and Mary right away or if I waited. I'm sure I wrote Michelle back—quickly, briefly—expressing my sympathy for what happened, for her having to carry this burden for so long. The words of her letter weighed heavy on my heart, settling there like muck.

The following month I traveled to Cincinnati for the wedding of my eldest brother's daughter, who was just a few years older than Michelle. Family members had flown in from all over the East Coast for the event, and we were staying in the same motel. John and Mary came and, to my surprise, had brought along Michelle. As we were sorting out our rooms, I caught a glimpse of her and waved.

Later, I met John on the sidewalk outside the motel. I hugged him, cautiously. "I know about the rape," I said. "I am so sorry." He said nothing, just nodded his head. His eyes looked beyond me and into the distance. He asked me if I had spoken with Michelle. I told him not yet.

"Talk to her, if you can," he said.

The next day, the morning of the ceremony, I met up with Michelle to go for a walk in a nearby park. We headed out into the bright, late spring morning. She wore a simple flowered dress over her thin body. Her shoulders sagged in their characteristic, world-weary slope. Her thick blonde hair hid half her face. She peered out at the world as if from behind a drape.

We walked in sync, our legs fitting each other's stride. We began by trading niceties, but that didn't last long.

"You know that letter I wrote you?" she asked. I nodded. A swell of compassion rose in my throat. How could I forget it?

"Well, there's more."

"More? Of what?"

"I've had more memories," she said. "About other bad stuff that happened."

"What bad stuff do you mean?" I asked.

"Well, I was in a therapy group at the hospital and I began having these . . . these memories. Like flashbacks."

"Flashbacks about what?"

"Of being abused. By other people. Not just those boys, I mean. It began a long time ago, when I was a kid."

"Abused? But by who?" I tried to calm the alarm in my voice. This was not the conversation I had expected us to have.

"I don't know who, exactly, " she said. "They were part of a cult. They were Satanists."

It was as if she had begun speaking in an alien dialect. I needed her to slow down. Way down. I took a breath.

"What on earth are you talking about?"

"Satanists. You know. People who worship Satan. People who do bad stuff, like hurting babies and kids and doing rituals and stuff."

They say the body grasps an emotional blow before the mind does. Mine did. I felt a lightness, as if gravity had suddenly let loose. Then a sucking down. Then nausea. The incomprehensible phrases ricocheted through my mind. A satanic cult? In Logan? In what I considered God's country?

If I had been paying more attention to the outside world, I would have been aware of the supposed uptick in satanic activity that had been reported around the country during the mid-1980s. But I hadn't seen the television talk shows on ritual

abuse. I hadn't watched the news segments on devil worship-
pers. I was marginally aware of the tawdry headlines about the
burgeoning McMartin Preschool case in California, where the
day care workers were accused of progressively more heinous
and debasing abuse of the children in their care. I didn't know
the charges had included satanic ritual abuse—I had never even
heard the term used. I certainly didn't know that the belief in
ritual abuse that had begun spreading in the early years of the
decade had, by the late 1980s, reached a full boil, or that the
existence of satanic cults that preyed on untold numbers of
children and young women was being taken in many communities as a given, not as rumor-driven paranoia. I didn't know
about the other childcare workers who were on trial or had
been convicted of grisly ritual abuse of their child clients. (1) I
didn't know that, for the most part, the media had aligned itself
against the accused, no matter how flimsy the evidence against
them. I didn't know that one journalist would later dub 1988 "a
seminal year" in the spread of the ritual abuse panic. I didn't
know any of it.

My thoughts whirled as I tried to relate to what Michelle was
saying. Words spilled from my mouth as if they could somehow dilute Michelle's horrific tale. "But . . . how could they have
done that?" I choked out. "Why you? And how could your parents not have known?"

She was ready with the answers. It had gone on since she
was a child, she said. They had come for her at night. They took
her to dim, secret places. They had sex with her. They hurt her
and made her hurt others. She remembered blood and sacrifices. She spoke in a deadly calm voice.

Outside of the tight net of words that enveloped us, I could
hear children playing on nearby swings. Birds chirped from the

leafy branches over our heads. I didn't look up. The ground beneath my feet felt tilted. I tried to hold on to her words one at a time. Sacrifices. Sex. Cult. Blood.

The memories were so horrible she had buried them in the back of her mind, she told me. But now they had surfaced. They came like darts—fast, sharp, and terrifying. Then they faded away. She couldn't hold on to faces, names, or places. The boys who attacked her may have been part of it. She wasn't sure.

As we circled the park, Michelle explained that now she understood what she had been fleeing from for so many years. But the realization didn't bring her any relief. She lived in a thicket of fear. She couldn't be alone. Her mom slept in her room at night because "they" might come back and Michelle was terrified she wouldn't be able to resist their power.

"I know it sounds unbelievable, but it happened," she said, her voice flat and matter-of-fact. "They warn us that, if we tell, people won't believe us. They'll think we're crazy."

I struggled to find something solid to hold on to. Could she be crazy? At the time, I wasn't ready to admit that. Traumatized, yes. A buried, forgotten rape can fester, break open, create chaos in someone's life. But abuse by Satanists? Taken away in the night? Ritual sacrifices? Impossible. But, I also thought, Michelle must have gone through something unspeakable— didn't her bulimia prove that? And these last few emotionally fraught years?

Right then, absolute truth didn't matter, I decided. The young woman in the cotton dress in front of me did.

I took a breath. "I'm so very sorry, Michelle, that this happened to you," I said, looking directly at her. I didn't allow a sliver of doubt to infect my tone. She nodded slightly and thanked me. We walked along the path back to the motel. My left arm could have brushed her thinner, whiter right arm, but I didn't let it. I considered her fragile as ash.

There are moments when you feel your personal world shift on its axis. Something in you realizes that life as you know it has irrevocably changed, that you will, from that moment forward, see the world through a drastically altered lens. This was one. As we walked back to the motel, I kept my eyes fixed on the cement path as if to keep me from sliding over some invisible edge.

A few hours later Michelle and I stood next to each other in the stately Catholic church where her cousin was being married. We got to our feet as the attendants and the white-draped bride walked up the aisle and took their places to hear Mass. I had rejected the belief behind the familiar words of the Catholic communion ritual, but the words had never before made me flinch. That day they intoned with a skewed resonance: *The body and blood of Christ. Washed in the blood of the lamb. Take this and eat.* I recalled how a priest at my childhood church used to end one prayer asking for protection from Satan, "who roams through the world seeking the ruin of souls."

When the ceremony closed, I kept a close eye on Michelle as her just-married cousin floated down the aisle, her tall, handsome husband by her side, her fairy-tale dress billowing with lace and netting and hope. Michelle barely moved, just flashed a shy smile. At that moment, I couldn't imagine Michelle walking down an aisle, her arm looped securely around the arm of a new husband, both of them fixed on the rosy future before them. She had slipped into a world few could—or would be willing to— share. I knew she must have felt utterly alienated from the scene she was watching. I knew I could do nothing to change that.

When it was our pew's turn to file out, I gripped the wooden bench in front of me, stood up, and followed Michelle out of the church to stand in the line to congratulate the happy newlyweds.

chapter 8
another michelle remembers

In June of 1989, two months after Michelle's implausible disclosure, I was back on the road heading to Logan. I chose to take the slower, northeastern route out of the Willamette Valley that winds over the Cascades, through the pine and juniper forests of Central Oregon, then skims along the ranch lands that reach to the Idaho border. I had taken the route so often by then that the sweeping curves and jagged, river-sliced gorges had become like friends. I knew which turnout offered the best vista of the spreading sagebrush hills, and where I could pull over to let out the dogs and cool my feet in a shady stream. I knew at what point I'd need to fidget, pinch my arms, and slap my face to fight off the bleary numbness that descended in midafternoon like a feathery dream.

I wasn't sure what I could do or say that could help John, Mary, or Michelle, but I wanted to try. The rape explained so much—her bulimia, her need for control, her ever-present anxiety. But I didn't believe her bizarre memories of being abused by what she said was a cult. I didn't know where they came from, but there was nothing to them—of that I was confident. Surely they were distortions created by years of repression and a desperate need to make sense of her wounded psyche.

A few weeks before I left for Utah, I had quit my job with the trade magazine, where I had grown restless and discontent. I had moved out of my shabby duplex and stashed my belongings in a friend's basement. It was time for a change, but I wasn't sure what direction to take. Before I went to journalism school, I had considered becoming a counselor, and in the late 1980s it certainly seemed there was a need for it. Most of my friends were seeing therapists, probing their pasts and digging up forgotten memories that would help explain their lingering anger, self-sabotaging behaviors, or fears of intimacy. When we got together, we didn't talk about politics, but instead about our childhoods and our unhealed wounds. Michelle's rape memory was extreme, but some of my friends, too, were recalling incidents of past sex abuse, which I believed had occurred. At the time, I had no idea that the therapeutic trend of probing the past for forgotten incidents of child sexual abuse was a facet of what was called the recovered memory movement. Like so much else, it would take years for me to see how the concept of recovered memory was related to the panic I was trying to understand, and to the memories that Michelle insisted were true. But back then, driving through the high desert landscape, I didn't question the therapeutic process. I told myself that as a counselor I could make a difference, not just write stories. I could help people live fuller lives. And I would begin with Michelle.

I sped along through the Ochoco Mountains, pumped up with my self-appointed mission. Noble ponderosa pines stood like sentries along both sides of the road. I rolled down the windows, breathing in the fresh mountain air. I kept an eye out for coyotes. Once along this route I had spotted one standing in a field, its slim, rufous head cocked and wary.

After several hours, I stopped for gas in the small mountain town of John Day. "What'll it be?" asked the capped gas station attendant.

"Fill it with regular," I said. I gave the dogs some water and stretched my back while they slurped away their thirst.

"Looks like you're on a trip," the attendant said, eyeing the tapes, maps, and water bottles piled in the passenger seat.

I was grateful for the superficial, anonymous banter that came with being on the road. "Yeah," I said. "On our way to Utah. Not enough space here in Oregon for the three of us."

I paid for the gas, bought a beer to drink during dinner, called the dogs, and drove into the nearby Malheur National Forest. Near the top of a steep pass I pulled into a familiar campground, let out the dogs, and set up my tent. We took a walk along a cushioned, pine-needled path that eased into an open pine forest. The dogs scurried from the base of one tree to another, intoxicated by strange, enticing smells. Back at our site, I fired up my camp stove to heat soup for dinner. I soaked in the simplicity of hunger, the waning light, my frosty beer.

The next morning, sunlight spread over the roof of my tent. I crawled out into the damp, sharp air and lit the stove to heat water for tea. Birds warbled unseen in the tops of the pines. Insects chirped from their hidden perches. I cupped my hands around my steaming mug of tea and lifted it to my lips. I wanted the moment to last forever.

Back on the road I descended out of the pine forest and into open pasture and farmland. Tractors kicked up dust in the fields. Cows huddled under clumps of leafy cottonwoods. Irrigated rows of crops shone green in the morning light. I crossed the border into Idaho, caught Interstate 84, and sped eastward along the state's broad southern base. My musings shifted in the harsher light of the late morning sun. It seemed glaringly wrong that I was once again unemployed and homeless, and yet had convinced

myself I could somehow help Michelle feel better, something neither John, Mary, nor a string of therapists had been able to do. I
was unsparing in grilling myself. Was I running toward her so I
could run from myself? What tools did I have to ease her emotional pain, or her bizarre memories? Who did I think I was?

I shifted in my seat and pressed on the accelerator. The
landscape stretched out flat, brown and empty on both sides of
the highway. The ache in my lower back had returned, throbbing either a warning or a remonstrance. My eyes burned from
the dry air and the bleached-out sky. Several hours after leaving
my peaceful campsite, I came to the exit for Utah. I flicked on
my turn signal and headed south.

When I arrived at Center Street, the Logan household looked
and felt familiar. The backyard grass was its usual lush, velvety
green. The family dog was tethered under a leafy tree near the
haphazard woodpile. The porch was littered with the familiar
jumble of lawn tools, muddy sneakers, fruit boxes, tennis balls
and bags of feed. The kitchen displayed its perennial clutter,
and the small living room with its stuffed chairs and scattered
books exuded a familiar, welcoming warmth.

Unlike the previous Christmas, when the atmosphere in
the house crackled with Michelle's combustible rage, the prevail-
ing mood during that visit was somber. Mary spoke in hushed,
pained tones. John, when he was home, was stern and focused.
Michelle spent hours huddled on the living room couch, an
oversized T-shirt and sweatpants engulfing her bony frame. Her
three anchors—her journal, the Bible, her Book of Mormon—lay
within close reach. "She is trying to figure out what God really is
to her," I wrote in a letter to one of my sisters. "Half the time she
is enraged at what she sees as God's abandonment of her. The rest
of the time she wants desperately to have that force on her side."

As painful and upsetting as Michelle's disclosure about the rape was, it gave John and Mary an explanation for their daughter's obsessive need for control, her rages, and her determination to hang on to her bulimia. It also provided a course of action—to identify and confront the perpetrators. But Michelle was foggy as to details. One night, Mary rounded up several high school yearbooks, and she and Michelle sat at the kitchen table poring over them. I was sitting in the living room, and I couldn't help but overhear them.

"Are any of these faces familiar? Do you remember any of these boys being there?" Mary asked, pointing at a photograph.

"Red hair. I remember one of them had red hair," Michelle said, her voice small and tentative.

"But which boy?" Mary pressed, naming two names. Michelle looked closely at the photos on the pages. "I think it was him," she said, pointing to one. She, too, wanted clarity. But the rape had occurred almost a decade earlier. By then, too many memories were colliding in her brain. She paused and looked away. "But I'm not sure, Mom. I'm just not sure."

John and Mary had reported the rape to the police. Later John told me he had gone to the homes of two of the boys Michelle thought were among those who attacked her. One father turned him away. The other father listened, but said he needed more information. I don't know if the responses eased John or frustrated him. At least he had been able to do something.

Michelle still binged, but her eating wasn't the focus it had been. Her disclosure about the rape had impacted John. He was less critical of her and more compassionate. He and Michelle engaged in conversations instead of sparring. Sometimes she chuckled at his jokes. He was silent about her memories of ritual abuse. He gave them wide berth, like he would an angry badger or a tree with hidden thorns.

Michelle's flashbacks of cult abuse were brief, terrifying

images of bloody sacrifices, tortured animals, and depraved sexual acts. When she spoke of those who hurt her, her eyes were steady and her voice rang with certainty. "They got me in the neck," she told me one day while she was sitting on the couch. She had stretched out the necklines of all her T-shirts, and they sagged loosely over her sharp, thin collarbones. "That's how they made me do things. They hurt me." She jabbed her index finger toward her neck. "Here. In the neck."

To me, Michelle's memories of abuse by a cult resembled a twisted, medieval fantasy—only later would I understand the 1980s social panic had a history reaching back centuries—not anything that had actually occurred. But in the few short months since Michelle had begun recalling her ritual abuse memories, Mary had, to my dismay, come to believe them. To her, the memories and the horrific reality they depicted—along with the rape—answered questions that had plagued her for years. Now she knew why Michelle's behavior had been so strange, so anguished. Now the bulimia made sense.

By the time of my visit, Mary had acquired a wealth of information about the "cult"—she was vague about her sources, but by then the topic had become media fodder—and in her mind it loomed epic and terrifyingly real. The cult was hugely powerful and incredibly savvy, she told me. Cult members were committed to spreading evil and to recruiting the innocent and unwary into its sinister fold. Few people understood how vastly powerful the cult was. She shared more details during our nightly walks around the edges of Logan, or when we were sitting around the kitchen table. "They are everywhere, but nobody realizes it. They pretend they are like everyone else. That's why nobody knows they're there," she said. The fact that no one wanted to believe the cult existed helped it to flourish. Nobody was putting up a fight.

Mary and I occupied opposite ends of the political spectrum. I could be staunch in what I believed, but Mary came close to being ferocious. She was a fan of conservative radio talk shows—she was a loyal Rush Limbaugh fan—and she listened intently as he used his soapbox to sow fears of a misguided culture on the brink of collapse. She subscribed to right-wing journals and took every word she read to heart. For her, the line between truth and rhetoric was indistinct. She was convinced the Mormon Church was one of the last bulwarks against the tide of immorality sweeping the nation. When Limbaugh or other broadcast fearmongers warned that the nation was being sabotaged by leftist-led excesses, she nodded in agreement. When their kids were growing up, she and John had strictly regulated what movies and television programs they could watch. Anything with swear words or intimations of premarital sex was taboo.

I was an emissary—maybe an alien—from the other side when I visited Logan. Early on in each of my visits, after the initial burst of welcome wore off, politics would surface like an underwater creature breaking through the calm of a lake. Mary would bring up a current issue that to her illustrated the dangers of liberal thinking. One year it was the wave of student demonstrations against apartheid that were held on college campuses across the country. She was adamant the students were following the dictates of an unnamed, unseen liberal provocateur. "They are just doing what they're told," she insisted as we washed and dried the dinner dishes.

I disagreed. "They might get their ideas from what's happening on other campuses," I said, "but no one is telling them what to do. College kids are young, idealistic. They are incensed about apartheid, how unfair it is. They want to express that." Mary didn't buy it. The idea of spontaneous outrage, even copycat behavior, didn't fly with her. In her worldview, power flowed from the top down. "They're being directed, Alice," she said. "They just don't realize it."

Our political clashes didn't last long. Once either of us felt the conversation heating up, we retreated to our respective corners. I was her husband's sister and, at the core of her beliefs, family trumped politics. For my part, I needed and loved my Logan family too much to let political differences sully my relationship with Mary.

But Michelle's claims of being abused by a cult ratcheted up the differences in Mary's and my worldviews. Much more than politics was at stake. On our evening walks, I was quiet while Mary talked about the nefarious cult. She explained the cult's operations the same way she had framed the college protests—as being directed by an inaccessible, unseeable top power down to the masses. Internally, I fought against my own skepticism. Who was I to challenge her? Despite my conviction that Mary was deluded, what evidence did I have that she was wrong? Back then, I didn't feel I could risk dismissing her or Michelle outright, no matter how far-fetched I thought their claims were. I straddled our two worlds as best I could.

"They would come for me in the night," Michelle said one night when she, Mary, and I were on a walk. Her shoulders hunched inward, and she had shortened her loping stride to match her mom's and mine. Her voice was quiet, but certain. "They made me eat disgusting stuff. They gave me drugs to make me confused. They said if I told anyone, people would think I was crazy, that I'd end up in a mental hospital." As frightening as they were, her descriptions of her memories had become repetitive, almost rote.

I probed carefully, like a surgeon incising around a nerve. Mary hadn't worked outside the home until the kids were older.

John kept an unpredictable schedule, popping in and out of the house at all hours, the screen or storm door banging to announce each entry and exit. Their upstairs was small and compact, the bedroom walls thin.

"But you and John were around the house all the time," I said to Mary later, as gently as I could. "Wouldn't you have noticed if Michelle was gone? Or if her hair was matted down, or her clothes a mess? If she had bruises or welts?"

My questions singed Mary's patience. Once again, I was a voice from the uninformed side. "You can't believe how secretive, how deft these people are," she replied, shaking her head. "They know how to hide their tracks. They knew how to hurt her without leaving marks. Then they would fix her back up as if nothing had happened. They'd bring her back looking just as she did when they took her."

Sometimes when the three of us were driving around town on an errand, Mary urged Michelle to point out homes, streets, abandoned buildings—anything she might remember that could provide a clue to who the cult members were or where they had taken her for rituals. Michelle would think a house looked familiar, then grow confused. For her, it was like trying to pin down a shadow.

One evening, Mary and Michelle took me to an old rock quarry not far from their house on Center Street. We walked among the hulks of abandoned machinery and concrete blocks scattered around the brushy hillside. They led me to a bunker-type structure that was open at one end. The walls were spray-painted with looping red, black, and green graffiti. Glass shards from broken beer bottles and cigarette butts littered the ground. Back in my own world, I would have seen the cave-like nook as an illicit clubhouse, a place where boys would come to smoke, chug beer, practice swear words, and look at dirty magazines. But in Mary's and Michelle's eyes, it was a place of defilement.

"They brought me here," Michelle said. "This is one of the places they did the rituals." I took in the graffiti, the acrid smell of urine, the dank, chilled air. For a second, I glimpsed the way Michelle and Mary had come to see the world. I shivered. Dread crept up my neck like an unwanted caress.

One night after Michelle had gone to bed, I asked Mary about Michelle's counseling. I wanted her to focus on Michelle's health, not her flashbacks. Mary told me she had taken Michelle to a psychologist at Utah State University who had put her through a series of tests. "He said she was disturbed at a very, very deep level—that she may never be OK again," she said, her voice breaking.

I refused to believe Michelle was so disjointed she couldn't be made whole.

"Nonsense," I snapped. "She'll be all right. I know she will. She just needs to find the right help."

During that visit I stayed in the two-room apartment John had built onto the house a few years earlier. I had set up camp in the living room, spreading my sleeping bag on top of the colorless rug. Broken lamps and boxes of household items were stacked in the corner. The familiar photos of Mormon elders hung on the wall.

At night, I retreated to my lair to sort through my thoughts. I wanted very much to believe the universe was held together by a generous, loving presence, not a patriarchal figure that used shame and fear to keep people in line. Despite the wars, per-secutions, and genocides that kept erupting all over the globe, I wanted to believe we—humanity—were all moving toward a better place, a clearer vision, a more compassionate acceptance of our differences. When I left Catholicism, I had tossed the devil out of my reality and all the fear and self-condemnation his image conveyed. That personification was an excuse, I thought, that people had created to avoid taking responsibility for desires, actions, or thoughts they considered taboo.

Yet there I was, decades later, tossing in my sleeping bag and trying to comprehend how an entity I refused to recognize had come to be so dominant in the lives of people I loved. I was painfully aware that my non-churched life was riddled with holes. I was months away from turning forty and was once again adrift. I kept a mental list of former friends I had split from. I was often unable to summon the love I wanted to feel surrounding me. The acceptance and protection Michelle sought from her God seemed to have forsaken her as well. I wanted to be a rational oasis for my niece. I wanted to challenge her belief in the cult and in the grisly memories she insisted were true. I wanted her to believe what I wanted to believe: that the kind of evil she feared didn't exist outside of her mind, that nothing could have power over us unless we gave it away. I wanted my spiritual convictions to be as bedrock certain as Mary's were for her. But the fact was, they weren't.

"So, here's the deal," John announced one day during lunch. He explained that Mary's brother had a cabin nestled in a canyon deep in the mountains. "Michelle would love it if the two of you drove up there, hiked around, and spent the night. It's pretty country. You'll like it."

He didn't leave me with any options. He knew Michelle's affinity for wild places, and I suspected he wanted to remind her of things she used to love to do—hiking and climbing. I, too, loved disappearing into the wilderness for hours at a time. I was confident hiking by myself. But the prospect of being alone in the wilderness with Michelle unnerved me. It was one thing to be skeptical of her memories. It was another to know what to do if she experienced one while we were together. What if she began wailing and shaking, like I had seen her do at home? What if she became desperate to binge? I was used to being an aunt and a compassionate ear, not a parental figure having to handle a crisis. Would I know what to say? What to do?

"Sure," I said, sounding more confident than I felt. "Sounds great."

Michelle wasn't completely paralyzed by her flashbacks. She would still cook dinner on occasion. She seemed to enjoy the attentions of a young man who often stopped by the house to see her. I didn't know how much she had told him, but I had watched them banter back and forth. One afternoon he had driven the three of us into the mountains to a place where it was rumored quartz crystal shards could be found lying between the chunks of granite rock. If someone had come upon us that afternoon, clambering from boulder to boulder, they wouldn't have suspected anything was amiss. Michelle was loose and easy. She danced up the rocks, finding tiny crevices with her toes and fingers and pulling herself up with her wiry arms. "Hi, Alice!" she called down to me as I searched below her, picking my way carefully around the boulders. "Find any yet?"

The morning we left for the cabin I followed John, Mary, and Michelle in my Toyota sedan. We drove far up the canyon and followed a winding dirt road for several miles. I lost my nerve trying to follow John's pickup up the final steep grade. I backed down and handed him my keys. He muscled my four-cylinder car up the hill and parked it near a path that cut through the woods. After they helped unload our supplies, he and Mary headed back to Logan. Either he or Wynlee would pick us up the next day. Michelle and I shouldered our day-packs and carried water, food, and our sleeping bags a short distance to the cabin. We dropped off what we didn't need for our hike and headed out to explore.

As we gained elevation, the tree canopy thinned and we emerged onto a barren ridge overlooking an expanse of high desert dotted with sparse, scrubby bushes. Hiking through the open landscape helped calm my fears. Maybe it relaxed Michelle as well. As we walked, she talked about going back to school in the fall, about her job as a house mother for disabled kids. And about a boy she had dated briefly a few years back, whom she would never forget, who would always be the perfect love that got away. "When I was with him, everything was OK," she told me. "We could talk for hours. I felt so safe with him."

I had felt that way a few times, but it had been a while. I wasn't going to tell her so. "I know what you mean," I said. "It's good you got to feel that, even if it didn't last. And you'll feel that way again, with someone else."

Her eyes were more used to the muted landscape than mine, and she spotted things I didn't—a hidden cave, a bird's nest woven into the thorny branches of a bush. She picked up a pair of smooth, curved antlers shed by a young deer. "You take them," she said, holding them out. "They're for you."

From the time we broke through the trees, a gray cloud had hovered over us, one of few in the mostly blue sky. I ignored it, even as it grew more ominous and threatening. Suddenly, a chill wind came up and pea-sized hail began to rain down, stinging our faces and hands and bouncing off the dirt at our feet.

I berated myself for not paying more attention to the weather, to my surroundings. I scanned the ground for any kind of shelter that would protect us. There were no trees, no bushes even, to hide under. Thunder rumbled across a nearby ridge. Hail poured down.

Uncertain what to do next, I looked over at Michelle. She was lying on the ground with her backpack covering her face. Tiny balls of hail had collected along the seams and in the grooves of the pack's zippers. Her blonde hair was spread away from her face. She was laughing, a sound I hadn't heard from her in a long time. She loved the zany, the unpredictable. "Come on down," she said.

I lay down beside her and placed my pack over my face. Hail pelted our legs and arms. I could hear the muffled rattle as the pellets hit my pack. Seen from above we would have looked like snow angels, or, as we had our arms folded tight across our chests to keep out the hail, more like snow mummies. The absurdity of the situation finally got to me. I began to chuckle. "You are brilliant," I told her. "Absolutely brilliant."

In telling me about the cult, Mary referred often to the book *Michelle Remembers*, the 1980 chronicle of a young Canadian woman's memories of childhood ritual abuse. "You should read it," Mary told me. "You'll learn a lot. Michelle is not by any means the only person this has happened to." One afternoon during that visit she dropped me off at Logan's library, then housed in a remodeled Sears department store. I found the book in the stacks and sat at a comfortable seat at a table. The atmosphere in the library was genial. The room was quiet and pleasantly warm. I opened the cover.

The book described in rambling but lurid detail the memories of abuse a young Canadian woman, Michelle Smith, said began when she was five years old. She had related the memories to her psychiatrist (her coauthor, and later husband) Lawrence Pazder. She described dark rooms lit by candles and being encircled by caped men and women chanting in unintelligible syllables. She recalled being confined in cellars and being forced to drink her own urine. She remembered her mother handing her over to the group, telling her, "I don't want you." She relayed scenes where young girls—always virgins—were sacrificed on X-shaped altars, their hearts cut out, their body parts tossed into a raging fire.

Pazder described his client's ordeal as nothing less than "a cosmic battle" between Satan and the forces of light. The battle went on for more than three hundred pages.

At first, when I read the grisly descriptions of rituals and bloody sacrifices, the words didn't compute, as if they were written in a language close to English, but different enough that they weren't intelligible. The fact was, I didn't want them to make sense. I thought I had things figured out: Michelle's bulimia and her memories were a product of years of repressing a traumatic rape. Mary's willingness to believe her daughter's memories of ritual abuse was a radical extension of her Mormon belief in the overwhelming power of Satan. Both Michelle and Mary were the sole victims of this religious-fueled delusion.

But the book *Michelle Remembers*, as much as it repulsed me, called my theories into question. Here somebody else—not a Mormon, but a Catholic—who lived hundreds of miles away was claiming similar memories, similar terror, similar violations as those my niece had described. The book's hyper-sensational tone was off-putting, but I had no basis for calling it fiction. I didn't know what to think. It felt like my internal rational compass had broken. The needle pointing to truth was spinning around and around, unable to find a resting point.

Years later I found a paperback copy of *Michelle Remembers* on a used bookstand at my local library. By then I knew the book had been denounced as a fraud (1) and was considered a "template" from which self-proclaimed ritual abuse survivors took their stories. But I wanted to reread parts of it to remind me of what I had read that summer afternoon in the Logan library, two decades earlier. I bought the book for twenty-five cents and took it home. A previous owner, also named Michelle, had written her name on the inside cover.

Reading the book all those years later, and from a sadder, more informed perspective, I winced at the hysterical chicanery that bled from words that by then I knew had helped fuel the decade-long panic over satanic ritual abuse.

> *She picked me up like a baby! I didn't want her to. She kept mumbling in that funny language and was sort of hissing and meowing, like a cat. . . . But then she turned me upside down. She made me keep my knees on my chest. And she hung onto me and moved me down really slowly. And all those ladies in black were hissing and meowing and dancing funny, like cats. . . . And she started licking me. . . . And then she laid down on the black thing with my head stuck between her legs, and she made me crawl out. Then I had to stand up. And she held out her arms and I had to come back to her. And she breathed into my mouth and my nose. What could I do? She said, "You're mine, Michelle. You're mine." She told me my new life was just beginning. I thought: Oh, God, I hope I die. (2)*

I noted how in the introduction, Pazder took great pains to defend the book's credibility, claiming Smith's recollections were from taped transcripts of therapy sessions. At one point in the book he explained to Smith why he believed completely in her memories and why they differed from delusion, which he described as mental hallucinations experienced by an unstable or emotionally unbalanced mind. He came to this conclusion, he said, because the memories "felt real."

> *You feel like you go to a place that is very real, and you go back to it, and the door begins to open, and*

you begin to remember things that happened. . . .
I hear you describe what you see, and I don't hear
it as a hallucination. It is too organized. Too long-
term. It fits into the pattern of your life too well.
You haven't been psychotic at any time. You aren't
delusional . . . You are struggling to work with what
you remember. That's very different from a person
who is delusional. (3)

It's an uncomfortable feeling when something you think you have no part of—want no part of—knocks at your door and insists you let it in. Suggests, even, that you share some history. Its clothes are stained. It has bad breath. Its voice is harsh and whiny. Your first inclination is to push it away, deny any kinship, and send it packing. That's how it was when I found myself having to deal with the phenomenon of satanic ritual abuse. The phrase repelled me. I wanted not to have to know about it. I wanted to lock the door and pretend I had never heard the knocking. But it kept coming back. The knocking became louder and more insistent. I finally realized I had to invite it in and hear what it had to say, no matter how ludicrous, how unthinkable.

When I began my research, I had no idea what a social panic, or hysteria, was. I soon learned. Sociologists describe it as a widespread, exaggerated reaction to a perceived social threat. Social panics—also called moral panics—have occurred for centuries, erupting when a powerful segment of society creates religious or racial scapegoats and blames them for social ills, or projects onto them the dominant group's fears, taboos, and suspicions. Supposed "victims" of these scapegoated groups are often children or young women, who are purportedly kidnapped and cruelly treated, often sexually. Social panics tend to surface without a lot of prelude, create a maelstrom of paranoia and worse, then die down and lie dormant until the next stew of cultural factors rouses them from sleep.

Sociologist Jeffrey Victor, one of the early researchers to analyze the 1980s panic, traced the modern satanic scare in part to an old "blood ritual myth" in which children are kidnapped and murdered by strangers—a story that resonates deeply with parents. In ancient Rome, early Christians were accused of kidnapping Roman children for secret ritual sacrifices; later the Greeks and Christians accused Jews of doing the same. The eighties panic, Victor wrote, combined that narrative with another ancient story—that of Satan, or evil, threatening God's moral order. This story emerged over the centuries in different guises, prompting the witch hunts that waxed and waned throughout medieval Europe in the fifteenth and sixteenth centuries and made their way to Salem, Massachusetts, in the 1690s. (4)

The intersection of these two narratives in the twentieth century created the "story" that members of satanic cults were kidnapping, torturing, and mentally programming thousands of children and young women, then releasing them back into society to do whatever evil the cult requested. Impassioned believers in the story broadcast the narrative, and the media helped them. The story spread from workshop to workshop, from task force to task force, from one supposed victim to another, from one media story to another, gathering strength and credibility with each repetition. Claims that today seem deranged and implausible—the sexual debasement of children and young women during satanic rituals, the ingestion of murdered infants, and the implanting of subconscious directives into victims' minds— were considered during that time not only probable, but likely. In an effective twist of mental manipulation, the stories were accompanied with the warning that to not believe them was, in some way, to be in league with the dark side.

Momentum for earlier hysterias over supposed satanic forces had come from religious and political institutions. But the panic over ritual abuse was promulgated by more secular authorities, many of whom were leaders in psychiatry, law enforcement, and social work—professions charged with the mission to guide their clients out of confusion, not into it. Pazder, for instance, was a Canadian psychiatrist, a fellow of Canada's Royal College of Physicians and Surgeons, a member of the American Psychiatric Association, and a Catholic. He coined the term satanic ritual abuse and became the first ritual abuse "specialist." He married Smith, and the couple traveled to the Vatican to alert the Catholic Church of the supposed satanic onslaught. He was a consultant for the McMartin Preschool trial, appeared in a 1985 ABC *20/20* report on ritual abuse, and spoke at venues across the United States where law enforcement personnel were educated about this new threat to the nation's children. (5)

I knew none of this the afternoon I spent reading the book in the Logan library in 1989. While the blinds over the windows slapped gently in the breeze, I forced myself to read a book that revolted me, trying to understand what had ensnared my niece and her mom in a bizarre and creepy web that I considered implausible and they insisted was utterly real. I didn't know what that web was. I didn't know it had a name. Had I come upon *Michelle Remembers* before my niece's stunning disclosure, I would have dismissed the book as sensational drivel, and badly written at that. But that day I was trying to stay open-minded, trying to consider all possibilities. I had learned from my college days that social institutions and those who ran them resisted facing our culture's downside. I remembered how police and the courts treated the first women who came forward with reports of domestic violence, and how incest survivors once had to fight to be believed. Was the culture now denying the existence of another despicable behavior foisted on young women and children? I couldn't deny that the incidents Smith recounted, the ways the cult operated, and its use of psychological control echoed many of Michelle's memories. Or Michelle's echoed hers. I didn't know which, if either, were true. Or what to do about any of it.

chapter 9
in the valley

Back in Oregon, I tried to push my thoughts of Michelle to the edges of my mind, but at night they crept up like cats and settled their dense weight on my chest. During the day I kept mostly to myself. I had a group of friends from graduate school, but that summer their lives revolved around 10K road races, their day jobs, and their kids' first teeth. The Masters Games—track competitions for the over-fifty set—were being held in Eugene that summer, and the social gatherings I attended buzzed with excited chatter I couldn't share.

I am a talker. I talk to puzzle out my feelings, clarify them, even to release them. But I couldn't imagine telling anyone in that group about the odious world I had been introduced to in Logan. I didn't want to admit any connection to it, much less bring it up in casual conversation. Most of my friends were journalists and rational skeptics who—like me, just a few months earlier—would likely dismiss Michelle's claims with a shake of their heads and a few caustic comments. The words I

couldn't say lodged in my throat like a lump of dirt I could neither swallow nor expel. I felt tarnished, heavy, old.

I found refuge with my elderly neighbor, Zilpha. That
summer, her arthritic knees were swollen to the size of egg-
plants. Because of her pain, she couldn't walk; because of mine,
I couldn't speak. We made a good twosome. When she asked
me to help sort through decades of clutter in her back shed, I
gladly took on the task. We spent hours rummaging through a
massive jumble of books, magazines, junk mail, photographs,
mildewed clothes, tangles of yarn, and dusty craft projects. As
we pawed through her past, she told me stories of her childhood
growing up in the mountains of Colorado. For many years she
was an only child, and her closest neighbors were miles away.
Her friends were the barn animals and the stray dogs that
showed up at her family's rural homestead.

"That donkey Nell was a mean one," she told me once,
chuckling. "I rode her to school, and some days she just didn't
want to go. I had to hit her with a stick. And there I was, this
scrawny seven-year-old beating on a big ol' donkey."

She spoke of finding buffalo bones on the stubbly range-
lands and of the long, desolate winters with thigh-high drifts
of snow and night skies bright with stars. For brief moments
I lost myself in her Western girlhood, envisioning her astride
that loping donkey, her blue eyes hopeful and eager, the rest of
her life spread in front of her like a beckoning promise. I could
only imagine that expansiveness in someone else's world, that
summer. Not in my own, not Mary's, not Michelle's.

I told myself I should go to the library to check out books
that might give me insight into the cult Mary and Michelle
described with such conviction. But I couldn't bring myself to
do it. I didn't want to read about animal sacrifices, figures in

hoods, or blood-smeared rituals—images that were multiplying like cancer in Mary's and Michelle's minds. I still was convinced Michelle's memories had more to do with her assault than any sort of satanic abuse. I thought Mary profoundly misguided and gullible in her willingness to accept not only Michelle's fractured memories, but also the cult she believed was infecting every tier of society.

It turned out I didn't need to go anywhere. The information I didn't want to find found me.

One Sunday that August, the *Register-Guard*, Eugene's daily newspaper, featured a long story addressing concerns over the growing number of occult-related crimes being reported throughout the Northwest. Reports of secretive, generations-old cults whose members were killing and abusing children had been surfacing throughout the country, the story said, including in Oregon.

"Let's be blunt about it," a state police detective told the reporter. "It's murder. It's been going on for a long time, and it will continue to do so." (1)

One high-profile crime the story discussed had occurred a year earlier in Springfield, the town across the river from the duplex I had lived in for several years. Two men had strangled a woman, and later told police the murder was a sacrifice to "a supposed occult god of chaos and evil." Officials in one community on the Oregon Coast suspected more than a dozen groups of being involved in occult activity. In some Oregon counties, law enforcement agencies had begun providing training in how to spot cult-related crimes. A Boise cult crime consultant for law enforcement agencies told the reporter that "deep-core" Satanists in the Pacific Northwest and other parts of the country had been getting away with ritualistic murder and sex crimes for years.

"This has been going on since ancient history," the consultant said. "The philosophy of Satanism has not changed in the last five thousand years. They were doing them [murders] then. Why should we not think they are doing them now?"

The story profiled an unnamed Portland woman who claimed that, when young, she had been abused by members of a cult that had been active in her family for generations. "I was victimized by ritualized torture and profound, prolonged sexual abuse," she said. The graphic scenarios she recalled were similar to Michelle's and to the ones in *Michelle Remembers*: candlelit ceremonies where she was cut with knives and made to drink the blood and eat body parts of sacrificed victims, both human and animal. The woman claimed she had seen children die from mutilation and torture. She spoke of young women who were kept in isolation and were used as "breeders" to produce fetuses for human sacrifice.

"We were programmed not to feel, taught that it is not OK to become angry," she said. Cult members told her, "Weak people cry. Weak people die."

The woman said she knew of twenty ritual abuse survivors in Oregon "and for every one I know, there are probably at least five others." She had dedicated her life to educating mental health professionals and police about cults and how they operate. Her goal, she said, was to convince others that "the horror stories told by her and other survivors of ritualized satanic abuse are true; that something must be done to help the victims and stop the Satanists."

Reading the story made me face the possibility that Mary and Michelle might not be the outliers I had thought them to be. Here in Oregon's Willamette Valley, another woman—not one in a lurid book, not a Mormon—was telling a story eerily similar to Michelle's. She, too, was adamant there were many more victims who were afraid to speak out.

The woman's words hung inside my brain like black flags. During my trip to Logan that June, Mary had grown impatient with my reluctance to accept the cult's existence, both in Logan and elsewhere. "'The Willamette Valley, where you live, is full of it,'" she had snapped. I had felt my face grow hot with denial and protest. My home in western Oregon—teeming with sharp minds, progressive politics, and spiritual seekers—riddled with cult activity? "How can you know that?" I had responded defensively. "Who says so?"

That summer, *The Oregonian,* the state's largest newspaper, also published a long feature story on rising concerns over Satanism. One rural sheriff had asked for state aid in investigating a rash of recent activities that included "grave-robbing, the drinking of animal blood and apparent mutilation of small animals." Throughout the Northwest, law enforcement agencies were holding seminars on how to recognize the signs and victims of satanic abuse. (2)

The story quoted a few skeptics. A former chief criminal deputy said he thought belief in Satanism was used by people looking to validate their antisocial behavior, and a Presbyterian minister said the extent of satanic activity was being exaggerated. But the story tilted toward those who believed the phenomenon was real. A member of a cult-awareness group warned of teenagers' vulnerability to becoming involved in ritual practices that progressed to serious crimes. A sidebar listed indicators of child ritual abuse from a manual compiled by a sheriff's department in the state of Washington. Signs to watch out for included a child's preoccupation with body wastes, fear of toilet training, aggressive play with a marked sadistic quality, and revulsion to anything resembling blood.

The night after Michelle had first shared her memories of abuse with me in Cincinnati, I repeated her story to my three sisters. My second eldest sister, Ellen, responded first. She is the most dramatic of the four of us, and we often laughed at how gullible she could be. But, as a physical therapist, she also has a cool, rational side. "I don't believe it," she said, after I finished recounting my conversation with Michelle. She had given her pillow a definitive *thwack*, turned her back, and settled down to sleep. My other two sisters and I looked at each other and shook our heads. Anne, who was a probation officer in upstate New York, hadn't heard anything about ritual abuse cases. But Caroline lived in Hamilton, Ontario, where a highly publicized ritual abuse case had surfaced four years earlier, in 1985. (3) Like me, she didn't know what to think.

Over the next few years, I would often recall Ellen's response that night. I envied her certainty. Before that summer's trip to Logan, I too had possessed a measure of certainty, even superiority, when it came to knowing what was "real." But by the end of that summer I was humbled. Now it was me fumbling through a maze of resistance and revulsion as I wrestled with the memories that Michelle—and by then, apparently, many others—swore were true. Now it was me floundering around, reaching into the muck, and trying to seize hold of a root of truth. At night my mind vacillated between disbelief and the creeping fear that Michelle's grisly memories could have more substance than I wanted to admit.

One afternoon I forced myself to go to the local library. After scanning the room to make sure no one I recognized was there, I searched the card catalogue for titles using words whose very sound I had come to detest. I wrote down the call numbers and headed for the stacks. The selection was small, and the books I needed most to read hadn't yet been written. I leafed through what was available. The books were printed on cheap paper; the print was large, the writing overwrought. The books offered little more than crude, graphic accounts of rituals that sought to scare rather than inform. They described satanic symbols—upended pentagrams, upside-down crosses, the number 666. They listed the dates of pagan holidays when ceremonies were most apt to be held. Some described lurid sexual assaults performed under the auspices of Satanism. My immediate inclination was to put them down. "Wait. Just find out what they have to say," I told myself. I tried. But after skimming a few chapters, I felt as if my mind had been swathed in oily scum. I shoved the books back on the shelf and left.

Michelle sent me one letter later that summer of 1989. It was upbeat, even feisty, but she still held fast to the belief that she had been ritually abused.

"I take pen in hand to assure you that all is well. All is also chaotic, disturbing and in continually shifting stages of upheaval, but still well. I alternately wish to burn, chop, shoot, crush and destroy those perpetrators, when part of me is not wishing to throw myself down at their feet and be in complete submission to them for fear of the consequences that are only too vivid and clear to the child inside me. The amount of abuse that went on is staggering, and my horrendous reactions and feelings are completely in context, though for all those years these things were hidden, or came out as 'warped' reactions to reality."

Even as she was grappling with her memories, she was trying to live a productive life, she wrote. She still had her job as a house parent at the home for disabled children. She was taking a class at the university on women in literature. "My brain synapses are snap-crackle-and-popping with excitement," she wrote. She had gone mountain biking in Moab and had begun attending a non-Mormon church, where she felt more comfortable. A new suitor had asked her to lunch. "It feels so good to let down my guard and be vulnerable again," she wrote. "To be able to accept kindness from someone."

Late that summer I received a windfall from my parents that I used to make a down payment on a small, fifty-year-old bungalow in Springfield. A realtor had showed me many units, but none of them drew me. I liked this house the minute I saw it. I noted it had an extra bedroom. Michelle could stay with me while she got the treatment she needed, I had thought.

The loan process took months. While I waited for the sale to close, my two dogs and I moved in with friends in a rural farming area north of Eugene. My friends' busy lives rarely crossed mine, and I spent most of the day by myself. In the mornings I pecked out freelance stories on my electric typewriter, which I had set up in their kitchen. In the late afternoons I rode my bicycle on the curving roads that wound along nearby cornfields and apple orchards.

I wasn't ready to accept my niece's memories of ritual abuse as true. But back then, I did believe that, on the edge of puberty, she had been raped by a group of boys, and that she was deeply wounded because of it. Her image was with me constantly, like a frail, rippling presence. The trees in the orchards I pedaled along were heavy with ripening fruit. I bent under the weight of my niece's ordeal, and the awareness of something I didn't want to acknowledge, that I had no answers for, and that went against what I wanted to believe about the world.

One afternoon I answered a knock on the front door. A group of teenagers was selling raffle tickets for some sort of event. As they made their appeal, I noticed a girl in the group had eyes like Michelle's, a similar hue of blue, the same sweet, pained vacancy. I tried not to stare. I told the kids I didn't want a ticket, thanked them, and shut the door. But immediately I realized I needed to look into that girl's eyes again. I grabbed my wallet and scurried down the walk after the group. "I decided to buy a ticket after all," I stammered when the girl turned to face me. She looked nothing like my niece.

A few days later, in the deep of the night, the novel I was reading described the brutal rape of a young woman. She too was an innocent at the brink of womanhood. Her attackers held her down, grabbing her arms and legs, sinking their fingers into her straining flesh. I should have put the book down, but I read the chapter through to the end. After I turned out the light, I drew my knees into my chest and rocked back and forth. Clearly, I was one of the weak ones.

That fall I became the editor of a newspaper for foster teens preparing to live on their own after they turned eighteen, the age when they left the state's care. The set-up of my new job seemed ideal. I knew one of the two owners of the business. The newspaper's purpose appealed to me. The office was located in an old house in downtown Eugene, and the staff was informal and upbeat. But I soon realized the impact of my months of self-imposed solitude. I had lost the knack of chiming in with carefree office banter. I was continually a beat behind the flow. One of my coworkers was cute, witty, and indisputably hip. I tried to keep up with her one-liners, but my words came out slow and halting, as if percolating through a slurry. One day I tried to respond with a quick comeback. It fell way short. "Uh, yeah," she mumbled, giving me a pained smile. "I guess. Something like that."

The loan on my house cleared that November. I retrieved the boxes and few pieces of furniture I had stowed in my friend's basement, took down the faded "Pending Sale" sign from my new living room window, and began life as a homeowner. My nine-hundred-square-foot house was squat and simple, but after years of living in a one-room studio and a summer spent holing up in a spare bedroom, it felt palatial. Everything about the interior suggested a new beginning. The kitchen had white countertops, white linoleum, and newly painted white walls. Every appliance was out-of-the-box new, shiny and stain-free. Five white doors lined the back hallway like an image from a hopeful dream. The first night I could barely sleep from excitement. What would these walls hold for me, I wondered. What life would I build here?

For weeks I slept on a sleeping bag and pad with my reading lamp perched on a wooden milk crate and my clothes layered on the floor in the bedroom closet. I was oblivious to the cheap wood paneling stapled on the bedroom wall and the budget carpeting that covered the floors like beige moss. As I arranged my few pieces of furniture, I thought again about Michelle coming to stay with me. Bright light poured into the small bedroom on the west side of the house. The room's other window looked out onto a huge, rustling cottonwood tree with a rough-hewn swing hanging from one of its branches.

Michelle had visited me just once in Oregon, when she and Wynlee had come through town on a high school band trip. They called me up and asked if they could stop by. Of course I said yes, but I had misgivings. The sagging half of the duplex I was renting then was situated behind a used tire store and a shabby, long-stay motel. My studio had a kitchen at one end, my rolled-up futon at the other. The flaking green paint on the walls of the minuscule bathroom shower resembled the lichen that hung from trees in the nearby woods. For furniture I had a desk, a cat-shredded armchair, a rickety kitchen table, and a couple of chairs. My décor consisted of rocks and feathers I had picked up on hikes into the backcountry. When Wynlee and Michelle arrived, they perched on the two straight-backed chairs and caught me up on family and school news. During a lull in the conversation Michelle took in my surroundings. "I like your house, Aunt Alice," she said. "It's like being outside, but with walls."

After I moved into my new house, I never extended the invitation to have her stay with me. As helpful as I wanted to be, I could not see a way to mesh her current life with mine. In fact, I had begun calling John and Mary less to inquire about her, not more. If John answered when I phoned, he immediately handed the phone to Mary—I suspected he was deliberately keeping his thoughts, maybe his doubts, about Michelle's claims of cult abuse to himself. Within minutes of speaking with Mary, I would be sucked into her and Michelle's nightmarish reality where a faceless cult now occupied center stage like an unending horror movie. The list of friends, acquaintances, and relatives who were experiencing "memories" of cult abuse expanded with each conversation. After listening for a while, I would try to steer the focus back to Michelle.

"How is she feeling?" I would ask, tentatively. "What does her therapist say?" Talking with Mary required an exacting exercise of diplomacy. Aligning with her meant swallowing the tarry paranoia over satanic cults as truth. Express skepticism and I risked losing her trust—and my link with Michelle. After I hung up, an opaque fog enveloped my mind for hours.

I rarely regretted my decision to not have children. Nevertheless, I had enormous respect for the task of mothering. Mary was often self-critical of her performance as a mom, but I knew no one was closer to Michelle than she was, no one as tenaciously on her daughter's side. She had withstood Michelle's childhood meltdowns, her prickly temperament, her adolescent battles with self-acceptance. She had lived through the years of bulimia, hearing the toilet flush, four, five times a day, week after week, month upon month. She comforted Michelle through her horrifying memories and episodic breakdowns. I knew I would never know how it felt to witness a beloved daughter trapped in a self-destructive cycle. I would not know what that helplessness felt like. I would not know the weight of that kind of love.

At the same time, I didn't agree with how Mary was handling Michelle's claims of being ritually abused. She stood so firmly with her daughter you couldn't see daylight between them. Mary couldn't entertain the notion of a symbolic or metaphoric interpretation of Michelle's memories—the possibility that they reflected an emotional imbalance not related to a physical reality. She refused to consider that the memories might be a product of Michelle's extreme suggestibility, or her mental illness. Maybe it was easier for her to blame her daughter's bulimia and emotional unraveling on an all-powerful cult than to accept that Michelle had an illness with no discernible cause and no foreseeable cure.

It never occurred to me—couldn't have occurred to me, then—that Mary and Michelle were caught up in a tide of hysteria that was far more real and powerful than the physical entity they were imagining. Their true tormentor, it turned out, wasn't a supposed massive "cult," but people's unquestioning belief in its existence, despite the absence of any demonstrable proof. When I finally learned about the panic that ate away at the underbelly of critical thinking and common sense during that decade, I better understood Michelle's fears and Mary's willingness to believe her memories were true. But I would also have to look at how the panic had affected me. Time after time in my conversations with Mary, I had chosen silence over confrontation. Had the panic leached away my ability to challenge beliefs and certainties that had no rational basis? Had the panic—not Mary, not my fear of losing contact with Michelle—somehow quelled my willingness to speak out?

That fall, Michelle checked herself into the hospital for a brief stay. Mary wrote a letter addressed to family members explaining what had happened. (Mary gave me a copy of the letter years later—I don't remember receiving it at the time.) She wrote that Michelle was programmed to remember particularly horrendous rituals at the time of year she was first introduced to them. On cue, Michelle had begun to experience vivid memories of her abuse in late September. "She was reliving the sacrifice and it was in awful detail—all the emotion and loss and helplessness and betrayal," Mary wrote. "It felt like the devil himself was after her. She was in so much pain that she was talking suicide just to put an end to it."

I don't know how long Michelle stayed in the hospital or how she fared on the unit—that particular record is missing from the medical files I had access to. When she left the hospital, she returned to her job at the group home. In the next letter she wrote me, she didn't refer to the hospital stay, but told me how much she appreciated the "no-nonsense, what-the-hell-do-you think-you're-doing" young woman she worked with at her job, who took Michelle's hospitalization in stride and gracefully tolerated her emotional swings. "She doesn't act like I'm the weird one from hell," Michelle wrote.

But Mary couldn't push aside what she had witnessed, and she decided to reach out further than she had previously dared. She wrote to an official high in the state hierarchy of the Mormon Church, telling him about Michelle's ordeal. She and John then met with him. "He told us they get this kind of report maybe once a week," Mary wrote me. "He said that my letter was obviously valid and it really got the attention of the men at the top, so that now this effort to recognize Satanism and handle it would be expedited."

Along with being embraced by the media, fundamentalist churches, and law enforcement, the ritual abuse hysteria attracted feminist and pro-female advocates. The year before, in 1988, the Los Angeles County Commission for Women created a Ritual Abuse Task Force, which published a thirty-one-page handbook detailing the particulars of ritual abuse, including mind control techniques, types of torture, and the effects of the abuse on victims' states of mind. The task force did not address the possibility that ritual abuse was the result of overblown fears or cultural anxieties. It did not use words such as "it is believed" or "it is possible that." Ritual abuse was real, the authors wrote. The mushrooming reports from victims were proof enough. People who thought otherwise were blind or in denial. And denial, they warned, would result in even more victims.

"Despite detailed evidence of ritual abuse coming from child victims and their families, from adult victims, and from the professionals working with them, and despite the remarkable consistency of these reports both nationally and internationally, society at large resists believing that ritual abuse really occurs," wrote task force chair Myra B. Riddell. "There remains the mistaken belief that satanic and other cult activity is isolated and rare." (4)

According to the task force, ritual abuse could occur at the hands of extended family members, but was also likely to occur in preschools, day care centers, churches, and summer camps. "The ritual abuse in such an institutional setting is not incidental to its operation, but is in fact intrinsic to it, the very reason for the institution's existence." (5) Along with torture and sexual abuse, the task force asserted, cult members used drugs, hypnosis, and suggestion to numb and confuse victims' minds and to program them with cult directives.

The handbook listed sixteen sources readers could consult for further information, including two titles released by a Christian publishing house in Eugene, Oregon, and the book *Michelle Remembers.* (6)

chapter 10

memory

I returned to Logan the next summer, August 1990. Even though I knew the visit wouldn't be easy, the trip was a good excuse to get out of town. The honeymoon stage of my job was long over. My boss and I were embroiled in a vexing power struggle—I considered him a pesky micromanager; he wanted me to defer to him more. We both needed a break. But that wasn't all. Earlier that spring I had attracted the attention of one of the few men in a choir I sang with. He began showing up in my dreams and in the seat beside me when we traveled to gigs. He painted with watercolors and had built his own home. In conversation he was shy and awkward, but he wrote out his favorite poems and sent them to me in letters along with photocopies of his sketches and paintings. We began exploring what we might be together. He thought I was who I appeared to be when I was with the choir—cheerful, outgoing, made-up. He had no way of knowing what that persona masked. One night, loosened and emboldened by his touch, I poured out my heart, telling him about Michelle—the rape, her memories, my quandary. He grew silent. Soon after, he quit calling. He no longer found a reason to brush by me during practice.

His withdrawal flattened me. There were other reasons, I came to realize. The weight of Michelle's situation plus mounting frustration at work had given me a prickly and defensive edge. He was the first man I had gone out with in years and that added to my wariness. He had emotional baggage of his own and had expectations I couldn't meet. Clearly I wasn't his type. But back then I felt as if the secret I was carrying radiated from me like a bad smell.

When I arrived in Logan the household felt as if it were in mourning. Michelle, withdrawn, pale, and swathed in bulky workout sweats, spent much of the day on the living room couch. Mary, quietly frantic, hovered around her. Their grief had become one. During our evening walks Mary shared yet more information she had learned about the cult and how it operated. Its power over its victims was absolute and impenetrable, she told me. Its genius was in twisting people's minds in order to control them. "You can't even imagine how intelligent, how devious they are at manipulating their victims," she said. During rituals, cult members gave their victims drugs to blur memories of the abuse. They planted coded messages into their victims' brains to ensure permanent control over them. The cult could summon victims back at any time, she said. No matter a victim's age, she or he would submit. "Once they've got you," she told me, "you can never get free."

I listened to her while watching the stars overhead and feeling the cool mountain air on my skin. Once again I felt a surreal disconnect between what I was seeing and the words I was hearing. When I first visited Logan in the mid-1970s, I considered the modest mountain town an earthly Eden. I marveled at its broad, trash-free thoroughfares and the irrigation canals brimming with snowmelt that ran along its residential streets. Police sirens rarely pierced the silence of the night. Compared to the blighted inner-city neighborhood of Boston where I had lived, Logan exuded calm and civility. Yes, I had chafed at the ubiquitous Mormon geniality, but it did a lot to make the town feel welcoming. And having the freedom to walk at night without fear had felt wonderfully freeing. All these years later, it was deeply disquieting to listen to Mary's stories about the evil she was convinced was worming through the core of the community. If a place like Logan could be a target—if indeed, it was—then what community was safe?

While Mary talked about how the cult had insinuated itself into all echelons of society—politics, hospitals, schools, and government—I stared down at the ground near my feet or up at the trees or sky. I wanted to be somewhere else and to be listening to different words. But I was where I was. I sealed my mouth to keep my opinions from slipping out. I feared the price of saying the wrong words. I felt like I was back on I-5 driving through the watery night, the way forward blurry and indistinct. I couldn't find traction.

John had changed in the year since I had last seen him. His aura had dimmed and the skin around his brilliant blue eyes had furrowed and deepened. He had grown gentler, sadder. In our brief nighttime conversations he didn't bring up the moral dilemmas he previously had enjoyed challenging me with. He steered clear of any talk about the cult. The lack of evidence to support Michelle's memories, I surmised, did not sit well with his logical mind.

Years later, he filled in what he hadn't told me at the time. He had gone to the houses of some of the people Michelle believed were members of the cult and had tried to get some answers, only to hit a dead end. "All of it was inconclusive," he said. Some people in the Logan community suspected one particular individual or another of having connections to the cult, and he tried to get the accusers to put their charges in writing. Or on tape. "But everyone backed down," he said. "No one would do it face-to-face." He had gone to conferences and sat through talks on ritual abuse. "Finally I said to myself, 'They don't know what they're talking about.'" But he stayed silent, he told me, because Mary was so convinced the cult was real. He admitted he had let her take the wheel when it came to Michelle's treatment. "What would I have done differently?" he told me. "I don't know if that would have been right, either."

One night during my visit he talked about how life had changed for him. Before Michelle became sick, he hadn't realized how much of a maze the mind could become. He hadn't fathomed the myriad ways it could twist, distort, and topple off course. Before Michelle became so ill, he hadn't experienced deep soul pain. Now he was ripped open and all he saw around him were people struggling with pain and trouble.

"I sit in church. The guy over here is miserable because his wife left him. The family over there has a son who does drugs. The guy next to them is so depressed he can't work. This woman sitting behind him has a husband who's an alcoholic. Everywhere you look, everyone's got problems—big problems."

He held out his callused hands, palms up, empty. His stared at me, unflinching. In the past he had been proud and assured, often righteous. When it came to moral choices, people knew what the right thing was and what they needed to do, he had insisted; they just didn't want to do it. But now he had come to see that sometimes things weren't so clear. No ethical signpost or high-minded platitude could show Michelle the way out of her confusion and fear. He and Mary had tried everything—patience, kindness, threats, God, counseling— and none of it made a difference.

One afternoon between tree service jobs John stopped at the house for lunch. Michelle came downstairs and begged him for a blessing. I was in the kitchen, but stopped my puttering to allow them silence. She wore her baggy sweats. He had on his work clothes—stained jeans and a white T-shirt. Sawdust and bits of bark clung to his board-tough forearms. It didn't matter. At least this was something he could do. He nodded his head. She stood in front of him, slight, hunched, and still. John's capable hands were used to building, doing, fixing. Now all he could do was raise them in blessing over his daughter's bowed head, and pray with the depth of faith he still had within him.

"Dear Heavenly Father," he began. Blessings are private and I did not try to hear his words. I'm sure he asked for peace for Michelle's agitated spirit, for strength to help her deal with her fears. He continued his simple, murmured prayer, and when he was done, he lifted his hands away. "Thanks, Dad," she said, giving him a wan smile. She turned and went back upstairs. He left to attend to his next job.

Once, while talking with me about how paranoid Michelle had become, John made a startling statement. "I know it's only a matter of time before she names me in this," he said. "I'm just waiting for it to happen."

Later it became clear that John was more vulnerable than either of us realized to being falsely accused, and not just because of Michelle's paranoia. During the 1970s, a therapeutic approach known as recovered memory had gained traction among therapists and social workers—feminists and evangelical Christians were among the early and fervent subscribers. Recovered memory theory held that a vast number of women (a common percentage quoted was one-third) had been sexually abused as children, but had buried the memories in their unconscious minds. The "repressed" memories nevertheless manifested negative effects, such as depression, or inability to form satisfying relationships. To heal from the effects of unremembered abuse, the theory was, women—usually with the help of a therapist—needed to recall the experiences, validate them, often relive them, and in some situations confront the perpetrator. The theory and approach was laid out in the 1988 book, *The Courage to Heal*, which became the bible of the recovered memory movement. (1)

To some degree, the theory addressed a historical failure of the psychotherapy field. Prior to the 1970s, the topic of sex abuse—and in particular abuse that occurred within families—wasn't spoken about openly. Children weren't taught about good and bad touch. There was no widespread cultural acceptance that girls or women (boys and men would have met with even more resistance) who disclosed that they were sexually abused were telling the truth. Girls and women who had been abused had few options: remain silent out of shame, confusion, or the fear of not being believed; question whether the abuse had truly occurred, particularly if the perpetrators were family members or trusted family friends; or "forget" it had happened. For many women who had actually been abused, and who had clear memories of it, the recovered memory movement gave them words for their experience, support for speaking out, and a path to possible healing. It was likely a godsend.

But the recovered memory movement also encompassed fundamental misconceptions about the mechanisms of memory and its vulnerability to suggestion and change. Supporters of the theory believed that "buried" memories retained accurate and intact reflections of the original events. Recovered memories, they believed, told the truth. But science looked at memory differently. Researchers by then had concluded that not only can memories deteriorate over time, but that they can also change, "becoming an amalgam of imagined and real events." And under certain influences, studies had found, memory can also be changed, or created. (2)

Despite this, recovered memory theory found wide public and professional acceptance. Bolstered by the theory's assumptions, some overzealous therapists used specific techniques to lead their clients to believe they had been abused, even if they didn't initially recall incidents of abuse, or had sought counseling for other concerns. To promote "recall," some practitioners used leading questions, hypnosis, or guided imagery. Others used "truth serum"–type drugs, such as sodium pentothol. In the course of therapy, many women came to believe they had experienced abuse based on little more than inference or hazy recall. Often, the longer the woman was in therapy, the more egregious the "remembered" abuse became. Some recovered memory practitioners encouraged clients to confront their suspected abuser. For women who were actually abused, confrontation may have been empowering (some therapists question the helpfulness of confronting an abuser). But in too many households, astounded fathers, uncles, grandfathers, and other male family members found themselves accused of sexual abuse they vehemently denied had occurred. (3)

The recovered memory movement eventually created a huge controversy in therapeutic circles and beyond—were recovered memories accurate depictions of the past, or were they re-creations fashioned to validate what the therapist expected to find? Many of those who have since analyzed the 1980s panic see the movement as helping create the cultural mindset that set the stage for the childcare abuse cases, the rise in diagnoses of multiple personality disorder, and the increased belief in satanic ritual abuse. In the course of the panic, recalled memories of sexual abuse—regardless of what techniques were used to recover them—were considered to be accurate reflections of what had occurred. Children, one theory held, never lie about being abused. In the day care abuse cases, the "memories" extracted from suspected victims during hours of interviews—no matter how preposterous or physically untenable—were accepted as true, and evidence of a suspect's guilt. Except in rare cases, juries, judges, and the public sided with the accusers.

I wasn't aware of the recovered memory movement that night as I listened to John in the living room, the tall clock ticking away each sad second. But I knew Michelle was so at the mercy of her "memories" she was capable of saying anything. I couldn't think of a word to say to ease his burdened heart. I couldn't tell him Michelle would never name him as a perpetrator. I couldn't tell him not to worry, that everything would work out for the best. I was confident that if she named John as one of her abusers, the accusation would fall on deaf ears in their local and church community, where he was well known and well liked. "My husband has more integrity in his little finger than most people have in their entire bodies," Mary was fond of saying. Still, even false accusations leave a mark.

During that 1990 visit, John, Mary, Michelle, and I went camping at a favorite family spot in the high desert, just over the state line in Wyoming. I rode with John in the camper; Michelle and Mary followed us in the family's well-worn Honda. From our remote campsite we took a hike up a desolate ridge where chunks of petrified wood littered the ground. Buffeting winds pushed against us. As we neared the top, John pointed to a golden eagle perched in a nest on a precarious rock ledge. We watched as she bent to feed her chick. Gusts of wind fluffed and flattened her feathers, but she didn't waver from her perch as she stuffed food down the chick's scrawny gullet. Back at camp we built a fire and cooked dinner as the purplish twilight seeped from the sky.

But as night descended, Michelle grew agitated. Her memories, or the voices she attached to the memories, had followed her to the desert. "It's not safe here," she said, in a small, scared voice. "They know where I am. I've got to go back." She begged John and Mary to return to Logan. They tried to reason with her, but she wouldn't be soothed. "If you don't take me back, I'll go anyway," she said. They knew she meant it—she had fled before when she felt pursued. Neither the lack of light nor the maze of winding dirt roads would stop her once she started to run. Some fears outweigh others.

My brother's face was drawn and spent. Mary wept. Without thinking, I opened my mouth and for once broke my self-imposed silence. "For heaven's sake, Michelle, just tell them, whoever they are, to butt out," I said. "Just stand up to them and tell them you're going to stay. You're stronger than they are. It's your life, not theirs. Don't let them push you around like that."

But if my words penetrated, Michelle didn't show it. She insisted on leaving. Mary, her voice weary and defeated, agreed to drive her back. They threw their sleeping bags and backpacks into the back of the Honda and drove off into the desert night. John and I stayed in the camper, sitting across the cramped table from each other in the light of a Coleman lantern. We didn't make conversation. We tried to read our books.

After a long while we heard a car approaching in the distance. We looked up at each other in surprise. We opened the camper's door and saw headlights coming toward us. I watched in disbelief as the Honda pulled up and stopped. Mary and Michelle hopped out. They were smiling.

"Michelle did what you said," Mary exulted. "She told them she was the one in control, not them. And she decided she could come back." Michelle nodded, clearly pleased with herself. I felt a warm, unfamiliar flush. Accomplishment? Headway? We settled in for the night under what felt like effervescent stars. One tiny triumph.

The victory was not long-lasting. The afternoon before I headed back to Oregon, Michelle and I went for a walk. Despite the brief reprieve in the desert, it had been hard to spend time alone with her. Mary constantly trailed Michelle while she was home, hovering close by when the two of us were together. I wondered if Mary's burgeoning paranoia now included me. I wondered if she suspected me of being one of "them."

But that last day she allowed us some space. As Michelle and I strolled through the nearby park, she talked about her memories and how they had come to dominate her life. Again, I encouraged her to push against the inner voices that so terrified her. I stressed that she was in charge of her own mind. For a while she was quiet. Then she began to speak.

"I know Mom and Dad were at some of the rituals. I saw them there," she said, her chapped, chewed lips quivering. "They couldn't save me. I know they wanted to."

There it was. Exactly as John had feared, only she didn't name just him. I felt a shuddering begin to rise from my gut. And the by-now familiar floundering for an appropriate response. Did one even exist?

"Don't tell them I told you. Please," she said. "I know they love me. It wasn't their fault—they couldn't help it. I've forgiven them."

I nodded. I hoped this would be the end. The final confession. The last unthinkable horror she would share.

But she wasn't done.

"Those people got me pregnant—you know, during the rituals. I had a baby."

She must have seen how stunned I looked.

"I did," she repeated, her voice ominously calm. "But they made me kill it. With a knife. Then . . ." Her voice dropped so low I could barely hear it. "They made me eat some of it. They made me eat pieces of my own child."

As Michelle spoke, I balled my fist and pressed it hard into my stomach. I didn't remember that eating parts of a newborn child had also been described by the Michelle who authored the grisly *Michelle Remembers*. I did not consider for a moment that Michelle was replaying a copycat scenario. My only thought was, here we are, plunging into yet another layer of hell. Was there no bottom to this nightmare?

"I remember the night it happened," she went on. Her voice grew stronger as she spoke. "After they let me go, I lay all night with my face in a ditch. I wanted to die. When I woke up, I knew I had to keep on living. Because what they wanted was for me to die. I got up, cleaned myself up, and went home."

You would think at this point I would have had enough. That I would have been adamant that she had crossed a line. That I would have told her in a firm but determined voice, "No, Michelle. This did not happen. I know you think it did, but it did not." But I didn't say any of that. It took years for me to ask myself why, on that August afternoon, with Mary nowhere around, I didn't challenge my niece. Was I afraid how she would react if I called her "memory" a delusion? Was I afraid of the rage or distancing such a statement might provoke? Or had I, like hundreds of others, been cowed by the panic I hadn't yet identified into a bewildered silence?

I had a personal precedent for not challenging abuse victims' stories. In the early 1970s, I volunteered at one of the country's first battered women's shelters in Boston. The issue of domestic violence was just emerging, and women who accused their husbands or partners of abuse often faced suspicion, along with condescension or ridicule, from police, the courts, and sometimes their extended families. At the shelter, we were taught to believe what clients told us without question. To voice doubt would be to abuse the victim all over again, we were instructed. Just believe them. (Recovered memory adherents, it turned out, held the same line, except regarding recall: If you remember abuse, it happened. If you challenge the veracity of a victim's memories, you become like an abuser. If you care for someone, you believe them.)

Today I realize there is a major difference between believing someone's story about being hurt by an identifiable abuser, and believing a story about improbable and heinous abuse that doesn't leave marks or identify a perpetrator, a place, or a time. But back when Michelle was in the grip of her memories, the line for me was less distinct, even when she told me something that was as patently unbelievable as that her parents had been present at satanic rituals, that she had ingested parts of her own child.

Don't double her pain, I told myself as we walked back toward her house. Don't salt her wounds. Don't let her see your doubt.

Instead, I sputtered out questions: How could people not know? Didn't John or Mary notice her stomach growing? What about the labor pains? As she had before, she had an explanation for everything: baggy clothes, the cult's talent for hiding telltale signs, the late-night disappearances while her parents slept. I stopped my probing once I realized my questions weren't doing any good.

"Please don't tell Mom and Dad," she begged again. "They don't know I saw them, you know, at the rituals."

"I won't say a word," I said, trying to sound reassuring. As we walked, a moment of rare clarity surfaced in my mind. If the rape or even one instance of ritual abuse was true, Michelle

144

had suffered an unthinkable ordeal. And if none of it were true, then something was terribly amiss in her psyche. Either way, she was undeniably ill.

The thought gave me some comfort. It released me from the grip of needing to figure out "the truth," at least right then. All I needed to do was show her I loved her and supported her, I decided. If I said anything, I knew it had to be real. I took a breath and spoke the only words that seemed true enough to utter.

"Thanks for sticking around. For not, you know, ending it all," I said. "You must have been tempted. This whole thing has been hell. No. Worse."

She paused. "I tried once or twice," she said. "But it didn't work. I think I'm past that now. I want to get better. I really do." We gave each other a quick hug, and walked into the house.

A few weeks after I returned to Oregon, in late September, Michelle checked herself into Logan Hospital. "She has been an established victim of a satanic cult with recurrent sexual abuse and intermittent out-of-control bulimia," the hospital record reads. "Patient states that . . . 'My life is in danger. I don't want to go back to the cult. I don't want to mess around. I want to live.'" The admitting doctor described Michelle as unkempt and gaunt, but alert and bright. "She is oriented in all spheres. . . . She is insightful. . . . There is no evidence of delusion, dementia, or delirium."

She had been bingeing for months. She was five feet, five inches tall and weighed 109 pounds. She was convinced she had given birth to a child and was made to consume parts of it. She walked out of the hospital the next day.

One of my sisters saved a letter I wrote after I returned from that 1990 visit to Logan. Even though what I remember from my time there is my helplessness at hearing Michelle's latest disclosures, and my realization about how ill she was, the letter mentions none of that. In fact, it is inexplicably upbeat. I refer to the issue of ritual abuse as a given, not as something whose credibility I was grappling with incessantly. I told my sister I thought it would be good for Michelle to get out of Logan and that I was busy cleaning my house because I had invited her to visit me in Springfield, even though I don't remember having done that. I told my sister I had spoken with a counselor in Portland "and she says a major step to healing is getting the person out of the town where it happened in the first place. I don't know what I can and can't handle as far as the eating goes and the fearfulness, but I'm willing to give it a try."

Reading the letter decades later, I am unsettled at its tone. Did I adopt my optimistic attitude to balance out Mary's increasing despondency? Was that my form of denial? What about the despair John had shared with me? What about Michelle's story about delivering and killing an infant, and my realization about her mental state? Was I so intent on believing Michelle could get better that I refused to give voice to deeper and more tangled concerns?

Memory isn't only affected by outside influences. We shape and remold it all on our own.

"I'm glad I don't know for sure if Michelle is coming," I wrote at the end of the letter. "Because if she wasn't I probably wouldn't be so industrious. Will send more when there's more to send."

chapter 11

voices

Later that fall, Michelle slipped deeper into psychic chaos. She agreed to be readmitted to Logan Hospital because of her bulimia, her incessant memories, and her increasingly suicidal thoughts. "She has considered leaving the area and 'healing' herself in a place where she does not know the cult members," the hospital record reads. By then, both Mary and Michelle's counselor were convinced Michelle was being targeted for speaking out against the cult. The counselor directed the hospital to keep Michelle from any contact with outsiders. She gave John and Mary a code name to use when they visited so the staff would know they were truly who they said they were.

"Patient feels obliged to do all she can to destroy the satanic cult," a nurse noted. "Patient fears she may be susceptible to satanic recruitment at this time."

After Michelle was released from the hospital, Mary and Michelle's therapist decided that Michelle needed to go underground. Mary had a plan. She had recently attended a talk on ritual abuse given by a Denver woman (I'll call her Jean) who identified herself as a survivor. Mary—who by this point was beyond desperate—had spoken with Jean after the talk and told her about Michelle. Jean told Mary she had worked with a psychologist who was skilled in treating ritual abuse victims and that she had learned the techniques. Jean had no professional credentials—I surmise now she had other skills, such as knowing the ritual abuse lingo and being able to spot an easy mark—but to Mary, she offered hope.

In January 1991, Mary drove Michelle, then twenty-two, to Jean's apartment in Denver. Mary stayed with them for a couple of weeks and then returned to Utah, leaving Michelle at the apartment with a car and a stocked bank account.

John never liked the plan, he told me later, even though he didn't intervene. He thought it would help Michelle to get out of Logan and live in a neutral environment. But the Colorado plan had left him wary. "I didn't trust those people," he said. "I didn't trust the type of person who said they can cure something like that."

He was right. Within a couple of days of Mary's leaving, Jean withdrew the money from Michelle's account. Michelle moved out of the apartment and soon after wrecked her car. She was found passed out on the street and was admitted to a hospital. She was transferred to a halfway house and ran away. At the time, Wynlee was a veterinary student at Colorado State University. Michelle found her way to the highway heading north to Fort Collins. She held out her thumb and hitched a ride.

From the time Michelle showed up at her apartment that night, Wynlee, then twenty-three, took on the role of courier, as Michelle frantically tried to find a place where she felt safe from the cult. It was a twist on the old Greek myth—Wynlee, as Michelle's Charon, was trying to ferry her sister *out* of the underworld.

"She'd call from Denver and say, 'Come get me,'" Wynlee told me. "She'd stay a few days, but then she'd want to leave again. We went back and forth several times." One night, Wynlee drove Michelle from Fort Collins to Logan in the middle of a snowstorm. I imagine them pushing through the mountain passes, snow flying at the windshield in a spray of white bullets, Wynlee focused and determined, Michelle silent and rigid in the passenger seat. But as they neared their hometown, Michelle faltered. She insisted the cult would track her there, that they had to return to Fort Collins. "So I turned around and drove her back," Wynlee said.

Despite being just fifteen months apart, the two hadn't been close growing up. Wynlee's inherent self-possession and Michelle's emotional neediness weren't a good fit. As children, they lived in different worlds even while sharing the same room. When Michelle reached her teens, her bingeing, purging, and flaring rages kept the family stirred up and on edge, and Wynlee, understandably, judged her for it. When Michelle was first admitted to the hospital in 1989, Wynlee couldn't muster much sympathy. "I thought she was just messing up terribly," Wynlee told me, years later. "I thought, 'Why does she do all these things? Why can't she just get along?'"

"I had a teenager mentality, then," she told me. "I deeply resented the suffering she was causing my parents. I was cruel to her. I would say, 'Why can't you live by the rules like everyone else? You're destroying Mom and Dad.'"

But witnessing her sister's emotional state during the harrowing winter of 1991 changed her. "I stopped being a teenager and became an adult about it," Wynlee said. "I finally realized how sick she was. I remember grasping onto any hope that she was going to be OK."

But that winter, Wynlee's hope flowed through her fingers like water. Michelle was desperate to find a safe place to land, but because the true source of her anxiety was internal, not external, there was no safety to be had. So she ran. When that didn't work, she tried to kill the pain. She stabbed herself with pencils, overdosed on drugs and ended up in yet another hospital, this time in Boulder.

Back in Oregon, I felt guilty about my reluctance to check in with John and Mary. But it wasn't just me who was being stand-offish. Mary was deliberately evasive about Michelle's where-abouts that winter. By then, she was so convinced of the cult's limitless power that she believed it could track Michelle wher-ever she went. She wouldn't specify where Michelle was living or how she was faring. It was years before I knew of that winter's nighttime ferrying between Colorado and Utah, the drug over-doses, the hospital admittances.

Maybe it was just as well. Ever since I'd returned from Logan the previous summer, concern over my niece hung on me like an invisible yoke. I was convinced no one was provid-ing Michelle with the help she needed, and I knew I didn't have the skills, either. I knew by then that others—not just a few, but dozens, maybe more—were coming forward claiming similar memories of ritual abuse. I lived in a twilight limbo, a murky space where I neither believed nor completely disbelieved in the ritual abuse phenomenon. I resisted believing that a massive, undetectable cult was scooping up armloads of children and programming them to do evil. But neither could I explain why so many other women were coming forward with similar, grue-some claims, or why my counselor had more questions than answers when it came to ritual abuse, or why local therapists had begun adding "RA survivors" among their lists of treat-ment specialties in their newspaper advertisements.

My job as editor of a monthly newspaper for foster youth

entailed interviewing foster teens across the country. I was well aware of the troubles hundreds of these kids went to bed with every night and woke up with the next morning—neglect, loss, usually some sort of abuse or mistreatment. The teens told me stories of living with parents who were addicted to drugs or alcohol, and their own struggles with substance abuse. They told me about being beaten and sexually molested, not by strangers in ceremonial robes but by family members or people they knew. They told me about white-hot rages they couldn't control, about failed placements with foster families and how it felt to love someone who couldn't love them back. The stories I wrote for my newspaper needed to sound upbeat, but I carried the weight of what they left out. I didn't want to accept the existence of yet another horrific reality that manufactured misery, but I felt the possibility hovering around me.

My boss hired a man about my age with a freshly minted PhD in psychology to be a consultant. I ached for this man to notice me, to want to know who I was, to want to hear my story. He didn't. My loneliness became like a stray pet I had invited inside that then wouldn't leave. The winter dragged on.

My one dependable source of comfort was singing with the community gospel choir I was part of. The majority of the choir was white, but our director was black and chose music from the traditional gospel vein or modern arrangements written by current gospel artists. Even though most of the members held the Christian beliefs I had rejected years earlier, singing with the choir provided sustenance I couldn't get anywhere else. I showed up for every rehearsal, every performance. Some of the words of the songs rankled me—I cringed when one lyric referred to "filthy sin"—but I kept returning. I was hungry for community and the music's spiritual boost. For a few hours a week I was willing to tolerate a characterization of God—and occasionally of the devil—that didn't fit what I believed. I envied choir members whose belief in God and the triumph of good-ness was simple and unconflicted. When John, our director, sang, his baritone voice resounded with bone-deep conviction. "You took my world that was torn apart, and you brought it all back together," one soloist sang with no quaver of ambivalence. At the end of particularly moving songs, the tenors on my left and the sopranos on my right would raise their arms in praise, thanksgiving, or joyful surrender. Week after week, my arms stayed rooted to my sides.

But occasionally, in the midst of the throng of other voices, I felt a presence greater than the dimension I lived in daily, and it bolstered me. Accompanied by a piano, an electric bass, and pounding drums, the sound of the choir vibrated with power and—I refused to let go of the word, despite its religious overtones—even grace. Our lusty volume threw a glimmer of light on the bleak sea that lapped at the back of my brain. "The Lord is my light and my salvation, whom shall I fear?" we sang. "Though I walk in the valley of, in the shadow of, darkness, I shall fear no evil." When I sang by myself, my voice was timid and small, but in the safety of the choir, my throat swelled. Every word that left my lips was pushed by all the words I had stowed unspoken. Longing, fear, and need poured from me. I leaned into the notes and they held me up.

In one of our conversations, Mary told me that Michelle had acquired a new diagnosis. Her previous diagnoses included post-traumatic stress disorder, bulimia, and borderline per-sonality disorder. This new one was called multiple personality disorder, or MPD.

When Mary told me, I was immediately skeptical. The very label sounded contrived. "I've never heard of it," I responded.

But even though I wasn't familiar with the term itself, I

was aware of the concept. I had seen the film *The Three Faces of Eve*, years after it first came out in 1957. Based on a book about a psychiatric case study, the story centered on a prim and proper woman, Eve White, who developed two secondary personalities, one of which was Eve Black, a provocative seductress who most often surfaced at night. (1) The actor Joanne Woodward, whom I adored, played the part of all three Eves and won an Academy Award for her performance.

I more vividly remembered the TV movie *Sybil*, which was based on a 1973 nonfiction book of the same name. The book chronicled the case of a young girl who was horribly abused by her mother and, in order to cope, developed sixteen different personalities. The 1976 movie starred Sally Field as Sybil and Woodward as Sybil's therapist, Dr. Cornelia Wilbur. I was among the viewers glued to the TV screen both nights the movie aired. I remember one haunting scene where the mother forced water into Sybil's bladder, and made her hold it in while her mom pounded out classical music on the piano. I remember the girl pleading, the mother's ringing refusal, and the liquid finally pooling on the floor.

Significant doubts have since surfaced as to the veracity of Sybil's multiple personality diagnosis. (2) But back then, I was among the public that accepted her story as true. The possibility that anything related to that eerie movie would touch my life was inconceivable to me, but Michelle's ordeal had spat out one inconceivable notion after another. I just listened. Briefly, Mary explained the theory, which I paraphrase here because I don't remember her exact words. MPD was brought on by severe childhood trauma, usually sexual. Because the child's developing psyche can't handle the abuse memories, they split off from the core personality, eventually becoming separate personalities, or alters. Some of the alters are protective; some hold the abuse memories; others are angry, or afraid. The alters come and go of their own accord; often the core personality isn't aware of them, or their behavior, which can be a marked contrast to that displayed by the core personality.

For Mary, the new diagnosis made sense. It explained why Michelle was so changeable, how she could be calm, rational, and accessible one minute, a hysterical child or an angry, curse-spewing adolescent the next. Those other personalities weren't the real Michelle. They were fragment selves.

I added the term MPD and its accompanying jargon to my growing lexicon of the confounding world Mary and Michelle now inhabited. People with MPD often referred to themselves as "multiples." The sub-personalities were called "alters," "adaptives," or "splinters." "Switching" was when a person with MPD changed from one alter to another. A "trigger" referred to a sight, sound, or smell that brought on memories of past trauma. "Triggers" often led to "switching."

In her 1999 book, *Creating Hysteria—Women and Multiple Personality Disorder,* Joan Acocella presents a nuanced and multilayered analysis of the MPD epidemic. The phenomenon of dissociation—a condition in which a person is disconnected from the present—and a spectrum of dissociative states had been identified by researchers. Until the 1970s, however, multiple personality disorder was a rare psychological phenomenon. But beginning in that decade, several factors—including, Acocella says, the momentum of the recovered memory movement, the child protection movement, the growing influence of television and other media, and practitioners' fascination with the phenomenon of alternate selves—brought MPD to wider social awareness, and acceptance. In 1980, the term multiple personality disorder, or MPD, was listed among dissociative disorders in the *Diagnostic and Statistical Manual of Mental Disorders* (DSMIII), the American Psychiatric Association's guide for treatment providers. Soon, MPD went from being a psychological anomaly to the decade's most trendy diagnosis. (3)

Therapists who espoused MPD theory operated on the premise that women who had been severely sexually abused in their childhoods—even if they had no memory of it—had developed alternate personalities to allow them to cope with the trauma. In order to heal their patients, they needed to contact the alters, because they held the memories of the abuse. The most zealous practitioners used whatever tools were necessary to uncover alters, from drugs and hypnosis to inpatient hospitalizations to outright threats and badgering. The process rarely stopped at finding just a few—the longer clients were in therapy, the more alters therapists found. Some practitioners cited cases where they identified more than two hundred alters.

Many of the most impassioned and high-profile MPD advocates promulgated their belief in the widespread existence of satanic cults, and satanic ritual abuse, or SRA. Acocella describes how the two epidemics overlapped: both were an outgrowth of recovered memory theory; both arose out of similar cultural stresses; both drew from the ranks of feminists and Christian fundamentalists; and both had a similar demographic profile: predominantly white, North American, females who came out of the offices of a relatively small number of therapists. "By the mid-eighties, SRA was not only like MPD; it was part of the MPD movement," she wrote. (4)

In February 1991, John and Mary drove to Boulder to pick up Michelle after she had again tried to hurt herself. Back in Logan, Michelle was admitted to Logan Hospital's Behavioral Health Unit. She was disheveled, anxious, hostile, and reluctant to talk.

"She is reportedly the victim of cult abuse including sexual abuse, animal mutilation and possibly human sacrifice," the admitting physician wrote. "She has fragmented into dozens, perhaps hundreds of personality 'alters' which she now refers to as 'splinters.'"

A few hours after being admitted, Michelle bolted from the unit, ran to a friend's house, and downed a handful of antihistamines. She was brought back, admitted to the Intensive Care Unit, and stabilized. The next day, she was placed in seclusion.

The caregivers on the unit were vigilant—her first day on the unit they produced six pages of logged comments. Michelle's emotional state ricocheted between terror, rage, despair, and exhausted apathy. She called John and Mary and begged them to come to the unit, but when they arrived, she refused to see them. When John tried to give her a blessing, she refused it, saying, "No, Michelle isn't here. It won't do any good. Go do it in my name for someone else."

Most of her caregivers seemed to believe her claims of being a ritual abuse victim. They commented on her acting out of "re-lives," where she would experience a flashback from the abuse and retreat to the ward's seclusion room to shriek and pound on the walls.

But a few were skeptical. One physician suggested she was capable of "some degree of psychiatric malingering." After seeing that Michelle's behavior didn't abate after several days, some of the staff set boundaries. "Patient was told that she could have a memory, but that she could not scream. She asked, 'What if I need to?' and was told she would have to wait until morning."

Another female patient who believed she was a ritual abuse survivor was admitted to the ward. "They shared MPD language. . . . I suspect some recruitment may be occurring," one nurse wrote. Another staffer tried to quell Michelle's anxiety by using gentle techniques. "Imagery work done. Safe place created. Patient sees the evil, programmed parts of herself as 'monsters.' [She] felt Michelle had been destroyed. She was able to rip open the monsters and liberate pieces of light. She put the indestructible part of Michelle—an image of a smooth white stone—in a box and put it in a safe place."

During the 1980s media outlets fed the public's fascination with MPD. Talk show hosts presented programs on it. Comedienne Roseanne Barr came out as having it. Several multiples wrote about it. *When Rabbit Howls*, written by "the Troops for Truddi Chase" in 1987, tells the story of a woman who began splitting at age two, and ended up with ninety-two personalities. In 1992, Sandra J. Hocking and Company published *Living with Your Selves*. ("Troops" and "Company" are both terms for a person's collection of alters.) It was followed by the 1994 book *Someone I Know Has Multiple Personalities*, authored by Hocking alone. In her 1992 book *Revolution from Within*, feminist icon Gloria Steinem proposed that women might be able to harness the vast creative potential of MPD without having to endure the trauma that gave rise to the condition. In 1993 she narrated an HBO television show on multiple personalities. (5)

But for some women, being diagnosed with MPD led them into a hellish existence with life-shattering consequences and no easy exit. Women who initially went into counseling for minor symptoms—mild depression, anxiety, or mood swings—were led to believe they had been horrendously abused as children and consequently had developed a roster of alters. In particularly egregious cases, women ended up believing they had been ritually abused, or were recruited into a cult, or had initiated their children into cult rituals. A handful of hospitals opened up special "dissociation" units where women spent months as inpatients, becoming sicker and sicker as their therapists discovered more and more alters and "memories" of abuse. Feeling worse, they were assured, was a necessary step in the healing process.

Years after Michelle died, a friend sent me a videotape of the award-winning 1993 documentary *Dialogues with Madwomen*, which featured the struggles of seven women who overcame or were living with emotional illness. (6) One of them identified herself as having had MPD and discussed her abusive childhood and her subsequent development of twenty-five alters. She described her MPD as protective and life-saving. "I know that I kept going because I was a multiple," she said. By the time she participated in the documentary, the woman had become "integrated," meaning her various personalities were under the control of her core personality. That might explain why her description of her relationship with her alters included an element of levity. In the film, she tells the story of how one Christmas her alters had bought presents for each other. "We lived in a very little apartment, though, and everyone was trying to buy Christmas presents and hide them, without anybody else knowing what was going on. The adults [alters] hid them really high up and the children [alters] hid them really low down."

I became increasingly agitated as I watched her section of the video. I couldn't dispute the woman's claims of having MPD, or how it helped her survive her difficult childhood. But levity hadn't been any part of Michelle's experience with MPD. Rather than saving her, her multiples plagued her. She spent the last year of her life trying to marshal or control the interior cacophony of voices that haunted her days and nights. I found these entries from one of her later journals.

Sharon—frightened half to death, alone. Vague memories of good things but infiltrated with terror. Has no hope. [The word "Ricks" is written in the margin.]

Helga—afraid of everyone and thing.

Brian—Homosexual. Quiet, downcast eyes. Sweet.

Wanda—Believes sex is all she is good for. Very ashamed. Children, I need your help. Please keep the death wish people under watch and please keep them as far away as you can for me. I want to feel human. I know you saved my life, and you are very important. I do need your help. Can you help me?

I feel enraged, furious and upset when I feel I haven't done what I want but let my feelings or adaptives get in charge, or when I haven't been able to switch back. I feel hopeless, upset, in despair and like I am cast off from God when I get disoriented, which happens a lot. I feel completely out of control and like there are no limits on what could happen or there is no rhyme or reason and never will be. I feel furious that what I thought was me was just a bunch of adaptives. Nights are bad because if I don't go to sleep being me I feel I have failed, and if I wake up being me I have a distinct impression I have to do something or remember something to make it stay. Plus feelings of despair, incredible anger, hopelessness and lostness haunt me.

. . . Tuesday I woke up. I felt a little more with it, but totally crummy. I tried talking [with my alters] but I couldn't keep them under control. I went on this drive. I made this rule, no one under 18 driving. I felt instantly clear. I could hear the music on the radio, the suicidal impulse was gone and I felt a lot more together. I could feel there were alters I hadn't met. I wrote down their names. They said we belong in

*college, they said to not let the children be in control,
that I didn't have to give them everything they wanted.
Mostly they just said, "Figure it out, Michelle."*

*I could suddenly see that I was separate from
my children and that I had a life separate from
theirs. I wondered why I had waited so long to see
this. I decided I would get on with my life, go to
college, hopefully some day get married and work
on this stuff slowly in the meantime. It seemed like
I had multitudes of parts of me that were ready. . . .
Immediately all my children quieted right up. They
had been wailing in my ears all night long for the past
two nights.*

After three weeks in the Logan Hospital, Michelle's mental
state did not improve. Her "re-lives" continued to prompt fits of
screaming and crying. Her conviction that she was a multiple
caused her to despair. "I don't remember any other life but this
pain. I'm still alive inside, but I can't reach her. I don't know
how to gain control."

In late March, her physician discharged her to the Utah
State Hospital in Provo. She was accompanied by sheriff dep-
uties who were advised to take extreme caution to protect
Michelle from harming herself.

A few months later, *The Oregonian* ran another Sunday feature
on satanic ritual abuse and the resulting development of multiple personalities. (7) The story from the McClatchy News Service, focused on a thirty-eight-year-old mother from Auburn,
Washington, who believed she was the victim of a multigenerational family cult. The woman, called Sophie, recalled being
"sadistically tortured, starved, locked in cages and hung upside

down, forced to have sex with animals." She reported witnessing and participating in human sacrifices and claimed to have fifty-two different personalities.

"Fifteen years ago her account might have earned Sophie a trip to the mental hospital and a diagnosis of delusional psychosis," the reporter Elizabeth Moore wrote. "But an increasing number of clergy and counselors say they can no longer ignore such stories. . . . Therapists aren't ready to champion the idea that there are satanic family cults, going back generations . . . but they're not ready to reject the stories, either."

By then, Moore wrote, several liberal church congregations that had once expressed skepticism over ritual abuse claims had dropped their denial. In Spokane, clergy and counselors had formed a support group to handle their growing fear of being targeted by cults for treating clients. Other clergy were saying prayers over empty coffins for newborn infants said to have been sacrificed in satanic rituals. "The services are performed at the request of the infants' mothers, some of whom told clergy they'd been forced to take part in the murders to save their own lives," Moore wrote. One counselor interviewed for the story said the center where she worked was treating fourteen patients with multiple personalities—many of whom relayed stories of familial satanic abuse—and that others had been turned away because there weren't enough counselors to treat them.

chapter 12

provo

On a bright Monday morning in August 1991, two days after Wynlee married her childhood sweetheart, Robert, in Logan, I followed the directions Mary had given me to the Utah State Hospital in Provo, about an hour south of Salt Lake City. I drove into the designated parking lot and turned off the ignition. I took a deep breath and let it out slowly. I took another, opened the door, and pushed myself out of the driver's seat.

When I got to the entrance Mary had specified, I rang the bell. An attendant answered. The day before, Michelle's counselor had approved my visit. I gave the attendant my name and told her why I was there. After checking her notes, she let me in. She led me down a hallway to a small, square room. I glimpsed the back of a slight figure, dressed in sweatpants and a baggy T-shirt, running a vacuum over the carpet. Michelle. I knew the bend of her bones by heart.

I waited. She turned and looked up. The nurses hadn't told her I was coming. A huge smile broke across her face.

"Aunt Alice!" she cried. She ran toward me. We hugged, Mormon-style, as I called it: a quick, chaste press from the shoulders up.

She sat down on a couch and folded her fawn-thin legs underneath her. I took the remaining chair. We weren't alone. Michelle was on twenty-four-hour suicide watch, and an attendant had to be with her at all times. He sat in a chair against the wall and thumbed through a magazine while I prepared to fill the drab, low-ceilinged room with as much life as I could.

"How was the reception?" Michelle asked. Wynlee and Robert had been married in the Temple; non-Mormons couldn't attend the ceremony, but we were invited to the reception that followed, which was held in a nearby park. I described the pink rose bower where Wynlee had stood greeting guests with her new husband. I told Michelle that her sister wore the same gauzy wedding dress my mother had worn when she was married six decades earlier. I tried to give her sensory descriptions: the raspberry meringue tarts and punch Mary and Wynlee had prepared for the guests, and the tiny cranes Wynlee had woven out of straw ribbons and given away as favors.

"Impressive for someone who's not all that domestic," I said. Michelle, who knew her sister well, smiled at my understatement.

I didn't mention the question that had plagued me throughout the wedding reception, despite the lovely setting: Was this the real Logan, the one that had so charmed me when I first saw it, all those years ago? Or was it a false front for a town with a nefarious secret rotting out its heart, as Mary and others had come to believe?

Wynlee looked radiant through the whole affair, I told Michelle, but she had to have emergency dental surgery—a root canal—as soon as the reception was over. "Just got her married and already she's falling apart," Mary had commented.

Michelle fought back another smile. She had once shared her mother's dry, rueful sense of humor. I hadn't heard a trace of it from her in a long time.

After I told Michelle about the reception, I moved on to my own life. I told her about the gospel music gig my choir had been part of the day before in Salt Lake City. I told her about my new dog, Bailey, a young, high-strung Border collie mix, and how she had spent most of the long drive to Logan sitting in the passenger seat, pawing at my arm to get me to play.

Michelle leaned forward as I spoke, her sun-starved arms folded tight against her chest. She seemed to be drinking in my every word. Her pale face flushed with a hint of pink. A stranger coming upon us would have thought her almost well.

When I finished with my news, an ominous silence settled between us. I fought the urge to fill it with more chat. I pointed at her T-shirt; huge letters spelled out a passage from the Bible. The Book of John, perhaps. Something about light. I didn't write it down. I didn't think there was any reason to.

"The cult knows I'm here. They know I'm speaking out," she said quietly, without much emotion. She pointed to the rumpled shirt. "This helps protect me." She made the conversational transition from the wedding to the cult effortlessly, as if the two realities existed side by side—an angel and the devil sitting down to supper, with Michelle as their host.

The pain and chaos of the past few years hung in the air between us like a raptor hovering in midair. The room felt both empty and full, ringing and silent. The attendant thumbed his magazine, keeping his eyes down. I imagined him numb with boredom.

Michelle broke the silence, and asked me the question that went beyond the paranoia over the cult or flashbacks of abuse to the core of her emotional distress: "Aunt Alice, inside you, how do you feel yourself? I mean, do you feel like you are just one person? Or are there other voices, other people in there, saying things, speaking to you?"

Those of us whose core is strong can identify and regulate the different aspects of our personalities—the fearful part, the assertive part, the wise part, the snarky part. But for those who have lost touch with that inner regulator, the central hub, the "I" that moves us through our days with a sense of solidity, corralling those different parts of the personality becomes impossible, even frightening. Is that why Michelle gave her "parts" names? Is that why she embraced a diagnosis that validated the chaos she felt inside? To me, she was the same individual, the same bundle of quirks and contradictions I had known for almost two decades. But to herself, she had become a stranger.

"I want so much to be a whole person again," she said. "That's what I want, more than anything."

I did not realize, then, that she was admitting a kind of defeat.

The attendant looked at his watch, then at me, and nodded. My time was up. We got up from our chairs. Michelle walked with me toward the door, turned, and spread her arms. This time it wasn't a Mormon hug. Her touch was hard and fierce as she pressed into my body. "Don't forget me," she whispered, her eyes welling up. "Please, please, don't forget me."

On the drive back to Logan I thought of my time working at the mental health center in Boston. Five days a week I took patients' vital signs, sat with them at meals, and ushered them to occupational therapy or on daily walks. I learned about manic-depressive disease, psychotic breaks, and paranoid delusions. I became familiar with the names of the drugs such as Haldol, Thorazine, and lithium that our patients were prescribed to help control their delusions and behavior. I listened as my patients ranted while they played pool or shuffled through the dayroom. I was on the alert to catch some kernels of universal truth they might utter from what I thought might be a higher plane, some spiritual insights my obedient, socialized brain couldn't summon on its own. Occasionally I thought I did.

But after I had worked on the ward for several months, my romantic notions of psychiatric illness dissipated. I realized my schizophrenic patients were confused, not dazzled, by the voices they heard speaking to them from inside their heads or from the radio or television. The medications they took to quiet the voices made their limbs heavy and turned their mouths into tight, dry caves. The patients with manic-depressive illness (now termed bipolar disorder) could be entertaining while manic, but we had little to offer them when the thick cloud of depression inevitably descended, leaving them mute and inert.

Most patients stayed with us for short stretches but some were regulars. There was curly-haired Betty who returned from her day passes off the ward smelling unwashed and with her shirt buttoned wrong. Muttering over and over, "I'm spoiled, spoiled," she turned over her arms to show me scars from a spate of self-cutting that marched up her skin like a diary of despair.

Rita, another regular, stood barely five feet tall, had gaps in her large, nicotine-stained teeth, and wore her hair in a wispy bun on top of her head. She spent her days pacing the hall, smoking, and yelling back at the voices she heard speaking to her through the large, sealed windows. Often, while waiting for a light for her cigarette, she marched in place, switching her weight from one foot to the other. One Sunday I made her come on an outing with the other patients to a nearby ocean beach. After some coaxing, she rolled up her jeans and waded out into the surf. I watched her squeal as the chilly water nipped at her pale, spindly legs. On the way home we bought fresh corn from a farm stand. Back at the unit I boiled it up and served it to them on the cob. The patients seemed calm and sated. A few days later Rita walked up to me, gave me a shy smile, waved an unlit cigarette in front of my face, and asked for a light. I found a lighter and lit it. She sucked in the smoke, blew it out, and focused her eyes on my face. "You're soft, you know," she said. "Soft as a fucking grape."

And there was rail-thin Robert, a smart young man with a shy smile, a bleak, gothic wit, and purplish hollows rimming his deep-set eyes. He fought valiantly against the depression that sucked him down into an eddy of hopelessness, day after day, week after week. The first time he jumped from the second floor to the cement landing below the unit, he broke both legs. We didn't see him for several months, but then he returned, laid low by another bout of depression. He jumped a second time, this time from a higher floor, assuring he wouldn't return.

It was clear to me then those patients were ill, but Michelle was different, I thought. The young woman I had just seen was ill, but she was almost the same Michelle I had always known. I wanted her to be reachable, salvageable. As I drove north on I-15 toward Logan, I felt her eyes boring into me beyond the periphery of my vision. Her hoarse whisper echoed in my mind like a chant.

Later that night, after John and Mary had gone to bed, I sat in a rocking chair under a lamp in their homey living room, a pile of Michelle's recent, spiral-bound journals at my feet. When I first noticed the notebooks stashed along the wall of the back bedroom, I had debated about reading them, not wanting to invade her privacy. But after my visit with her I felt compelled to know more about what was going on in her mind. John and Mary were asleep, but they had trusted me to visit her. I didn't think they'd mind. I leaned over and picked up the top note-book from the pile.

Initially, the writing was vintage Michelle, but with a bitter twist.

I love anybody who ever dissociated under the influence of too much Diet Coke, a too-sweet cookie and the wrong trigger. I love anyone who ever ran out into the parking lot buck naked and screamed "I love Jesus" while jumping up and down on someone else's car. I love anyone who ever sneezed right in the middle of an intense, powerful satanic chant. I love anyone who ever walked for days and days and weeks and weeks and for two years trying to find the sun. That's me. I love her.

But soon the notebook documented her descent into the chamber of horrors she believed was her past. Memories of the rape blurred with descriptions of bloody sacrifices. In contrast to the silence surrounding me, her words blared and screeched. On page after page she scrawled out her rage, her feelings of betrayal, and her desire for revenge. It was hard to tell if she raged at the boys she believed had raped her, or at the ritual abusers—perhaps they had all become one. Some of the voices speaking from the pages were harsh and accusing. Others promised healing. Sometimes they merged in a discordant chorus.

You are not alone. Now I am here. I am with you. I stand with you and I am by your side. I give to you the power, yourself, to kill those boys. To slice them to bits. My power is now yours and you are not helpless, you are not powerless, your trapped screaming is stopped, because now you have power. Use it. Kill those fuckers dead. They are bastards and beasts and it is your right. . . . Michelle, for God's sake, see them as they are. Strip away their lies from your eyes, see their filth, their disgustingness. Those people hurt you. It was not one it was four. See their filthiness and kill them.

Another voice was that of a magnanimous healer.

Look into me and see the enormous reserves of healing and power. They exist in embryo in you, and now I give them back fully formed. They will heal you. You can speak. I validate you. I was the silent witness and now I am the healer. Now you will be heard and I can hold you forever. What you need I will give. Only Michelle, you must speak.

After finishing one notebook, I picked up another. In this one, her handwriting morphed from adult longhand to child-like printing to ramblings that shot diagonally across the page. She repeated bizarre incantations and nonsensical rhymes. Various voices threatened, cajoled, bullied. Words I had never heard her use—"Fuck," "cunt," "bitch"—shouted from the blue-lined paper. She pleaded for help. She prayed to be cleansed, forgiven, delivered.

"Help me. Won't somebody please, please, please help me?" she wrote in huge black letters. "God—where are you? Why won't you help me?"

On another page she wrote in a small, tight script these chilling thoughts:

I have to kill my mom and dad because if I don't I will be killed and I have to stay alive to protect the baby. I get to keep the baby if I cut up and kill my parents and family. I'll rip them up, I'll pretend I like it. . . . I like to be this disgusting and gross because it makes everybody laugh and I do it so well, but I hurt. I hurt because nobody knows. Nobody knows I am really like this. They think I am just OK Michelle. But I'm not. I do the most gross and disgusting things.

And then:

Do you see my hand reaching, reaching, reaching for life? For beauty. Can you see it. Can you see it.

I tunneled through one notebook after another. My hope for my niece diminished with each turn of the thin pages. The notebooks chronicled a mind at war with itself, so fragmented and chaotic that it had lost any sense of cohesion or oneness. "That's what I want, more than anything," she had told me. To be a whole person.

The clock chimed 3:00 a.m. My eyes burning, I piled the journals on top of each other and groped my way to bed.

I left for Oregon the next day. The drive back was grueling. Michelle's scrawled words flashed in my mind like neon signs, calling and repelling me. Despite the bright summer sun, I wanted to sink into blackness. But I could not escape my own mind, or hers. I had finally witnessed how truly split Michelle was internally, whether or not a cult existed, whether or not she had undergone the abuse she believed she had, whether or not she had this thing called MPD. I had seen her handwriting morph from childlike printing to prim, analytic cursive to a desperate scrawl. I had seen her flaming rage, the throng of voices crowding her mind, her pleas for help. Whatever denial I had left in me flaked away like old paint. The niece I had once delighted in was gone. In her place was someone so broken into pieces I could not imagine her returning to her former self.

I drove relentlessly to keep the inevitable at bay. I pushed west through Idaho and crossed the border into Oregon, where the road narrowed to two lanes. I wound through the familiar red rock canyons and dusty wheat fields. I shoved a tape into the cassette player and tried to sing along, but my voice came out reedy and thin, like a prayer drained of faith.

chapter 13
obituary

Michelle Tallmadge, 23, died early Saturday morning, Nov. 16, 1991, in Logan.

A pretty girl with sparkling wit, Michelle brightened the lives of all who knew her. She showed her compassionate nature by working as a housemother for several severely handicapped children. Michelle graduated from Logan High School in 1986 and attended Ricks College on a music scholarship.

In her childhood, Michelle was subject to severe ritualistic abuse. When these memories surfaced at a later age she was never able to resolve the memories with who she wanted to be. After four years of unbearable pain, she left this life of her own accord.

—Logan Herald Journal
(Written by John)

chapter 14
keening

Arriving home after the funeral, I was hit with the welter of bewildering sensations that huddle under the name of grief. I had imagined mourning as a sober, dignified state, not a swirl of crimson anger potholed by disappointment and feelings of betrayal. My nerves were raw as flayed skin. A disquieting rage seethed beneath my surface. If I had given it voice, it would have sounded like a brassy shriek.

I was short-tempered with my housemate and with strangers. When I called a friend for support, and she didn't remember about my niece's funeral, I cut her off in the middle of her fumbling apology and hung up. When reprints of a photo of Michelle I had ordered came back cropped wrong, the clerk at the store told me the redo would take several days because of the holiday rush. "I don't care about that," I barked at her. "This was your mistake. Fix it." When I learned I hadn't been chosen to be part of a small holiday choir performance, I demanded to know why. "Because you missed two practices," my section leader told me.

I fought the urge to clamp my hands on her thick, bowed shoulders and shake her. She knew I rarely missed practice. Couldn't she tell I was mired in loss? "I was at a family funeral," I told her, each syllable hot with righteous anger.

Even my grief, I felt then, was contaminated.

Each morning, as soon as my feet touched the floor, the awareness of Michelle's death flooded me. A dull fog hovered over my brain for the rest of the day. My counselor urged me to attend a support group for family members of suicide victims. I balked. Michelle's death was only part of it, I told her. It was the reason for the suicide that demanded silence. "I can't bring that satanic stuff up to people," I said. "They have enough to deal with without hearing about that."

I rummaged through my desk drawers to find letters from Michelle. I scoured my journals for entries that mentioned her name. I had not thought to keep her letters or my reflections in one particular place. I hadn't imagined a time when I would want so much to find them.

Among the scraps I found was a copy of a letter I had written recounting the guidance I had received from the *I Ching* after returning from Logan in 1989, the summer Michelle had begun recalling her memories of ritual abuse. I had been at a loss of what to do or how to help her, so I had turned to the wisest counsel I knew. Over the years I had performed the ritual of tossing coins to guide me to one of the *I Ching*'s sixty-four hexagrams that would help me with whatever issue I was facing. The *I Ching* was cryptic but helpful. The hexagram I had received regarding Michelle was "Preponderance of the Great."

I didn't remember the interpretation of the hexagram, so I found my copy and looked it up. "The weight of the great is excessive. The load is too heavy for the strength of the supports," the reading said. "It is an exceptional time and situation." At first I felt comforted rereading the words. The *I Ching* acknowledges but does not sugarcoat difficult times. Then I came to the last paragraph.

"Here is a situation in which the unusual has reached a climax. One is courageous and wishes to accomplish one's task, no matter what happens. This leads into danger. The water rises over one's head. This is the misfortune. But one incurs no blame in giving up one's life that the good and the right may prevail. There are things that are more important than life."

The words jolted me. Had the *I Ching* predicted that Michelle would sacrifice her life for the sake of a greater mission? Was her suicide a call for people to take action against the supposed cult that so terrified her? What was it that was more important than her life?

I spent my days in front of the computer tapping out stories for a local weekly newspaper and my nights nursing a hole I didn't know how to fill. I craved sympathy and attention, but to get them required revealing more about my niece than I wanted to. Opaque oil. Weeping water. They did not mix. My grief turned into a needy, demanding child. She wanted attention and comfort. But I couldn't muster them. I didn't know how to soothe her.

Catherine, my renter, tried to be sympathetic, but Christmas, her favorite holiday, was beckoning. She nagged me to decorate the house, but I couldn't summon interest in twinkly lights or a festive tree. I was relieved the morning she finally left for her vacation, but even that was short-lived. A few hours later, I slammed a door on my thumb. The pain was fierce. Within minutes, my thumb began to swell, and by the time I left for choir practice, it had become a throbbing, purple bulb. I didn't think of applying ice or taking aspirin. I realized now I wanted sympathy more than relief, but I didn't know that then. During our break, I approached a small group of tenors who were talking amongst themselves. I inserted myself into their huddle and waited for a moment to break in. "Look what I did today," I announced, waving my fat, distended thumb in front of their faces. Each of them looked at me blankly. After a pause they continued their banter as if I hadn't said a thing. Mortified, I brought the aching knob back down to my side, curled my other fingers around it, and made my way back to the other side of the room.

Does grieving count if no one sees it? Is it genuine if it is pierced with anger and a craving to be noticed? Sometimes I couldn't even decide what to grieve—Michelle's lonely, self-chosen death, her last few miserable years of life, or the burden of questions she left behind for which I had no answers. For the last two years I had tried to focus on her healing. But now that healing wasn't an option, the questions I had held at bay cascaded down like water over a breached dam: What if the ritual abuse—even a part of it—had been real? What if, as Mary feared, Michelle had been punished for speaking out about it? Had I failed my niece in not believing her? In letting her think I believed her? Should I have intervened—sooner, stronger, louder?

Sometime in her last chaotic years Michelle sent me a card that I had tacked up on the wall of my home office. Inside she had written, "Life has been tough but it is certainly getting better, Yes, even my eating, with all rapidity." On the front was a quote from an ancient Asian poet: "My barn having burned to the ground, I can now see the moon." But that's not the way I felt in the weeks after she died. Yes, the barn was in ashes. But I had yet to glimpse even a glimmer of the moon.

Despite my discomfort with the unanswered questions surrounding my niece, I didn't seek out answers. I didn't consult the indexes of newspapers or magazines to see what else had been written about ritual abuse. I didn't seek out local therapists besides my own for more information about satanic crimes, MPD, the whole tangled deal. Even in my grief I didn't want to be associated with ritual abuse claims and their lurid aura of sadism, horror, and paranoia.

But, in fact, I was. Even without searching them out, stories about ritual abuse crept into my life. A friend who was an attorney told me she had heard of ritual abuse cases surfacing in rural areas in Western Oregon. I remembered Mary's declaration two years earlier about the Willamette Valley being "riddled" with cult activity, and my immediate, blazing denial. Another acquaintance who had become convinced she was a victim of ritual abuse wrote me a note after I sent her a copy of Michelle's obituary.

"I often think and read about the Holocaust and have lately begun to feel there is a Holocaust happening to children, a very hidden Holocaust," she wrote. "I am sorry your niece did not survive it, and am glad your family let the world know what she suffered."

In January, Mary forwarded me a letter from one of Michelle's nurses at the Behavioral Health Unit at the Logan Hospital. "I have seen many patients come and go, but only a few become a part of a nurse's heart," she wrote. "Michelle was one of those." She described my niece's honesty and integrity, her vibrancy, energy, and wit. "But most of all, the profound pain she suffered touched me deeply. She taught me much about MPD, ritual abuse and the resiliency of the human spirit. I now work at [another facility] and have six patients in my caseload like Michelle. I could not have been able to diagnose and begin to treat them without the knowledge I gained from her."

The nurse wrote that she had collected twenty-four signatures for a Ritual Abuse Taskforce petition that would be presented to the governor to drive home the severity of the issue.

The doctor who asked for her help was astounded at the number of signatures obtained from Logan, she wrote. "Michelle taught many of us the stark reality of the war between God and Satan—we shall not forget."

For the first time, the cultural practice of wearing black while in mourning made sense to me. Grief, I discovered, saps your energy for day-to-day decisions, such as selecting what clothes to pull on or what food to eat. That winter I wore the same outfit almost every day, a pair of black stretch pants and a bulky knit sweater with a huge red-and-blue bird woven into the design. I had bought the sweater at a thrift store in the surreal, unhinged hours following Michelle's funeral. As the winter dragged on, the pants wore thin and bagged at the knees. The sweater cuffs sagged loose and ragged from my wrists. "Is that your uniform or something?" someone in my section finally asked, with a teasing grin. I nodded, saying nothing. I'm sure my lips, always pursed to some degree, pinched even tighter. To myself I said what I couldn't say aloud: they are my badge of mourning, my keening clothes.

Our concerts usually included some amount of preaching. Sometimes it would be the pastor of the church who had invited us to perform. Other times our director took the microphone. One night during a concert I felt moved to say something to the audience about what my niece had suffered through. I remember walking over to the microphone and speaking, but I don't recall the words I said. Maybe I don't want to remember. I doubt I equivocated. I doubt I said a family member committed suicide because she "thought" she was the victim of ritual abuse. Some people were listening. In the weeks that followed, two choir members came to me privately and said a friend or family member had begun experiencing memories similar to Michelle's. Their confidences made me feel ill.

I continued to draw comfort from singing. I still kept my arms rigidly by my side when those around me raised theirs. I would only mouth lyrics that included the words "Satan" or "evil" or "sin." But I was learning that true need knows no denomination. "Speak to my heart, Lord, give me your holy word," I sang with deliberate force. "If I can hear from you, then I'll know what to do."

But if words were sent, I couldn't hear them. As the winter deepened, so did my isolation. Grief burrowed into my bones. Occasionally I called Mary and John, but the emotional price of each phone call was steep. Mary's way of dealing with Michelle's death was to dig deeper into the twisted workings of the cult, and she would relate ever more tales and reports about the creeping evil worming its way through Logan and beyond. She was convinced the cult had punished Michelle for speaking out, and that it was infiltrating her extended family. Mary by then suspected she herself likely had cult connections she wasn't aware of, and wondered if, in some dissociated state, she had unwittingly led the cult to Michelle. Delivered her up, so to speak.

I listened to her, but said little. Did believing even more strongly in the cult give her some kind of proximity to Michelle, or provide some acceptable explanation for her daughter's death? Mary had lost her daughter over and over; but this time Michelle wasn't coming back. Even if I thought I had an answer, was it my role to make Mary see she was tumbling down a tunnel with no bottom, no end? To challenge the one explanation that seemed to offer an answer, no matter how terrible? I clicked the phone down after those calls, more forlorn than when I had first dialed.

One Saturday morning in the early days of writing this book, I heard loud, raucous cawing coming from a neighbor's tree.

After the racket had gone on for several minutes, I took my binoculars and went to investigate. Dozens of crows were perched in nearby branches, squawking in alarm. They took turns swooping down into the tree's leafy crown and rising back up. After some searching I spotted the source of the birds' upset: a hawk was perched on the edge of an almost hidden nest, its beak bobbing up and down as, one by one, it devoured the clutch of chicks inside. The bloody feast took several minutes. After the hawk ate its fill, it flew away, and one by one, the army of crows that had responded to the alarmed cries dispersed. In the end, just one crow remained. Its lonely, solitary cries echoed throughout the neighborhood for hours. The cries could have been from any one of us, I thought then. For Michelle and her years of unrelenting loneliness, terror, and mounting despair. For Mary and her doomed struggle to save her daughter from a force they both believed was too powerful to vanquish. Or it could have been the sound of my own internal wailing in those months after Michelle's death, not knowing what to think, who to call, where to turn.

When snow finally began disappearing from the Cascade foothills that spring, I headed for my favorite hiking trails. I needed to get out of the valley, to breathe hard, and to sweat. I needed to smell the awakening forest floor and feel the wind riffling down from the cloud-shrouded mountain peaks. I had tried hiking with friends, but their social chatter grated on my nerves. I preferred to be by myself.

One Sunday I drove to a familiar trailhead, locked the car, and slipped my arms through my pack. For hours my dog Bailey and I pushed through wet branches and climbed over downed trees that had fallen across the path during the winter storms. At about five thousand feet—a little higher than the elevation of Logan, a little lower than the pass Michelle was crossing the night she died—I stepped off the trail, climbed on top of a huge, horizontal fir, and lay down. There, under the protection of the surrounding trees, memories rose up like butterflies.

Michelle, ten or eleven, is lying on her stomach, reading, on the floor of the living room, oblivious to the pile of sheets and towels she is supposed to be folding. She is peering into the dining room mirror, using a curling iron to coax her stubborn hair to curl before Sunday church. She is perched on a chair in my tiny, crowded studio. She is blowing into her clarinet, fingering the keys into clear, dancing notes. We are running on an empty road that skirts a field of brown, dry grass. We are strolling through the park under a crescent moon, talking, wondering, probing. And then we are sitting in the front seat of John's pickup. It is hot. John and Mary are supposed to meet up with us but they are late. Michelle is absent, withdrawn, and fearful. She has chewed her lips raw. Our conversation has run dry. She stares out the windshield. The silence between us is an invisible wall: I cannot reach in; she cannot reach out.

Lying on the log, I watched the tops of fir trees swaying in the wind, but where I was, the air was still and silent. I could cry there and I did, as if the elevation and sighing trees opened something in me the valley could not. I stayed for a long time in the cradle of the massive log, and when I felt a chill, I stood up, knocked the debris from my pants, gave Bailey a treat, and got back on the path. This is where Michelle and I can meet, I thought. Where the air is clear and sharp. Where no words get in the way. Where absence is as simple as wind toppling a weakened branch.

A member of my choir was dying of a progressive lung disease that spring. Byron, just forty-two, had a hearty spirit, a great sense of humor, and a resonant tenor voice. The previous fall he had begun breathing through a machine that funneled oxygen into his nose via a tiny plastic tube. Still, he laughed and told his corny jokes to anyone who would listen. Throughout the winter he had been increasingly absent from practice. By April he was fighting to coax whispers of breath from his fading lungs.

Byron's wife, Sherrie, was a bright, cheerful woman whose clear soprano voice made me shiver. When Byron's disease approached its final stage, she opened his dying process to any of us who wanted to be part of it. One night during practice she stood in front of the choir and asked us for help—food, money, time, whatever we could spare. She hated to ask, she said, but they needed the help. Choir members responded by showering them with food, cards, company, and prayers.

I admired and cared for Byron and Sherrie, but my caring was tainted. I also envied their public struggle and the support they got from the choir. Byron's death would be difficult, but it would be clear, expected, and aboveboard, I thought. He would not die alone and Sherrie would not grieve alone. Alongside my compassion I felt competitive, jealous, and riddled with hypocrisy.

One afternoon I visited Byron at their small house. A hospital bed dominated the living room. Bottles of pills, tubing, drinking glasses, cards and books, lotions, and tissues were piled on the tables and chairs surrounding his bed. Byron lay in the midst of the chaos, projecting wisdom, love, and remorse with equal passion. I listened as he raged at the death he didn't want and couldn't prevent. He cracked jokes and he shared his regrets—mostly for the times he had failed to love enough.

"What matters is, us. This. Here. Now," he said in a hoarse whisper, waving his arms wide as he labored to suck in each breath. His body had withered to a pale, bony frame. His large, square glasses had slid forward to the end of his nose. His brown hair was greasy, his cheeks a bright, spotty pink. The sheets parted to show his penis, lying without apology against his pale, bluish thigh. He neither blushed nor covered it up.

I sat in a chair next to the bed, my knees rigid, my hands gripped together, and my throat thick and tight. I felt I would collapse if I loosened my hold. He was exhorting me to live, not knowing how deeply I was immersed in another death, one he knew little about and one I was still struggling to accept. Would I ever be able to feel anything cleanly again? Would my craving for attention and sympathy ever abate?

After Byron fell asleep, I walked through the kitchen on my way to the door. The kitchen table was crowded with messages of caring, vases of spring flowers, and plates of food. I ran my finger along the rims of the curved plates, poked at the cookies and the loaves of homemade bread wrapped in aluminum foil. The coil of my own, unseen grief unfurled within me like an alien bloom. I wasn't hungry, but I grabbed a cracker and choked it down. Then another. And another. They tasted stale and flat. I grabbed a handful of cookies, stuffed them into my pocket, walked out the door, and drove home.

chapter 15

marionette

Outside the huddle of grief I lived in, the panic over ritual abuse continued to spread, fueled by media coverage as well as symposiums, conferences, and workshops where treatment professionals, social workers, law enforcement officials, and child protection advocates supported each other and warned attendees of the threat of ritual abuse.

In June 1992, Dr. Corydon Hammond, a psychologist, a University of Utah School of Medicine professor and hypnosis expert, gave a talk at a ritual abuse conference expounding on his belief in the existence of a worldwide satanic cult. He explained in detail where the cult originated, how it operated, and how it programmed its victims. (1)

Hammond said he was convinced the ritual abuse phenomenon was much more than a rumor gone amok. "So I have gone from someone kind of neutral and not knowing what to think about it all to someone who clearly believes ritual abuse is real and that the people who say it isn't are either naïve, like people who didn't want to believe the Holocaust, or they're dirty," he said, meaning that unbelievers likely had cult connections.

He described his take on the convoluted history of a worldwide cult that included satanic Nazis, use of mind control techniques, and other bizarre elements. The purpose of the cult, he said, "is that they want an army of Manchurian candidates—tens of thousands of mental robots who will do prostitution, do child pornography, smuggle drugs, engage in international arms smuggling, do snuff films, all sorts of lucrative things and do their bidding. And eventually, the megalomaniacs at the top believe, [they will] create a satanic order that will rule the world."

He continued in this same vein. "Basically in the programming the child will be put typically on a gurney. They will have an IV in one hand or arm. They'll be strapped down, typically naked," he told the audience. "There'll be wires attached to their head to monitor electro-encephalograph patterns. They will see a pulsing light, most often described as red, occasionally white or blue. They'll be given, most commonly I believe, Demerol. . . . after a suitable period when they're in a certain brainwave state, they will begin programming oriented to self-destruction and debasement of the person."

Hammond did not proclaim his theories from the fringes of mainstream psychology. He was the first president of the American Society of Clinical Hypnosis and the editor of several books, including a textbook on hypnosis. (2) In a different time—one that hadn't seen day care workers charged with gross sexual abuse of their child charges, that hadn't seen skyrocketing diagnoses of multiple personality disorder and burgeoning claims of ritual abuse—Hammond's address would likely have been seen as the workings of a mind that was either overexposed to conspiracy fantasies or had temporarily derailed. But in the skewed cultural climate of that era, his audience apparently saw no reason to challenge his bizarre assertions that linked former Nazi collaborators, mind control, the government, conspiracy theories, and Satanism.

Hammond was among the more-credentialed advocates of the belief in cults, but there were others. In January 1993, *Ms.* magazine published a first-person story by a woman who claimed she had grown up in a family that was part of a secret satanic cult. (3) The writer, who used the pseudonym Elizabeth Rose, wrote about rituals involving girls and sadistic sex. She described in detail how her pregnant mother's labor was induced by the cult, which then sacrificed the infant. She, too, described a cult that was so clever it knew how to hurt children without leaving marks or scars: torture with pins and needles, use of mind-altering drugs, and forced ingestion of feces or urine. Like her counterparts, Rose insisted the most important step in stopping cult abuse was to believe it existed, despite a consistent lack of physical evidence supporting the supposed abuse. "If we want to stop ritual abuse, the first step must be to believe that these brutal crimes occur. Society's denial makes recovery much more difficult for survivors. . . . It is only by taking this unbelievable reality out of the shadows and into the sunlight that we can begin to wake up—and put an end to it," she wrote. (4)

Ritual abuse survivors shared their experiences in journals and books published by both small and mainstream presses. Professional voices chimed in as well. In 1993, James Glass, a professor of political philosophy at the University of Maryland, published *Shattered Selves—Multiple Personality in a Postmodern World*, based on years of researching mental disorders at Sheppard and Enoch Pratt Hospital, a psychiatric facility in Baltimore. During his research, Glass wrote, he listened to the stories of several women who claimed to be victims of cult abuse.

"Clinicians dispute the authenticity of stories of cult abuse," Glass wrote. "[But] if even a small percentage of what I heard is 'true,' that is terrible enough. . . . The cult produces terror; it thrives on terror; it is an instrument of terror. . . . In my sixteen years of research at Sheppard Pratt, I have never before encountered such a confounding and ultimately unknowable form of human experience." (5)

The Logan counselor who worked with Michelle after she began remembering episodes of satanic abuse declined to speak with me. But I was able to speak with the therapist who had treated Michelle when her main symptom was bulimia and extreme social anxiety. The therapist, SB, recalled the late 1980s as a chaotic and paranoid time for counselors, most of whom found themselves ill-equipped to handle the stories they were hearing from their clients about ritual abuse and personality alters. Popular embrace of the recovered memory movement made challenging the "memories" difficult, he said, because the approach "presented a conundrum which said, 'this might have happened to you, but you wouldn't know it because you couldn't remember it.'"

When it came to treating individuals who believed they had developed multiple personalities, SB said he had tried getting clients into a dissociated state—a state of mind where the individual is emotionally unattached to the current moment—so he could contact some of the alters. But over time, he observed that with this approach, his clients became more, not less, fractured.

"The further clients go into [those experiences], the more . . . they have," he said. "It just grows." He also noted how members of a therapy group would often absorb and take on each other's stories. "There was a muddying of memories and experiences," he said.

Looking back, SB said therapists should have concentrated more on integrating their clients' psyches into a whole, rather than trying to contact the various alters and thereby imbuing them with more credibility. "It was kind of like digging in a manure pile thinking we were going to find a pony," he said.

The ritual abuse component complicated things further, including the role of the therapist. Some saw themselves as their clients' rescuer or savior, and rather than remaining objective, turned themselves into detectives charged with proving that their clients' memories were valid. "There was a blurring of boundaries because of the time," he said. "Some therapists lost their way."

As I would discover, the most egregious practitioners did far more than simply lose their way. They created, then immersed themselves in contrived theories that justified what, in saner times, would have been indefensible. They supported each other's claims regarding the existence of satanic cults and the connection between ritual abuse and multiple personality disorder. They referred to each other's "work" in journal articles and "consulted" in treating each other's patients. They used drugs, suggestion, power, and even threats to confuse and manipulate patients.

I was able to get a glimpse of what these manipulation dynamics may have sounded like. After Michelle's death, Mary sent me an audiotape of a session she had with a counselor who had worked with Michelle at the Utah State Hospital. The counselor, M., believed a satanic cult was operating throughout the country. She believed Michelle's memories about being ritually abused as a child, and that she had developed several alters as a result. She was convinced the cult had "accessed"—meaning it had made contact with—Michelle while she was at the hospital.

On the tape, M's voice is low, hypnotic, and self-assured. She talks with Mary about a particularly vicious torture

Michelle had described to her that she called "The Marionette." M. sets the scene according to what Michelle had told her: Michelle is lying on a table in a large, dimly lit room. Around her, several people are chanting in unison. Michelle looks from face to face and realizes no one is going to help her.

"There was just this glare of evil and kind of excited anticipation of what they were going to see," M. says. "That's when they hooked her up. . . . they attached these electrodes to her. It hurt really, really bad," M. says, adopting the high, breathy voice of a terrified child. "They were really bad people. I just thought they would stop but they wouldn't."

M's voice returns to its adult tone. "I asked, 'So what else are they doing, Michelle?'"

Her voice changes to reflect a young Michelle. Her words come faster and faster as she replicates a whispery, frightened tone. "They've got wires on all of my joints. These wires do something to me, and my bones go in every direction, and the more it does the more people are chanting and they're really excited."

M. stops to explain the child's voice to Mary. Although this particular torture ostensibly happened when Michelle was older (both she and Mary believed it occurred while she was at Ricks College), a younger personality, M. asserts, had emerged to shoulder the experience. "When they [the other personalities] had their fill, they created another one that took the pain," she says, with authority.

M. tells Mary that, generally, the cult performed this torture on children. Even then it is very painful, she says, but bearable. But when it is done to adults, when the bones are more firmly held in their sockets, the pain rises to an unimaginable level.

Again, M. adopts Michelle's voice.

"I had to go through excruciating pain. My bones were set, but my joints were going in every direction."

M. then addresses Mary, reverting to her own hypnotic

voice. "She said it was so frightening to stand there and see her knees go backwards, and all of this stuff."

After relating the details of the torture, M. shifts her focus from Michelle to her sister. Why, she asks Mary, was Wynlee not at Michelle's funeral?

Mary is clearly taken aback. "She was there," she responds, confidently.

"I saw her husband, but where was she?" M. asks again, her voice intimate and low.

"I don't know where she sat, but she was there," Mary says. "You're sure?"

Mary pauses. "Well, I thought she was," she says, doubt creeping into her tone.

M. explains that she drove to John and Mary's house right after the funeral to drop off Michelle's possessions. Wynlee, she says, came to the door dressed in a pair of old jeans, not in the funeral attire one would expect.

"You're kidding me," Mary says, clearly caught unaware.

M. continues. "And I said to my husband, 'Why do you suppose Wynlee didn't go to her sister's funeral? I mean, she would have had to be on a dead run to get over to that house.'"

"Maybe Wynlee doesn't remember not being there," Mary says, her voice now small and perplexed. "I was so out of it that I don't know who was there and who wasn't." (Wynlee had, in fact, attended the funeral.)

M. offers more details, building her case that there was no way Michelle's sister could have been at the funeral. M. goes on to suggest that Wynlee, too, was likely accessed by the cult.

Mary was fully aware that Wynlee had driven Michelle over the mountains in the depth of winter nights, had fetched her from various hospital emergency rooms, and later lambasted herself for not being kinder to her sister. But under the spell of M's insistence, Mary lost hold of her own convictions.

When M. finishes, Mary is quiet for a few seconds. "Well, M., you've raised more questions than you've answered," she says, with a nervous laugh.

M. answers, "I'd never in this world hurt you. I wouldn't do it for that purpose at all."

Mary opens up to M. about her overwhelming feelings of incompetence, her inability to embrace some of the church's teachings since Michelle's death, her compulsion to have a supply of Diet Coke available at all times.

"You're going to be a piece of cake [for the cult] to get," M. tells Mary. "Now you are this crazy old lady."

Hearing M. on the tape infuriates me. She seemed to relish relaying sadistic details of Michelle's torture, having the power to knock Mary off her center, then pretending to be a trusted confidant. I am sure the tactics of the most egregious practitioners during the hysteria were similar. I am sure they, too, got a sick enjoyment from ratcheting up their patients' suffering. I am sure they derived pleasure from acting like a savior who was saving their clients from Satan, all the while having to know their therapy was pure bunk.

M. has passed away, but it doesn't matter. When I listen to the tape or transcribe her words, I have to get up from my desk and walk around the house. I go to the kitchen and find something I can grind with my teeth, like toast or nuts.

An entry from Michelle's medical records on March 1991, a week before she was admitted to the Utah State Hospital, reads: "Patient began posturing as if a marionette (puppet on a string). Then fell to floor throwing herself about. Patient was assisted to the seclusion room where she continued to posture with verbal outburst."

Later that night, hospital personnel found Michelle lying on the floor, thrashing violently, "arms and legs swinging and banging her head on the floors and walls." Nurses placed her in four-point restraints and gave her Haldol, an antipsychotic medication. She vomited a small amount, then cried out, "They made me eat a rat! Is it still there? Can you see it?"

I try to imagine how it must have felt to Michelle when her psychological core—her singular self—began turning soft and yielding, slipping away from her like pieces of a dream. What it must have been like to no longer feel she had a solid self, to know that when she woke each day, she would face a small army of other "selves" and their demanding voices, or a barrage of terrifying memories. I think of how unspeakably lonely it must have been to express her fears of the cult and memories of abuse to therapists and hospital staff, and instead of assuring her that her memories were the product of illness and unbalanced chemistry, to have them agree that her delusions were real, her paranoia justified. To be told by her caregivers, those entrusted to deliver objective medical science, that, yes, the cult she so feared did indeed exist, that it was mercilessly vengeful, that she could never escape it, and if she tried, she would pay the price. I don't want to lay blame. Most of them were likely well intentioned. They had no idea they were in the grip of a social panic. They thought they were in a pitched battle with evil. Still, how utterly lost and alone she must have felt. No place could have been safe. No wonder she ran and ran.

chapter 16
good death/bad death

In mid-February 1993 I pulled into a space in the long-term parking area at Portland International Airport, turned off the ignition, and burst into tears. "We made it, Edgar," I sobbed into the wet, streaked windshield. "I'll make it to your funeral."

My father had finally succumbed to the weak heart that for the last two years had rendered him tired, weak, and, as he put it, "without ambition." The day before, when I had made my reservations to fly to upstate New York for his funeral, the Willamette Valley had been cold and cloudy but dry. But an atypical snowstorm descended in the early morning, and I had spent several harrowing hours on I-5 trying to keep from sliding off the road. My car was in the repair shop, and I had borrowed a friend's small pickup truck. I knew the rear tires had little traction despite the cement blocks I had thrown into the back. As I drove, heavy flakes collected on my windshield wipers in mushy globs. I could barely distinguish the road from the shoulder. The median strip was dotted with cars whose front ends were buried in snow. I flinched when larger vehicles with chained tires zoomed by me in the passing lane, splattering my windshield with even more slush.

"Are you with me, Edgar?" I had called out, my fingers latched on to the steering wheel as if they could secure the truck to the road. "I need you now. You'd better help me get through this."

My father had few likes, and driving and snow were among them. Living in upstate New York, we were subject to several snow dumps throughout the winter. He loved to ski, and my sisters and I loved to go with him. Driving to and from the ski area, he kept up a steady fifty miles per hour regardless of the road conditions. He never used chains. He also eschewed contracts with snowplow operators who would have cleared our driveway whenever it snowed. Instead, whenever a snowstorm descended, he got up early or stayed up late to shovel out our driveway. My brothers helped out when they were home, but once they left for college, I was next in line. "Now who wants to come and shovel snow with me?" he'd call out. My sisters weren't game, but I was a reliable volunteer, especially at night. I pulled on an assortment of outerwear and bounced out the door behind him. When the flakes were large and feathery, we each pushed a wide-blade snow shovel. If there was a layer of ice beneath the snow, he used a flat-edged spade to chop up the ice into pieces. I followed along with my snow shovel, scooping up the chunks and heaving them to the side. We barely spoke as we worked, just shoveled and scraped as the snow whirled down around us, the shiny flakes pirouetting against the night sky.

I'd last seen him the previous November, after his first major heart attack. The doctors had prescribed daily walks. My mother was a dedicated caregiver, but walking wasn't her thing. I gladly stepped in. Each day of my visit my father and I ambled, arm in arm, mostly in silence, through the older sub-urban neighborhood he had lived in for almost fifty years. He was frail and his gait tentative. Occasionally I felt his weight slump against my arm. One morning I stopped to arrange his scarf and zip his down vest to keep out the late-fall breeze. He waited as I fussed, a familiar, tolerant expression on his lean, lined face. I took a breath. I had planned for such a moment.

"I want to say thank you," I told him, looking into his tired brown eyes. I spoke quickly so my discomfort at putting my feelings into words wouldn't make me stop too soon. "For everything. How you've helped me out. How you've been so patient. I know it wasn't always easy." Even though he didn't understand my politics or my work ethic, I knew he was on my side. He had sent me occasional checks that had helped me out in lean times, always making it clear they were gifts, not loans. In his later years he had struggled with depression and he was often gruff and critical. He looked forward to his after-noon cocktail, but his declining health had altered his ability to handle alcohol. He grew groggy, slurred his words, and often nodded off before dinner. I missed his dry Midwestern humor and the dad he used to be.

But at that moment, standing on the sidewalk in the late autumn sun, he was awake, and he heard my every word. After I finished, he didn't miss a beat. "Well, you probably deserved more," he said, giving his head a decisive nod. "So there." The matter settled, I gave him a quick kiss and we resumed our walk, my stronger heart fluttering sweetly inside my chest.

The morning of the funeral, the streets of my childhood home were covered with glistening, powdery snow—I smiled at my father's last, quiet goodbye. At the service my siblings and I laughed, cried, and told stories. Afterward, a stream of people showed up at my mother's house and shared even more stories. His was a good death, I thought.

By then I had begun classifying deaths into "good" and "bad" categories. It wasn't that good deaths weren't sad. But they were deaths that were expected, where those of us who would be left behind could prepare, say our goodbyes, and afterward celebrate a life well lived. My father's passing was the third "good death" I had gone through in twelve months. Byron, from the choir, was the first, earlier that May. At the moment he died, he was surrounded by friends and family. I was sure a host of angels had squired him home. A few months later, my hiking mentor died suddenly. Doug had been a Forest Service fire lookout, a cross-country skier, a photographer, and a journalist. He had overcome childhood polio, but at age forty he had contracted post-polio, a condition that affected his breathing and his heart. He underwent a tracheotomy, and when he wanted to speak, he covered the tube in his throat with his fingers to force air over his vocal cords. Still, he kept on hiking.

That summer his chest had grown thick and puffy. When the trail took us uphill, he attached a plastic bottle to his throat tube and squeezed it to push more air into his lungs. But his calves remained strong as sprung steel, and it was Doug who was the first one to reach the top of whatever mountain we were headed for. It was Doug who carried a pack loaded with survival essentials, who showed the less sure-footed among us how to hop rocks across a fast-moving stream, who treated us all to ice-cold drinks from his cooler when we got back to the trailhead. He died during the night in a motel room when the portable respirator he was using to help him breathe malfunctioned. That evening he had attended a reunion of former Forest Service lookouts. Just a few weeks earlier, our informal hiking group had honored him for being our leader for so many years. His death was sudden, but the way I saw it, he left life feeling worthy and loved by his community. Another good death.

Good deaths, I had come to think, were ones that didn't gnaw away at the insides of your loved ones. They weren't marred by relentless questions and searing doubts. With good deaths there were no secrets, no questions lurking behind the smiles of sympathy. Good deaths weren't tinged with creepy details people spoke of in hushed tones, or in a coded language only certain individuals could understand.

Taboos, even if self-imposed, amass a lot of weight. My roommate during the year of those deaths was a bright, energetic graduate student. She was what she was supposed to be—excited about life, upbeat, hungry for fun. Her optimism chafed against my prickly depression, but I needed the rental income too much to ask her to leave. I set my jaw when she told her stories and glared at her when she left her belongings scattered around the house. I was unfair and unkind. Her only sin was being so damn joyful. So full of life.

Talking with John and Mary by phone remained frustrating. They had never agreed on how to deal with Michelle while she was alive; after her death, the gap between them became a chasm. Mary was deep in the clutches of a social panic, but didn't know it. None of us did. She still spent hours talking with acquaintances and others who by then believed they, too, had been accessed by the cult. I think she saw herself as trying to put out a forest fire with a tin bucket. John doubted whether a fire was even burning and wouldn't lend a hand. His take was that Michelle had a mental problem, not a cult problem. "She had a glitch in her mind that was never diagnosed and certainly never repaired," he told me once. "Something happened and it just sort of twisted something in her and it never got fixed. And nobody was equipped to do anything about it."

I didn't want to imagine what their days and nights were

like at the small, worn house on Center Street. Two rock walls facing each other, split by a river of loss.

When I spoke with the supervisor at the home for disabled children where Michelle had worked, she said that Michelle's suicide had provided grist for Logan's churning rumor mill. Some people speculated "that something or someone made her take the aspirin and that she tried to tell that to the paramedics." Another rumor was that no aspirin had been found in her system. (Hospital records show that aspirin was clearly present.) "People thought she died of not any kind of earthly thing," she said. "And I can see how something like that can take root, be fed into, because of Michelle's past."

The woman was sure Michelle had suffered some sort of abuse. She recognized the symptoms, she said, regardless of whether a cult was involved. And, she went on, severe sexual abuse, no matter the context, can destroy a person's soul. In her mind, that was ultimately what killed Michelle.

"I don't believe it was a suicide," she said. "Either she developed an alter ego or a multiple personality. But the Michelle we knew as Michelle was a victim. Whether other [people] were involved because she was trying to expose a cult, I have no idea."

Mary, too, came to question what occurred that night on the mountain pass, and how doctors responded to Michelle in the emergency room. "I don't think Michelle killed herself," she told me. "I think she acquiesced in her death."

Michelle's friend Tammy was convinced that Michelle did not commit suicide. Before Michelle was taken to the state hospital, the two had a conversation about what both sensed would be inevitable. Michelle told Tammy she was speaking out about the cult to protect would-be victims. She knew the price, Tammy said.

"She said her life would be taken, that it would be staged to look like a suicide," Tammy said. "She looked me straight in the eye and said, 'I'm not suicidal and I don't want to die.'" Michelle had explained to Tammy that her suicidal impulses were a result of the cult programming her to believe she would be punished if she spoke out against it. Michelle knew her death would be a great loss to Tammy, and tried to prepare her. "But she was adamant that when it occurred, it would not be suicide," Tammy told me.

Bad deaths, I thought then, were ones where the split edges of grief never quite knit, where lingering questions deny peace to those who remain.

chapter 17
witness

Maybe the need to impose order on a small part of the world is a natural response to sudden loss. For me, it emerged as the only option. Once I got over the initial, paralyzing grief of losing Michelle, I needed to do something with the energy that buzzed inside me. I wanted my loss to lead somewhere, build something. The solution I came up with wasn't necessarily logical, but it fit the way I felt: I decided to write a handbook for juvenile sex offenders who were entering treatment for their behavior.

My idea gestated over several months. I remained undecided about my niece's ritual abuse claims, but I believed the rape she recounted could likely have occurred. I wanted to see what an offender looked like, hear his voice, listen to what he had to say. I wanted to know what he told himself about his crimes. I wanted to know why he did what he did, and how he lived with himself afterward. I wanted to get inside his skin.

In my previous job with the foster teen newspaper, we had used a peer-to-peer approach to deliver information to our audience—instead of us, as adults, telling our teen readers what worked and didn't work in various situations, we had teens share their experiences with each other, via interviews. My plan was to do something similar—I would interview offenders who were far along in their treatment, using their stories and insights to introduce recently charged offenders to issues they'd be facing in their process.

I was confident the format would work. I was also convinced I was the perfect person for the project. Nothing any of these offenders would tell me could top the content of Michelle's memories or what I had read in her journals, I told myself. I had become tempered. Immune.

To prepare for the interviews, I submerged myself in learning the particulars of sex offender treatment and becoming familiar with its vocabulary. I wound through the necessary bureaucratic hoops to get permission to interview young, incarcerated offenders. I sought out a therapist who worked with sex offenders to help me formulate interview questions—I would ask the offenders how long they had been abusing others before they were caught, how many victims they had, how long it took them to stop denying their behavior.

In April 1993, two months after my father's death, I sat in a small anteroom at MacLaren Youth Correctional Facility, a state institution for young male criminal offenders near Salem, Oregon, about an hour north of Eugene. The unit I was visiting housed youths who had been convicted of sex crimes. The room was painted an institutional gray-beige and outfitted with a small table and some chairs. As I waited, I stared out the window at the prison grounds—green lawn and wire fencing under a leaden sky.

The first interviewee entered the room accompanied by

the unit's director, an unkempt, bulky woman with hooded eyes and loose, puckered skin who had a reputation for keeping even the toughest kids in line. She knew her charges well and had selected the candidates for me to interview. She introduced us and left the room.

The young man took a seat across from me. He was eighteen years old, tall, red-haired, and thickly built. He wore loose correctional garb—slippers, drawstring cotton pants, short-sleeved T-shirt. His doughy face had the dull pallor that comes from spending too much time indoors. I noted the large window in the wall between the anteroom and a small office where an attendant sat at a desk. It comforted me to know she could see us just by raising her head.

I explained the purpose of the interview. I positioned the tape recorder so that the microphone faced the young man. I pressed the record button and started at the top of my list of questions.

"What was your attitude like when you first came into treatment?" I asked him. "How long did it take for you to be open and honest about all your offending behavior?"

His answers were simple and direct. I took notes as he spoke in case the tape recorder malfunctioned, plus it allowed me to look down at my notebook instead of at his face. His offenses had begun with fondling young girls but had grown more intrusive as time went on. After coming into treatment, he minimized his offending behavior for eighteen months. It took nine polygraphs—the tests couldn't be submitted as evidence in court, but were used in the treatment process to gauge an offender's truthfulness—before he came clean about all his offending behavior.

I made my way down the list. "And how many victims do you have?" I asked.

He paused, then answered, almost in a whisper. "About two hundred."

I locked my eyes on my notebook, scratching words with my pen. My mind blurred and I felt a flush rise up my neck. "You've heard worse," I reminded myself. I took a deep breath and asked the next question. For the next few minutes I let the tape recorder do the remembering.

As editor of the newspaper for foster teens I had often needed to address the issue of sex abuse. It is among the reasons many kids end up in foster care. But back then I was interviewing victims, not perpetrators. We spoke on the phone so I didn't see their faces, the angle of their chins, or the color of their hair. When we spoke, no one's eyes looked into my own. Now I carried more searing images in my mind: Michelle's pleading whisper, her pained eyes, an open coffin. I imagined a line of two hundred girls, holding hands, propping each other up. I thought of the shock of abuse, how a girl wakes up one morning vibrant in her skin and goes to bed that night, stunned and confused, shame coursing through her like blood.

Early on in developing my plan for the book, I met with two administrators at a local social service agency and asked them to be partners in developing the handbook. (They later declined.) In preparing for the meeting, I had shed my oversized sweater and baggy stretch pants and dressed in a crisp black pantsuit. I summoned up the professional aura of someone who knew what she wanted. I relegated to another dimension the person who sat in front of the television all night long, who bridled at her housemate's slightest gaffe, who cadged food from a dying person's kitchen table. The two administrators had warmed to my idea, and we discussed various approaches. At one point in the discussion one of them looked at me sternly. "If you are doing this to deal with your own victimization, it won't work," he said. I had looked back at him with what I hoped was a cool, even eye. "Don't worry," I said. "I'm not."

The red-haired teen stared at the floor as he answered my questions. I asked how he felt about himself when he was offending and no one knew about it. I asked him how he got caught. "How did it feel when you talked about your offenses in front of the other guys?" I asked.

Scary, he said, because he had more victims than anyone else there. He didn't like to think about them. "It just makes me sick to think of all those people that I hurt," he told me.

I interviewed a few more offenders that day, and a few weeks later I returned to the facility to interview a second group. I was more familiar with my questions by then, and more prepared for the answers. The last young man I spoke with was sixteen years old. He had a wiry build and eyes the color of wet earth. "I'm a power rapist," he told me. His fourteen victims, male and female, included his younger sister. His mother still didn't know he had abused his sibling. He planned to tell her in the next couple of weeks, but he was afraid she would disown him when she found out. "I wouldn't blame her if she did," he said.

I listened while he spun out his story: a violent family, the white-hot anger that churned inside him, his own childhood assault by an uncle. As a kid he had been beaten, thrown around by the hair of his head. He started raping younger kids at age twelve, the same year he was attacked. "I was holding all my anger at that abuse inside me," he told me. "When you feel so rejected and powerless, and you are a sex offender, the only thing to do to get the power and control back is rape."

He chose mostly victims who were mentally slow, who wouldn't understand what was going on when he began grooming them, he told me. He had learned to portray himself as a victim to avoid taking responsibility for what he had done.

Instead of being put off by his disclosures, I was oddly drawn to him. For years I had aligned myself with victims and underdogs. I had written about people, mostly women, ground down by poverty, illness, abusive childhoods, domestic violence, or substance abuse. This project was my first foray into exploring the psyches of perpetrators. The cottage director had warned me that manipulation and lying were as familiar as breathing for many sex offenders, even younger ones. I knew I was at risk of being conned or "played," so over time I had adopted a brusque, impersonal tone in my interviews. I pressed the young offenders whenever I thought they were too blasé or too facile in their answers. I suspected a couple of them had told me what they thought I wanted to hear, but I didn't feel that way about this last young man. Maybe it was his quiet delivery or his lack of bravado. Maybe it was the insights he had come to about himself, or that he made me see that some perpetrators were themselves victims. I felt he was sincere when he spoke of wrestling with his demons, of how hard he was working to change his behavior. There was a stillness about him, an openness, that drew me in.

"Before, I didn't have empathy for any of my victims," he told me. "Now I do. Now I want every one of them to get help."

At the end of our interview I thanked him, turned off the tape recorder, and began packing up. He asked if he could ask me a question. I nodded. "Why," he said, "are you writing this book?"

His question caught me off guard. Before I knew it, Michelle's story—not the ritual abuse aspect, because that was untellable—but the rest of it came tumbling out. The bulimia, the rape, her unraveling. As I spoke, I was alarmed that I was blurring the boundary between interviewer and interviewee, researcher and subject, professional and personal. But I couldn't stop myself. During the course of our interview in that drab, anonymous space, we had created something church-like between us, a confessional, a space of disclosure and forgiveness. It was my turn.

"What happened to her?" he asked. I told him, meeting his directness with my own.

"She didn't make it," I said, pausing to settle my voice. "She killed herself."

He was silent. "I'm sorry," he said finally, his eyes looking straight into mine. The staff member on the other side of the window motioned that it was time for the interview to be over.

We shook hands goodbye. I wished him luck as he turned to go back to his regimented life. I thanked the unit director and walked to the parking lot. I felt lighter than I had in a long time.

Over the next few years, I began to rejoin the outside world. I stepped up my freelance writing for a local alternative weekly newspaper and eventually joined the staff as a reporter and associate editor. The demands of the job forced me out of my self-imposed shell. I wrote about issues I had previously been too preoccupied to pay attention to—land-use squabbles, environmental controversies, women's health, low-income housing, local politics, the fallout from the overuse of chemical pesticides and herbicides. I interviewed strangers, conversed with coworkers, edited copy, and wrote stories. I found a publisher for my handbook and tackled the lengthy peer-reviewed suggestions. Work became my antidote.

Gradually, my grief over Michelle seemed to recede. Days would go by without me thinking about her, but occasionally someone would make a remark or I would read a story that sent my emotions tumbling backward. One day, a reader who was angry about a story I had written—I don't recall what it was about—called me at home. When I answered, she lit into me. "I'm thinking you must be involved in some kind of witch's group," she said. "Or something worse."

For an instant, the dormant coals of my paranoia flamed hot. Mary, Michelle, and I shared the same last name. Was this the payback Mary had warned about? Was it my turn? But as the caller railed on, my fear turned to anger. Usually I maintained a professional reserve when someone complained about one of my stories. Not this time.

"How dare you associate me with something like that?" I demanded. She tried to speak, but I cut her off. "I'll contact a lawyer if you ever try to publicly link me with witchcraft or anything remotely connected to it," I told her, surprising myself with my vehemence. "I'll sue you for slander. Don't for a minute think I won't." I was shaking as I hung up the phone. She didn't call again.

Working at the paper provided a steady flow of drama: a controversial ballot measure over homosexuality, rogue police, racism, and the occasional crime article. I could immerse myself in these stories—they were about real issues and real events. They had names, a paper trail, sometimes real tragedy. In May 1998, Kip Kinkel, a fifteen-year-old high school sophomore, showed up at Thurston High School in east Springfield, about three miles from my home, with a rifle under his trench coat and a Glock pistol tucked into the waistband of his pants. He killed two students and wounded twenty-two others before being tackled and disarmed by other students. Later that day investigators discovered he had fatally shot his parents in the family's upscale home. At the paper we scrambled to redo the next issue, jostling with the swarm of reporters and television broadcasting vans that descended on Springfield overnight from national media organizations like an incursion of brightly lit aliens. We wrote reams of stories dissecting how and why this could have happened. We published articles on the availability of handguns, bullying, and the lack of mental health resources for adolescents. A few weeks later, President Bill Clinton came to Springfield to meet with traumatized students and their families. I stood with dozens of others on the curb as his motorcade sped by, all of us craning our necks to catch a glimpse of his thick hair and bulb-bright smile.

After almost a two-year delay and a second round of excruciating edits, my book, *Tell It Like It Is,* was finally published. But emotionally I kept people at a distance. Intimacy requires honesty and revelation, and I didn't know how to tell who would be able to listen to what I felt I needed to reveal. Over time, my pain had changed shape. By then I felt that wherever Michelle was, she was in a good place. Now my pain was about me—what I had seen, heard, and been party to. It was about being saddled with the impossible weight of Michelle's whole thorny saga. It was about the weight of witnessing some kind of disaster unfold and not knowing what it was or what to do about it. It was about not knowing where I stood, about having to pinch back my words for months on end, terrified that saying the wrong ones would have unalterable consequences.

When I write this, I cringe at how close I come to self-pity or a maudlin self-involvement. But back then I hadn't put words to my feelings. I didn't know I was wallowing. I didn't feel I had the ability to lessen the isolation I felt imprisoned by. My unspoken burden kept me apart from my younger coworkers. On weekdays it mostly remained at bay, but on weekends it became my constant companion, like an invisible pet. I hauled it up mountains and took it on long walks along the river. I took it with me shopping for things I didn't need. It went with me to movies and to staff picnics. "If you only knew what I've been through," I'd think to myself when in the midst of a crowd of seemingly carefree folks. "If you only knew my story."

By the spring of 1999, the relationship had worn thin. I was stuck. I was tired of being alone and feeling sad. I wanted to be somewhere else. To feel something else. And that's why on a blustery Sunday in March I was lying on a mat in the spacious living room of a house across the street from the Pacific Ocean, my limbs bent in a fetal fold. My throat ached from the force of the sobs that reverberated from my throat.

I, along with several other women, had signed up for a weekend workshop that was intended to put us in touch with our inner child, or our inner joy, or whatever it was that was preventing us from living the lives we wanted to live. Two friends had encouraged me to go. Saturday's agenda had included a session on releasing anger and an exercise in putting different endings on stories from our past to help release us from their hold. But I hadn't been able to come up with versions I could believe in. There was no changing the narrative about Michelle, no different outcome that could break its hold over me. My emotional self felt like it was sitting outside a locked gate. Behind it lay what I imagined was a sense of belonging, an ease in walking the earth without dragging a heavy weight. I just couldn't get the damn gate to open.

On Sunday morning we had come together in the large, airy room after breakfast. I was convinced that, for me, the workshop had been a bust. No cloud had lifted. None of the exercises had led me to a new way of seeing or feeling. My "story" felt as weighty as a river stone. The workshop leader had us lie on our mats and began leading us in a visualization. Her voice was soothing and low. Quiet music played in the background.

I know now that the workshop leaders used versions of what I would learn were called "recovered memory" techniques— guided imagery, light trances, visualization—that contributed to the number of false memories reported during the late 1980s. But back then it wasn't the techniques themselves that were at fault—it was the misuse of them. I trusted the women who led the workshop and was confident they wanted to help each of us wade through our layers of experience and beliefs to release whatever was keeping us from finding freedom and clarity. I believed in them.

As I lay on my mat with my eyes closed, images of Michelle appeared in my mind along with the familiar sadness that welled up whenever I thought of her stunted life. I watched as her movie unwound, reel by reel, to its inevitable end. But at some point, the movie shifted focus and became about me. I felt my sense of helplessness, of being powerless to prevent her unraveling or to quell the terror that ruled her last frenzied years. I felt again my months of fumbling to find a way through the confounding labyrinth of belief, memory, reason, love. I felt the dome of silence I had lived within all those months after her death. Me, the talker, who had heard throughout my childhood, "Alice, your mouth." Me, whose lips had grown tiny puckered lines from keeping in the story that lay silent within me, like an unborn child.

I don't know how long I lay weeping—for Michelle and for myself. Ten minutes? Twenty? Forty? I lost track of time, the day, the others in the room. At some point the workshop leader brought us back from our individual reveries. She had us feel the weight of our legs, spine, and head. She instructed us to move our toes and fingers. She asked us to sit up, slowly. As I pushed up from the floor, I was hit by a quiet, unbidden realization. Almost wordless. *Michelle was the one who died that November night. Not you. You are very much alive. You have a life to live.*

The words beckoned, like an invitation.

A few weeks before the workshop, I had run into the man who had been the consultant on my book. He told me he had recently divorced and that it had been a congenial decoupling. He and I had met occasionally to share the modest royalties from the book over lunch, but he rarely discussed his personal life. Since then we had met up a couple of times, but I had turned down his last request. I sensed I could trust him, but I hadn't been ready to test it. After I returned home from the coast, I gave him a call. We went out again. Not long after, he lay in my bed and listened as I told him about Michelle. He held me the entire time. He asked the right questions. He said the right words. He didn't stop calling.

chapter 18
backstory

On a blustery February evening in the mid-2000s, I drove to a workshop led by Portland writer and memoirist Sallie Tisdale. Few cars were out on the road. A rogue weather front had funneled buffeting winds into the Eugene area, causing trees to shuck their weakest limbs and power lines to fail. The weather caused the cancellation of a host of meetings that night, but I wanted to hear Tisdale's talk so badly I refused to call ahead to check if the workshop was still on.

I turned into the lot of the community center where the talk was scheduled, and noted several parked cars. A handwritten sign was posted on the front door. I walked down a hall to the designated room and pushed open the door. Apparently Tisdale's fans were as determined as I, and more punctual. More than a dozen people sat in chairs facing the self-possessed woman speaking at the front of the room. Tisdale didn't miss a beat as I sidled in and slunk into a chair.

"What I want you to do now," Tisdale was saying as I settled down, "is to write down on a sheet of paper 'I can't write about [blank] because of [blank].' Then fill it in. What is keeping you from writing the memoir you want to write?"

I flipped open my small notebook and without hesitation encapsulated years of dithering into two words: "Michelle" and "family." Writing the words down gave them an unexpected authority and a truth I couldn't look away from. By then my niece, Michelle, had been gone for more than a decade. By then I had found the trove of letters I hadn't realized I'd kept. But until I jotted down those two words, I had not identified what was keeping me from moving ahead with writing about her life, and about that time.

Tisdale asked some of us to read off what we had written in our blanks. Our reasons were similar—we were afraid of bringing secrets to light, of exposing the pain in our hearts, of hurting those we love. She challenged us. There is no such thing as an objective memoir, she insisted, only the subjective version of our experience. She likened the experience of writing memoir to two boxers—one the material, the other the writer—engaged in a high-stakes bout. "They circle and circle each other," she said. "The moment of engaging is fraught with peril."

Tisdale's words helped expose the truth of my procrastination. I wanted to know more about Michelle's last years, but I was afraid to know more, afraid of what that knowledge might cost. I loved my brother and sister-in-law dearly. I saw up close the pain Michelle had brought them. To write a memoir, I would have to speak with them. I would have to ask difficult questions and listen to their answers. I feared betraying their trust. I feared losing their love. By then they were healing. John was playing tennis, and winning. Mary seemed lighter, warmer. They had begun to make each other smile. What right did I have to dig into their scarred and tender past?

That is a memoirist's only job, Tisdale said. To write his or her truth.

That night, amongst a roomful of strangers, I gave my fear a name and naming it gave it a shape I could wrestle with. Uncovering the truth would be my job. By the time I drove back home, the wind had eased, the trees were standing upright, and the traffic lights were back in working order. Except for a scattering of twigs and branches on the roadside, little evidence remained of the earlier storm. But things were not as they had been. Something inside me had shifted.

With Tisdale's tacit permission, I slowly began looking into the whirlpool that had sucked in Michelle, Mary, and, as I would discover, hundreds of others during the 1980s. Before I began my research, I didn't realize that Michelle's "memories" of ritual abuse had a connection to the childcare abuse cases of the early 1980s. I didn't realize how far the tentacles of the hysteria had reached, how many lives it had touched, how many families were thrown into chaos. I didn't know about the inpatient units set up in hospitals to treat women who had been manipulated and drugged into believing they harbored scores of alters or had been subjected to years of horrific ritual abuse. I knew nothing of the phalanx of impassioned psychiatrists, therapists, social workers, and others who had done the convincing. I was about to learn.

By then, refinements to the Internet made it possible for me to research archived articles and studies at the local library. Hunched over a keyboard, I typed in the words I had resisted for so long—satanic ritual abuse—and spent hours following wherever the cyber threads led me. My mission was silent, secretive, intermittent. I didn't tell friends, colleagues, or, initially, John and Mary, about my project. I wasn't ready to share. Part of me was drawn to know more; part of me resisted the material as if it were a contaminant. I found reasons to avoid continuing the research—I misplaced my notebook, I had errands to run, I had to mow the lawn. Part of my ambivalence was the profound "ick" factor that characterized the stories and rumors that had surfaced during the panic. Part of it was fear of discovering yet another headshaking travesty that had transpired during that time. One afternoon, after reading about a particularly egregious case of a woman being manipulated by a practitioner to believe she was the victim of ritual torture, a flash of white-hot anger rippled through me, blotting out the text on the screen. I shut my notebook and scuttled out the door. I didn't return for weeks.

I rationalized that my day job was demanding, that I had a relationship to figure out, a post-9/11 reality to adjust to. Now I think I also procrastinated because I needed time to assimilate all I was taking in. I needed to cultivate a mental toughness that could handle facing how the human psyche—even that of highly educated, supposedly savvy professionals—can be swept up in paranoia that, although dressed up in modern-day jargon, echoes the same irrational fears and projections that for centuries and across cultures have given rise to genocide, witch hunts, and cultural scapegoating.

I delayed. I dithered. But I kept on. Eventually I discovered that, in fact, a few journalists and others had tried early on to quench the fires of the creeping panic over child sex abuse, but they had been drowned out by the cultural din that surrounded them.

In 1987, the *Village Voice* published a story by investigative journalist Debbie Nathan on the convictions of two female El Paso day care workers for the abuse and rape of their child charges. Gayle Dove had received three life sentences plus sixty years; Michelle Noble was given life plus 311 years. The next year, Nathan wrote a story on Kelly Michaels, a twenty-three-year-old New Jersey day care worker who in 1988 was found guilty of 115 counts of child abuse and was sentenced to forty-seven years in prison. Nathan was one of the first journalists to question the approach used to interview supposed child victims, and to ask whether suggestion and manipulation had led to the testimonies that resulted in so many convictions. (1)

Nathan's stories challenged the widespread outrage over supposed abuse in childcare centers, but she wasn't seen as an investigative hero. Later, Nathan described how, following the publication of one of her stories questioning the conviction of a day care worker, someone made an anonymous call to police accusing her of child maltreatment. (2)

In May 1990, *Harper's* published a story by journalist Dorothy Rabinowitz, who concluded, like Nathan, that Kelly Michaels was innocent. Rabinowitz had originally written the story for *Vanity Fair*, but the magazine killed the piece because her editors feared her defense of Michaels was too controversial. (3)

In January 1990, the sensational McMartin Preschool case that had riveted the nation since 1984 came to a close. At its height in the mid-1980s, almost four hundred children were alleged to have been molested, including some being subjected to grotesque ritual abuse. By the time the case went to trial in 1987, charges had been dropped against all the suspects except Ray Buckey, a teacher at the school, and his mother, Peggy McMartin Buckey, who had helped run the school. The three-year, $15 million trial—at the time the longest and most expensive criminal trial in US history—ended after nine weeks of jury deliberation. Peggy McMartin Buckey was acquitted of all charges. Ray Buckey, who by then had spent five years in jail, was acquitted of fifty-two of sixty-five charges; the remaining charges against him were eventually dropped. (4)

A few weeks after the McMartin case concluded, *Los Angeles Times* staffer David Shaw lambasted the media coverage of the case—including that of his own paper—in a series of columns.

"In the early months of the case in particular, reporters and editors often abandoned two of their most cherished and widely trumpeted traditions—fairness and skepticism," Shaw wrote. Most of the media unwittingly bought into the skewed thinking that helped fuel the panic over ritual abuse, he wrote, by assuming "that responsible authorities just wouldn't charge people with such horrendous acts if the suspects were not indisputably guilty." (5) His columns won him a Pulitzer Prize for criticism in 1991.

In 1991, *The Economist* reported on the dismissal of a satanic sex abuse case in Hanover Park, a suburb of Chicago, for lack of evidence. The young female "victim" had been counseled by a self-avowed expert in satanic ritual abuse who had previously given lectures about the issue in England, leading to a panicked reaction in at least two communities. The story referenced Richard Gardner, a child psychiatrist and professor at Columbia University's medical school, who had written about the scare and concluded that the case "had all the hallmarks of mass hysteria similar to that which took place at the time of the Salem witch trials in 1692." (6)

Also in 1991, former police officer Robert Hicks published *In Pursuit of Satan: The Police and the Occult.* Hicks said he wrote the book to quell the ritual abuse hysteria he saw infecting law enforcement agencies around the country. After combing through scores of cases, Hicks wrote that he found no evidence of a nationwide satanic network. What he did find was a modern-day resurgence of the centuries-old struggle of good versus evil, or what he called "The Other." Throughout history, "The Other" has appeared in many guises, Hicks wrote. But regardless of when and where it surfaces, "The Other" is always seen as "an assault on stability, purity and innocence. It threatens the cornerstones of society. It is considered immensely powerful and pervasive. And it is empowered by a hysteric, collective psychology that eschews critical thinking." (7)

"I did not enjoy writing this book," Hicks wrote in the first lines of his preface.

By then I knew exactly what he meant.

The next year, the FBI weighed in with a similar conclusion. Agent Kenneth Lanning had spent several years examining ritual abuse cases, including those that purportedly occurred in day care centers. A longtime child abuse investigator, he knew certain individuals were capable of depraved, grisly crimes. The surfacing of so many reports of ritual abuse and allegations of cult activity in the early eighties spurred him to investigate. He thought the reports might be credible. In 1985, he convened a meeting at FBI headquarters for district attorney representatives and child protection agencies to discuss ritual abuse cases. Later that year he testified to the Meese Commission that ritual abusers acted from violent, not sexual, impulses. (8) But by 1992 he had reversed course. After being unable to uncover any evidence to back up hundreds of ritual abuse claims, Lanning, too, had concluded that the spike in ritual abuse reports arose from psychological influences.

"For at least eight years American law enforcement has been aggressively investigating the allegations of victims of ritual abuse," he wrote. "There is little or no evidence for the portion of their allegations that deals with large-scale baby breeding, human sacrifice, and organized satanic conspiracies. Now it is up to mental health professionals, not law enforcement, to explain why victims are alleging things that don't seem to have happened." (9)

It took a few more years, but once enough holes were punched in its credibility, the bloated panic over ritual abuse began to deflate. Researchers and journalists published analyses and theories about why the panic had surfaced and why it lasted so long. Sociologist Jeffrey Victor framed the eighties panic as a narrative that reached back centuries, in which accusations of ritual infant murder and cannibalism were used as propaganda against a supposed enemy. Such stories, he wrote, "have been passed down in the written and oral propaganda of past times as part of the folk culture of Western societies." Victor credited *Michelle Remembers* and other imitators with disseminating the satanic cult myth, along with prominent psychiatrists who championed belief in it and spread their theories via their publications, training conferences, and seminars.

Blind belief in ideology also helped spread the panic, Victor wrote. Christian therapists were "too quick to find the agents of Satan at work in the minds of their patients." And feminist therapists "have been too quick to see ritual abuse as one more example of the hidden sexual victimization of women and children." (10)

In 1993, *New Yorker* writer Lawrence Wright wrote a two-part story investigating the case of Paul Ingram, a devout Christian and a sheriff's deputy in Olympia, Washington, whose daughters had accused him of sexual abuse. Under prolonged questioning by investigators, Ingram confessed to extreme sexual violation of his daughters, including participation in satanic rituals. In reality, he had never committed any of the acts he confessed to. Lawrence turned his investigation into a book, detailing how Ingram's case—along with similar cases that had risen during the 1980s—was distorted by the belief on the part of detectives, therapists, prosecutors, and their clients that repressed "memories," once unearthed via loaded questioning, are a reliable and accurate accounting of actual events.

"Whatever the value of repression as a scientific concept or a therapeutic tool, unquestioning belief in it has become as dangerous as a belief in witches," Wright concluded. "One idea is modern and the other an artifact of what we like to think of as a credulous age, but the consequences are depressingly the same." (11)

Journalist Nathan continued covering the day care worker/ritual abuse phenomenon. She teamed up with a Portland, Oregon, attorney, Michael Snedeker, and together they wrote *Satan's Silence—Ritual Abuse and the Making of a Modern American Witch Hunt*, published in 1995. When I learned about the book, I ordered a copy. When the brown padded envelope appeared in the mail, I tore it open and pulled out a 317-page tome. The title on the cover was printed in red over a murky gray, from which the eyes of a child peered directly at the reader. The book contained forty-eight pages of footnotes and a twelve-page index.

Given what I thought I was after, it would have made sense for me to have immediately devoured the book from beginning to end. But it remained on my desk, unopened, for days. I circled it warily, oddly afraid of its heft, of all that it might say, of the weight of its truth.

"Writing this book has been hard for us," Nathan and Snedeker wrote in the preface. "There was a time when publicly expressing skepticism about small children being ceremonially raped and tortured by organized groups was, as one journalist put it, practically an indictable stance. Several years later, the national mood has changed."

Nathan and Snedeker tracked the origins of the ritual abuse panic in exhaustive, infuriating detail, starting with the wave of childcare abuse cases in Southern California during the early 1980s. They traced the McMartin Preschool case to a psychologically unstable woman whose untreated paranoia led her to suspect her two-year-old son had been abused by his day care teacher, Ray Buckey. Her suspicions became the spark that lit cultural tinder that, for a host of reasons, was primed to catch fire. Within months, day care abuse reports began to surface, first throughout Southern California and soon across the nation. Eventually those suspicions morphed into reports of ritual abuse that, the authors wrote, "erupted like lesions across the country."

Nathan and Snedeker culled reams of information from police files, newspapers, interviews, court documents, and federal committee meetings. They provided names, dates, and damning evidence that, during the 1980s, segments of the culture traditionally imbued with the expectation of rational thought had embraced as truth fears that had no basis in scientific or legal fact.

"Indeed, this is the way belief in ritual abuse spread: via an impassioned, nation-wide crusade conducted by social workers, therapists, physicians, victimology researchers, police, criminal prosecutors, fundamentalist Christians, ambitious politicians, anti-pornography activists, feminists, and the media," they wrote. "It was a powerful effort that did not come together overnight. But as it took shape, a veritable industry developed around the effort to demonstrate the existence of ritual abuse." (12)

Reading *Satan's Silence*, I felt like one who, after wandering for years in a foreign land, finally arrives in a place where the language was familiar, where the thinking made sense, where the water was safe to drink. But years of pent-up emotion rendered me anxious and tentative. I could only read a few pages at a time before feeling restless and edgy. I'd get up and rummage through the pantry, or brew yet another mug of tea, or take the dog for yet another walk in the rain. I'd come back, sit down, and read some more.

Over time, the text in my copy of *Satan's Silence* glowed with yellow highlighter; the pages fluttered with purple, blue, and yellow Post-its. The reading was difficult, maddening, strengthening. The "thing" that had entrapped Michelle and Mary, and that had confounded me for so long, was a real cultural and political phenomenon. It had a history, a cast of characters, and an edge-of-the-seat narrative. It would have made great fiction. It wasn't. Nathan and Snedeker investigated the panic's cultural and political roots, showing how cultural factors—including legalized abortion, the rise in numbers of babies born to unwed mothers, high divorce rates, women entering the workforce in unprecedented numbers—fueled social anxiety about sexual behaviors and gender roles. They traced the evolution of the 1970s child protection movement, which gave rise to more awareness about child sexual abuse but little actual training in how to identify it, interview children about it, or treat offenders. They showed how a handful of self-described child advocates—most of whom were likely well-meaning initially, but unschooled in critical thinking and emotionally swayed by the lurid scandal they believed they were fighting—influenced laws, policies, law enforcement attitudes, and criminal prosecutions.

I began keeping a list of names of individuals who surfaced as major energizers of the panic, those who prioritized proving the validity of their theories about MPD and ritual abuse over their clients' well being or any scientifically valid proof. Chief among them was Dr. Bennett Braun, head of the Dissociative Disorders unit at Rush Presbyterian-St. Luke's Hospital in Chicago. Braun was a passionate believer in the existence of multiple personality disorder and satanic ritual abuse. He was joined by his cohorts Roberta Sachs, the unit's training director, and Elva Poznanski, chief of child and adolescent psychiatry at the unit.

Braun's methods, which included housing patients in inpatient units for months at a time and using daily therapy as well as copious amounts of drugs to "help" them uncover their memories of abuse, were ethically unsupportable. The 1995 *Frontline* documentary, "The Search for Satan," examined in excruciating detail the cases of two of Braun's former patients, Patricia Burgus and Mary Shanley.

Braun treated Burgus from 1986, when she was twenty-nine,

until 1992. When Burgus first entered treatment, she believed she had developed some MPD alters. Under Braun's care, she was persuaded to believe she possessed more than three hundred personalities, was a satanic high priestess, had eaten human flesh, and had sexually molested her two young sons. The cost of her treatment (and that of her sons, who were hospitalized for three years) came to more than $3 million.

Shanley, an elementary school teacher, was also a patient of Braun's. Under the care of Braun and his colleague, Roberta Sachs, Shanley said she became convinced she was part of a multigenerational satanic cult and that she hosted more than a dozen alters. Braun prescribed an array of drugs and pressured her to name her cult contacts in the community. Shanley was eventually transferred to Spring Shadows Glen, a private psychiatric hospital in Houston, and put under the care of psychologist Judith Peterson, the clinical director of the hospital's Dissociative Disorders Treatment Program who was considered a "specialist" in using hypnosis to assist patients in retrieving memories of childhood sexual abuse. Shanley remained there for two years, at a cost of more than $1 million. (13)

Besides Braun, Poznanski, Sachs, and Peterson, my list included hypnosis specialist and case consultant Corydon Hammond, ritual abuse expert Roland Summit, and Colin Ross, a Canadian physician and early MPD advocate. Hammond's 1992 address on the machinations of the "cult" was cited in Chapter 15. Summit's theories included the idea that children never lie about childhood sexual abuse and should always be believed, except when they retracted initial disclosures of abuse. Summit also suggested that people who did not believe in ritual abuse claims were possibly complicit with perpetrators. (14) Ross's early writings included texts on diagnosing and treating multiple personality disorder and ritual abuse. (15)

I also discovered the 1994 *Making Monsters—False Memories, Psychotherapy and Sexual Hysteria,* by Pulitzer Prize–winning journalist and social psychology professor Richard Ofshe, an expert on the subject of coercion, and freelance writer Ethan Watters. It seemed the book was written to answer most of my questions, even those I hadn't yet formulated. Ofshe and Watters were unsparing in their attack on the triumvirate of fallacious beliefs that nurtured the 1980s social panic, in particular the recovered memory movement. "We will argue that the practice of uncovering repressed memories, along with the attendant theories of multiple personality disorder and satanic cult abuse, are fads as widespread and as damaging as any the mental health field has produced this century," they wrote. "We will show that recovered memory therapists are not . . . brave healers but professionals who have built a pseudoscience out of an unfounded consensus about how the mind reacts to sexual trauma. In the process they have slipped the ties that bind their professions to scientific method and sound research." (16)

The controversy over recovered memories unexpectedly hit close to home. In 1990, University of Oregon psychology professor Jennifer Freyd recalled forgotten incidents of alleged sexual abuse by her father, but not as a result of techniques used in recovered memory therapy. Her parents, Peter Freyd, a mathematics professor at the University of Pennsylvania, and Pamela Freyd, an education researcher at the same institution, vigorously denied their daughter's claims. In 1992 they founded the False Memory Syndrome Foundation, the first organized voice challenging the factual validity of recovered memories. (17)

While affirming that child abuse was intolerable, the False Memory Syndrome Foundation (FMSF) accused recovered memory practitioners of using unproven techniques to help "recover" abuse memories that hadn't happened, leading to false accusations and the shattering of families. At a time when courts and the media were focused on accusers, the foundation became an important source of information, advocacy, and community for those who believed they had been falsely accused of sex abuse based on recovered memories. The foundation kept track of lawsuits filed around the country, maintained a library, submitted friend-of-the-court briefs, sponsored continuing education programs, and marshaled the help of lawyers who helped accused family members defend themselves in court. By 1998, according to Pamela Freyd, the foundation had been contacted by twenty thousand families. (18)

Detractors accused the foundation of being one-sided, of giving shelter to perpetrators who were in denial about their abusive behavior, and of having board members who held conservative or extremist leanings, including some who held fast to the ritual abuse narrative. However, according to Nathan and Snedeker, the FMSF board also included a number of prestigious psychologists and academics. Richard Ofshe was an early member of the board. (19)

By the mid-1990s, the panic was on the wane, but it would not die quietly. In 1994, a barrage of accusations concerning child abuse sex rings roiled the town of Wenatchee, Washington, about one hundred miles east of Seattle. At its height, forty-three adults were arrested on 29,726 charges of child sex abuse—including ritualistic orgies—involving sixty children, many of whom were removed from their homes and relocated in foster homes. A pastor who publicly criticized the investigation was arrested, along with his wife, on child abuse charges, including abuse of their daughter. Of those charged, twenty-six were convicted of felonies. (20)

Also in 1994, three Arkansas teenagers, Jason Baldwin, Damien Echols, and Jessie Misskelley Jr., dubbed the West Memphis Three, were convicted of murdering three eight-year-old boys in what prosecutors asserted was a satanic crime. Echols was sentenced to death, Baldwin received life imprisonment, and Misskelley was sentenced to life imprisonment plus two twenty-year sentences. (21)

But for the most part, the jig was up. The fourth edition of the *Diagnostic and Statistical Manual of Mental Disorders*, published in 1994, replaced the term "multiple personality disorder" with the more neutral term dissociative identity disorder, or DID. The term, practitioners explained, better reflected that the condition "is characterized by a fragmentation of identity, rather than the proliferation of separate identities." (22) By then, judges had overturned many—but not all—of the guilty verdicts in the raft of childcare abuse cases from the 1980s. (More convictions would be overturned in subsequent years.) By 2000, the eighteen adults in the Wenatchee panic who had been incarcerated were either released, had their convictions overturned, or pleaded guilty to lesser, unrelated charges. (23)

Once willing to accept the claim of "recovered memories" as evidence in childhood sex abuse cases, courts began rejecting those memories as proof a crime had occurred. In one high-profile case, recovered memory was the basis on which California resident George Franklin was found guilty in 1990 of the rape and murder of his daughter's eight-year-old friend. The evidence against him was the recovered memory of his daughter, who recalled the incident twenty years after she said she witnessed it. In 1996, a judge overturned Franklin's conviction.

Most of the legal action, however, was via civil suits against therapists and other practitioners. From the mid-1990s and into the 2000s, more and more plaintiffs—from California, Oregon, Illinois, Minnesota, Texas, Wisconsin, and Washington—filed lawsuits saying their treatment providers persuaded them they were victims of ritual abuse or had developed MPD, or both.

In 1994, an Oregon woman successfully sued two Portland-area psychologists for convincing her that she and her children had been subject to severe ritual abuse. In 1995, a former patient of St. Paul, Minnesota-based psychiatrist Diane Humenansky, Vynnette Hamanne, won a $2.6 million settlement in a jury trial against the therapist. Hamanne claimed Humenansky told her she had developed multiple personality disorder, had been repeatedly sexually assaulted by family members, and that in order to heal needed to recover memories of the abuse. In 1996, Elizabeth Carlson, another former patient of Humenansky's, was awarded $2.5 million in a lawsuit that made similar claims. The judge who presided in both trials ruled "that the theory that humans are capable of 'repressing' or 'dissociating' memories of numerous traumas in childhood was not a credible scientific theory" and thus could not be presented to the jury. (24)

In 1997, Burgus won a $10.6 million settlement against Braun, Poznanski, and Rush Presbyterian-St. Luke's Hospital (now Rush University Medical Center.) Shanley settled her case against Braun for an undisclosed amount. (25) In 1999, Braun's Illinois medical license was suspended for two years, after which he was prohibited from treating patients with multiple personality disorder or dissociative identity disorder for five years. (26)

In 1998, a former patient filed a suit against recovered memory advocate Dr. Renee Fredrickson, a St. Paul, Minnesota-based psychologist and author of the 1992 book, *A Journey to Recovery from Sexual Abuse,* accusing the psychologist of implanting her with false memories. The case was settled out of court for $175,000. (27)

Two of Colin Ross's former patients filed suits against him. Each woman claimed Ross had used drugs and other techniques to persuade her to believe she had been severely abused by a cult, and each had developed multiple personalities as a result. One case, brought by a woman in Manitoba, did not make it through the court system; the second suit, brought by Dallas resident Martha Tyo, named Ross, several practitioners, and the Charter Behavioral Health System, where Ross was the head of the MPD unit. While in treatment from 1990 to 1997, Tyo said she came to believe her family was part of a multigenerational cult that participated in the torture, murder, and cannibalism of numerous adults and children. She was convinced that, in the guise of an alter ego, she had abused her own son. She had severed ties with her children, attempted suicide, and ended her marriage. Tyo's case was settled out of court in 1998 for an undisclosed amount. (28)

In 2004, former psychiatric patient Elizabeth Gale won a $7.5 million settlement in a case against Rush North Shore Medical Center, where Braun had been director of the dissociative disorders program. Under the care of Braun and others, Gale, who had initially sought treatment for depression, spent two thousand days in psychiatric hospitals from 1986 to 1997. In her lawsuit, Gale said that Braun and his colleagues—including Roberta Sachs and Corydon Hammond—convinced her that her family indoctrinated her as a child so she would make babies for cult sacrifices. Gale changed her name three times, underwent sterilization, left her job, and fled her home to escape detection by the supposed satanic cult. None of the practitioners or the institutions named in the suit admitted to wrongdoing. (29)

In August 2011, new DNA evidence, recanted testimonies, several investigative documentaries, critical findings by outside investigators regarding police and court procedures, and the untiring efforts of a corps of supporters—including musicians and the movie director Peter Jackson—led to the release of the West Memphis Three. For legal reasons, all three entered Alford pleas, but after being incarcerated for seventeen years, all are essentially out of the prison system. (30)

In 2013, Fran and Dave Keller, among the last of those incarcerated in the high-profile childcare abuse cases, were released from prison. In 1992 the Kellers were each convicted of aggravated assault and sentenced to forty-eight years; the offenses they were charged with at their Austin-area day care center included ritual abuse. During Fran Keller's 2013 appeals hearing, the ER physician who had examined one of the alleged child victims repudiated his initial diagnosis of abuse, and a prosecution witness was accused of having been shown to be "a charlatan and a crackpot." The appeal claimed that "a 21st century court ought to be able to recognize a 20th century witchhunt and render justice accordingly." Both of the Kellers spent twenty-one years behind bars. (31)

I have glossed over complex details and analyses and omitted many names in this cursory review of the 1980s hysteria. And I realize the issues the panic raised are layered, complex, and significant. Child sexual abuse—ritualized or in any other form—is a heinous crime that warrants investigation, intervention, and prevention measures. Child predators are real. And institutional denial and cover-up of sex abuse is, sadly, very real, as evidenced by the Catholic Church pedophile priest scandal, and recent complaints brought against private boarding schools and some universities.

But the unfortunate realities of sexual predators and institutional denial do not of themselves create a social panic. A social panic—and those who foster it—manipulates complex social issues to fuel a grotesque, distorted way of looking at the world. In the case of the 1980s panic over child sex abuse, a core of individuals revived fears that can be traced to pre-Christian times, medieval demonology, Jewish persecutions, and the Salem witch trials. A host of social, political, and religious factors conjoined to create a cultural mindset that enabled widespread segments of the public—treatment providers, law enforcement, courts, the media, religious clergy, feminists, parents—to see those baseless fears as real and imminent.

I don't know what fueled the panic's most fevered advocates. Their reasons for promoting belief in satanic ritual abuse are as confounding as the "evil" they accused the supposed cult members of promoting. If there was a malevolent force afoot during that decade, it was these individuals' commitment to promoting the panic, not any satanic presence. Michelle was undoubtedly ill before she got caught up in her ritual abuse memories and became lost in the maze of her supposed multiple personalities. But the panic intensified her mental instability and her feelings of terror, desperation, and isolation. I'm sure many others were similarly affected. I didn't try to find them. There are limits, I discovered, to what I want to know.

chapter 19
unplugged

Malcolm Gladwell's 2000 book *The Tipping Point* takes an innovative look at the phenomenon of social trends—fads, buying trends, crime waves—and how they spread. When I heard about the book, I was curious as to whether his theories might be applied to the 1980s social panic, and I bought a copy to find out. Midway through the introduction, I began to think it did. By the end of the first chapter, I was convinced. I reached for my pad of sticky notes.

Gladwell never refers to that decade's raft of day care child abuse cases, the hysteria over ritual abuse, or the spike in diagnoses of multiple personality disorder, but I made my own connections. By the time I finished the book, it, too, was festooned with yellow, purple, and green tags.

Gladwell identifies three requirements for an idea or trend to gain traction. The first is "The Law of the Few," in which a potent core of well-connected individuals have the status and standing to promote an idea or trend. Second is a "Stickiness Factor," which makes the idea lodge in people's minds and prompts them to action. The third is a specific set of cultural conditions—the "Power of Context"—that allows the idea to flourish. (1)

In my mind, the 1980s panic qualified in each category. Consider "The Law of the Few." The individuals who first postulated the existence of a widespread cult and those who advocated the MPD phenomenon were professionals who were savvy about broadcasting and disseminating their theories to the networks they created. They certainly had status and standing—they included psychiatrists and social workers, clinicians, law enforcement personnel, and heads of child advocacy groups, as well as individuals associated with the high-profile McMartin Preschool case. They wrote books on their theories and addressed audiences at symposiums and conferences.

As for the "Stickiness Factor," the hysteria over abuse in day care centers, the ritual abuse epidemic, and the furor over multiple personality disorder had it in spades. The episodes of cult abuse that were described in *Michelle Remembers* and became a template for subsequent "victims" were lurid and horrifying. Criminal cases brought against childcare workers for gross sexual abuse of their clients were widely reported, as were the convictions. Society's supposed inability to protect its children spurred those working in the child protection arena— social workers, therapists, psychiatrists, attorneys, clergy, law enforcement—to act. It motivated conservative Christians who considered it their mission to vanquish the devil in all its forms. It motivated feminist practitioners who saw yet another instance of society being blind to an evil being perpetrated on women and children. The stickiness was resilient and unyielding. The consistent lack of physical evidence in both the day care and ritual abuse cases wasn't a deterrent.

The bizarre but fascinating diagnosis of multiple personality disorder had an undeniable stickiness factor. The movies

The Three Faces of Eve and *Sybil*, both marketed as being based on actual case studies, had a high stickiness quotient from the get-go. The theory that MPD was an attempt by survivors to cope with childhood trauma (usually sexual abuse) created more stickiness, as did the parade of high-profile "multiples" who appeared on national TV talk shows throughout the eighties. As the panic evolved, MPD and ritual abuse stuck to each other, tightly.

Finally comes Gladwell's "Power of Context." Nathan and Snedeker, Victor, Acocella, and others enumerated a slew of cultural factors that created a cultural mindset ripe for embracing the 1980s fear-based epidemic. Among them were the rise of fundamentalist religions, anxiety about the loss of traditional values and changes in sexual mores, the swell of women entering the workforce, the proliferation of day care centers, the rise of the recovered memory movement, and the effect of feminism on cultural values. I wondered, too, if that decade's slow awakening to and fear of the creeping AIDS epidemic might have contributed to a general sense of cultural anxiety. For some it might have been more palatable to focus on egregious satanic abuse or an unusual psychological diagnosis than to deal with the indisputable tragedy of AIDS. Wrestling with false devils can be a distraction from facing what is clear, present, and seemingly uncontrollable.

One important component of "context," Gladwell wrote, is the power that small, close-knit groups have "to magnify the epidemic potential of a message or idea," another close fit with the eighties hysteria. (2) The professional communities that promoted the idea of the MPD and ritual abuse epidemics were potent clusters of advocacy. Practitioners who believed in the prevalence of ritual abuse and associated case of multiple personality did not critique one another's theories or research. They did not set rigorous scientific standards for one another.

Instead, they were co-conspirators. As colleagues, they created a nucleus of credibility that radiated outward across the country. In 1984, Braun and others formed the International Society for the Study of Multiple Personality and Dissociation, which attracted hundreds of like-minded practitioners. Beginning in 1988, the group published the journal *Dissociation*, which further disseminated their ideas. (3) The more MPD and ritual abuse advocates spoke at conferences and seminars across the country, the more people they drew into their fold. Membership in the club grew exponentially throughout those years. The only requirement of belonging was to believe without question.

I have simplified Gladwell's theory, but I found his basic template immensely helpful. I had begun my research hoping to find a cause or explanation that would shed light on the paranoia that had consumed Michelle and Mary. I didn't expect to find so many intertwining threads or such a mind-boggling tangle of cultural causes and effects. Each new study provided more perspective on the turmoil that had upended my niece's life and that of her parents and countless others. Gladwell provided yet one more way of looking at the 1980s social panic, and how it was able to spread as far and last as long as it did.

But one thing Gladwell didn't discuss in *The Tipping Point* was how people extricate themselves from a belief system they have bought into or been affected by. He didn't identify the steps a person needs to take to regain the power they have ceded to an ideological hysteria. He didn't explore the possibility that some individuals are more drawn into social hysterias than are others, or that a person could be affected by an epidemic but not realize it until years later.

One blustery, sun-dappled spring afternoon several years into my research, I took a long walk along the Willamette River. I needed to walk to calm down. That morning I had spoken with a woman who believed she had been subjected to cult abuse in her childhood. By then I was in agreement with what researchers had deduced about the 1980s panic—that it was a massive, rumor-infested hoax fed by fear, manipulation, and gross abuses of power. That it was an irrational reaction to a host of cultural changes. That it was a remnant of a cultural narrative that reached back centuries.

That is what I thought, but my hours of research had involved reading about, not speaking with, those who believed themselves to be ritual abuse survivors. I wanted to speak with someone who at some point believed she had been a survivor. I wanted to know if she had come to the same conclusion I had about the panic.

This woman had not.

She began our conversation tentatively, even questioning her own memories. But her voice became stronger as her memories assumed a familiar shape. She described exacting details not only about physical torture she believed she had endured by cult members, but also about mind control techniques they had used to keep her quiet and obedient. I don't have permission to share details of her story, but as she spoke, I felt the familiar dread response return to my body: heat radiated from my face; my stomach churned. Her details were more specific than anything I had come across in my reading, and they seemed targeted to her personally, not a rehash of other people's claims. Near the end of our talk, she made a comment that had an uncanny connection to Michelle's experience. I was in no shape to tell her that. I focused on masking my increasingly agitated state of mind. I had not expected our talk to go the way that it did—for me, a hairpin turn back into confusion.

I hadn't wanted anything to do with the ritual abuse phenomenon, but it had wormed its way into my life. For years I fought against it, even as it roiled my thoughts and tumbled through my dreams. While Michelle was alive, and afterward, her and her mother's staunch belief in a widespread satanic cult and its sadistic machinations became an indigestible clump that I gnawed on in the deep of the night. But resistance, I came to understand, can be as binding as an embrace, because you become so entwined with what you push against. To be free of it, I eventually realized I had to face it. I made myself read, research, and read some more. I learned about what a social panic was, what gave rise to it, and who it entrapped. I read about the people who cultivated this particular panic and about the cultural mindset that allowed it to spread. I kept on reading even when the words made the nape of my neck prickle or my jaw clench with anger. I kept on reading in my mind even when the words weren't in front of me.

By the time I talked with the woman that morning, I thought I knew where I stood. Most of me did. But, I think on a level I wasn't as aware of, a part of my brain was still hooked into unexplored fears that had fed the panic in the first place. Research and writing were necessary steps to learning about the panic, but they weren't enough. My information gathering hadn't clarified what my part was in that whole conundrum, or why it had affected me so deeply. Something in me was holding on to the oppressive confusion of those years. I didn't know its name. I didn't know its reasons. I felt it deep within me, in the part of me that registers what my mind isn't ready to grasp or admit.

I believe now that the part of me that was holding on is a part of my brain—of all our brains—that is primitive, emotional, and wired for survival, not for analysis or critical thinking. Brain researchers call it the amygdala. It is our first responder to sensory or emotional stimuli in our environment, and instantly engages when it senses a possible threat to our survival or to our feeling of being in control, regardless of the context. Our amygdalae hold on to illogical fears that can be rooted in personal experience or in religious, cultural, community, or familial belief systems. It prompts us to believe that, in order to maintain our world order, we must demonize the new or unfamiliar, including anything or anyone that challenges our beliefs. The amygdala's trigger response spurs us to reject the outsider, or the prophet with a new message, and hold fast to whatever our "group" declares to be true. It has no interest in rational thinking, or logic or anything that might jeopardize our sense of belonging or acceptance by our tribe, our families, or our peers. It is fight or flight, rule or be ruled. For me, it is my 4:00 a.m. mind, when the dark is most profound, when my worst suspicions hold sway and my fears appear real and absolute, not exaggerated or out of context.

The rule of this primitive part of our brains is not new. Over the centuries one culture after another has scapegoated, hunted down, and slaughtered untold numbers of individuals in order to gain or maintain a sense of control or dominance that, in truth, can never be permanently realized. Victims run the gamut—people with different-hued skins, who speak in strange tongues or worship different gods, come from unknown places or are suspected to have supernatural or demonic powers. Our collective fears of being overtaken are as stubborn as they are groundless. Their hold on us is fierce. They are enshrined in our religions, our national identities, our communities and families. They retain the power to push aside not only common sense and decency, but centuries of enlightened thought, as they did just four decades ago.

That, I feel, is the part of me that got hooked by the ritual abuse epidemic. It is what kept me from objecting—openly, confidently, without reservation—to Michelle's memories, to Mary's unswerving belief in the cult, to the whole sweep of the panic that now seems so ridiculous, so beyond the pale, so patently fraudulent and absurd. Yes, I was fearful of losing my connection to Michelle and to her mom. Yes, there were plenty of others who didn't know what to make of the ritual abuse phenomenon, either. But for me, there was more to it. I didn't have enough faith in the beliefs that I had tried to cobble together after leaving my childhood religion, or in the critical thinking I had cultivated through my years of schooling. I professed to believe in the light of consciousness, awareness, tolerance, and informed insight. I was proud of where I stood. If you had asked, I would have told you that ours is a difficult, challenging but wondrous world. That we are held by a loving presence with an infinitely forgiving and generous spirit. I would have said that most of what is termed "evil" in our world is not an entity but a void— the absence of love, of connection, of awareness, of respect for ourselves and for others. But the fact was, when my beliefs were challenged, I didn't step up. I kept silent. I gave myself over to fear and confusion and the kernel of paranoia that lay in a tiny fold deep in my consciousness. That was my one sin: I didn't hold on to what I professed to believe. I turned away from my own light. I bowed to an unnamed fear, and granted it power.

As I walked along the glittering river, I tried to breathe in its bubbly zest. Ducks bobbed along the banks looking for food. The willows were beginning to green out. The sweet scent of cottonwood suffused the air. The river rushed by, swollen with spring runoff. Everything seemed about to burst.

I didn't know what to make of the woman's memories. Clearly she had been traumatized. The desire to control others has

always been part of the human psyche. If professional therapists could manipulate adult women into believing they were
priestesses in satanic cults, had endured grievous physical torture, betrayed their children, and developed scores of alter personalities, couldn't amateurs use similar techniques to control
a terrified child?

Memory is susceptible to change, I knew by then, but what
about memories that remain fixed? Did her recollection, as precise as it was, mean the sadistic abuse had actually occurred?
Are repeated memories a more accurate mirroring of the truth,
or, as many researchers believe, are we simply more convinced
in the story we want those memories to tell?

And what if her memories were emotional images, not
reflections of a past physical reality? Did it even matter? Surely
we can suffer from a false memory we believe to be true as
much as we can from one that accurately reflects a past event. A
therapist once told me, "If a client comes in with a memory, we
start from there." Not to ascertain the truth of it, but to explore
its ramifications and help the person in pain regain a degree
of power over his or her life. Whatever had happened to this
woman, whatever the objective truth of her memories, for years
she felt she had been robbed of her self-determination, of belief
in her innate goodness. If that is how she was made to feel, does
it matter how the belief arose?

Likewise, I would never know what had broken in
Michelle, the specifics of her disrupted brain chemistry, or
the cause of her emotional pain. I would never know whether
the bulimia that dogged her through adolescence was rooted
in mental illness or in the traumatic rape she had disclosed. I
would never know why she, in particular, was drawn so completely into the 1980s panic.

But what I finally understood that afternoon was that it
wasn't up to me to discern the truth of my niece's memories,

or those of the woman I had spoken with. It wasn't my place to fit either of them into a category. It was my place to have compassion for the loneliness and pain they had faced from living in constant fear, from feeling "other," from being separated from their own light. Our lives and psyches have aspects that will never be knowable to others, maybe not even to ourselves. Truth and memory are forever entwined in a changing current of time, circumstance, and perspective. The flow can carry us or overwhelm us. Most of us have a choice as to which it will be.

That morning, as the woman shared her memories, I felt a pull sucking me back toward a vortex I thought I was free of. It was the ancient call of a dark lord. Not the devil of my Catholic upbringing or the Satan named in the panic. It was the gravitational pull of humanity's dark side—confusion, doubt, oppression, victimhood—the siren call of a lightless world calling me back. It didn't want to let me go. It wanted me to be fearful. It wanted me to give it dominion. It had followed me to the river. It wanted, again, to become my shadow.

I didn't have all these words that day. But I felt them. That afternoon, as swiftly as the river running next to me, as gently as the wind rustling through the cottonwood trees along its banks, I made a decision. I said No. No more. I didn't say no just in my mind, but throughout all of me, a river's breadth of me, as deep and as far as I felt myself reach. I unplugged from all of it—the grisly stories, my niece's vacant eyes, her scrawled and pleading journals, my doubt, my helplessness, my silence, my judgment, my need to have all the answers. Along that river, in the shimmer of the early spring sun, I said no. And quick as a blink, I set myself free.

chapter 20
epilogue

My brother John and his wife, Mary, still live in their home on Center Street. Their daughter Wynlee, her husband, Robert, and their two teenage children live in a town close by. Their son, Greg, and his wife have four children and live in Texas. John and Mary have tight bonds with all their grandchildren. Mary continues to believe that the memories that plagued Michelle arose out of real-life events. She does not agree with the findings of this book. She is as gracious and kind to me as ever.

In 2011, Lisa Nasseff, a former patient at Castlewood Treatment Center, a St. Louis-based facility that treats eating disorders, filed a lawsuit against her psychologist, Mark Schwartz, who with his wife, Lori Galperin, founded the clinic. Nasseff, a clinic patient for fifteen months, accused Schwartz of brainwashing her into believing she had multiple personalities, was abused by a satanic cult, and had herself committed abusive acts. Three other former patients came forward with similar claims.

Nasseff's case was dismissed in 2013; her attorney said the case "was resolved favorably for both sides." Schwartz and his wife left the clinic; a Castlewood spokesperson said their departure was not related to the allegations. Castlewood denied the allegations of brainwashing and said no therapist at the center had ever created false memories or hypnotized clients. (1)

Researchers and practitioners continue to study the mechanisms of memory, and the effect of early trauma on an individual, including delayed memories and the development of dissociative identity disorder. Disagreement persists over the validity of recovered memories—many practitioners believe them to be true; some researchers remain skeptical. How the memories are uncovered is an important factor. Stories continue to surface about memory's vulnerability to external influences, including authority and expectation. The *New Yorker* recently ran a story about several individuals who not only pleaded guilty to a 1989 murder they did not commit, but remembered and were tormented by physical details of the assault they were not part of. The suspects with the most vivid memories of the crime had been interviewed by the same psychologist, who subscribed to recovered memory theory. (2) At the other end of the recovered memory spectrum a 2017 Netflix documentary, *The Keepers*, examines the experiences of a woman who remembered her own repeated sexual abuse by a priest at her all-girls Catholic high school—twenty years after it had reportedly occurred. (3)

Austin day care operators Fran and Dan Keller were fully exonerated in June 2017. The former district attorney, who had been involved in the initial case, declined to exonerate them, which had made their lives difficult. Their exoneration is the first out of a conviction integrity unit of the Travis County (Texas) District Attorney's Office under a new district attorney. The Kellers will each receive $1.7 million for the twenty-one years they were incarcerated. (4)

I should mention the forget-me-nots. They started showing up in my yard several years ago while I was working on this book. They have spread, which is their wildflower nature. I find them in my bulb pots and mixed in with the tomato and kale plants in the backyard planting box. They take root in the cracks between the laundry room and the driveway, among the white iris and the daisies, at the base of the azalea bush, and in any pots containing dirt. Their tiny blooms appear where the lawn meets the walkway, among the rocks in the front garden, and along the fence. In the spring and early summer, my front and side yards are flecked with blue. I try not to disturb their roots when I mow or weed around them. Some wildflowers come and go. I want the forget-me-nots to keep coming back.

chapter notes

chapter 2: ticker

1. Debbie Nathan and Michael Snedeker, *Satan's Silence: Ritual Abuse and the Making of a Modern American Witch Hunt*. See Chapter 3, Beginnings: Mary Ann Barbour. All references to her work are by permission of the author.
2. Michelle Smith and Lawrence Pazder, M.D., *Michelle Remembers* (paperback by Pocket Books, 1981). Now seen as a fraud, the book in the 1980s was considered by many to be a prime energizer of the satanic ritual abuse panic.

chapter 7: wedding day

1. Communities/states where day care sex abuse cases surfaced include Miami (Little Rascals); Malden, Massachusetts (Fells Acre Day Care Center); El Paso (East Valley YMCA Daycare Center); Pittsfield, Massachusetts (Early Childhood Development Center); Austin, Texas (Oak Hill); Carson City, Nevada (private babysitting service); Maplewood, New Jersey (Wee Care Nursery School); Edenton, North Carolina (Little Rascals); Memphis, Tennessee (Georgia Hills Early Childhood Center); and the Bronx (Praca Day Care).

chapter 8: another michelle remembers

1. Early skeptics could not find corroboration for many of Smith's claims, but the momentum of the book was too strong to be stopped by factual shortcomings. Over time more doubters surfaced. A September 1990 story in the *Mail on Sunday*, sister paper to Britain's *Daily Mail*, interviewed Smith's father, who said Smith's "memories" were not supported by real events. (https://en.wikipedia.org/wiki/Michelle_Remembers *Michelle Remembers*)

2. *Michelle Remembers*, pp. 100–101.

3. *Michelle Remembers*, p. 244.

4. *The Satanic Scare*, edited by James Richardson, Joel Best, and David Bromley, p. 232.

5. Publisher's Note in *Michelle Remembers* and https://en.wikipedia.org/wiki/Michelle_Remembers, under "Results."

chapter 9: in the valley

1. "Police keep eye on occult," *The Register-Guard*, Eugene, Oregon, August 20, 1989.

2. "Satanism in Oregon," *The Oregonian*, Portland, Oregon, August 13, 1989.

3. In 1985, two young girls from Hamilton, Ontario, claimed they were victims of grisly ritual sexual abuse, including cannibalism, perpetrated by their parents and their mother's boyfriend. Freelance journalist Kevin Marron, who wrote for the Toronto newspaper the *Globe and Mail*, was one of a handful of journalists admitted to the eighteen-month guardianship trial, which ran from 1985 to 1987. In 1988, Marron published *Ritual Abuse: Canada's Most Infamous Trial on Child Abuse*. Despite the lack of physical evidence supporting the girls' claims, Marron wrote that the girls' descriptions of their abuse "could only have been based on experience, and that their accounts of ritual violence had the same ring of authen-

ticity." The presiding judge ruled that abuse had occurred and ordered the girls to be removed from their parents' care, but did not rule on charges of ritual abuse, and did not criminally charge the adults. (p. xii; p. 244)

4. Handbook Introduction, Los Angeles County Commission for Women's Ritual Abuse Task Force, 1991. (https://sites. google.com/site/mcrais/ritualab, accessed January 20, 2017.)

5. Task Force handbook, under "Descriptive Definitions."

6. One of the titles, *Satan's Underground: The Extraordinary Story of One Woman's Escape,* by Lauren Stratford, was a supposedly autobiographical account by a survivor of ritual abuse. The book was later found to have been fabricated. Harvest House withdrew it from its list in 1990 but sold it to Pelican Publishing in Louisiana. Stratford's birth name was Laurel Willson; Stratford/Willson later adopted the name Laura Grabowski and posed as a Holocaust survivor. (http://www.answers.org/ satan/stratford.html, accessed July 3, 2017.)

chapter 10: memory

1. Ellen Bass and Laura Davis, *The Courage to Heal*, 1994.

2. Richard Ofshe and Ethan Watters, *Making Monsters— False Memories, Psychotherapy, and Sexual Hysteria*, p. 38.

3. Several books about victims of the recovered memory movement were published in the mid-1990s. Mark Pendergrast's 1995 *Victims of Memory: Sex Abuse Accusations and Shattered Lives* includes interviews with more than a dozen individuals who said family members falsely accused them of sexual abuse. It also includes interviews with several women and one man who retracted their accusations. The 1997 *Lost Daughters: Recovered Memory Therapy & The People It Hurts*, by Reinder Van Til, tells the stories of five sets of parents— including the author—whose daughters accused them of childhood sexual abuse based on recovered memories.

In 2010, Meredith Maran authored *My Lie: A True Story of False Memory*, which chronicles Maran's involvement with the recovered memory movement, during which she became convinced her father had molested her when she was a child. Maran, a feminist and a journalist, came to this conclusion even though she had no specific recollection of the abuse. Her memoir takes readers through her initial suspicions, her accusations against her father, and, over time, her growing doubts about her accusations. Maran eventually retracted them and was able to reconcile with her father.

chapter 11: voices

1. The nonfiction book *The Three Faces of Eve* was based on the case of Chris Costner Sizemore, a patient of psychiatrists Corbett Thigpen and Hervey Cleckley. Sizemore also wrote a book on her multiplicity.
2. The book *Sybil* sold six million copies. Debbie Nathan's 2011 book, *Sybil Exposed: The Extraordinary Story Behind the Famous Multiple Personality Case*, explores the entwined relationship between Sybil, whose real name was Shirley Mason, and her psychiatrist, Cornelia Wilbur. Nathan's research raises significant doubt about the veracity of Mason's multiple personalities, and questions Wilbur's ethics as a practitioner. Nathan attributes Mason's "alter" episodes to her overly dependent relationship on Wilbur, and the drugs—antipsychotics, psychedelics, and Pentothal—that Wilbur administered to her client for more than two decades. The film included several fictionalized scenes, which Nathan posits were the television film writer's attempt to make sense of what was, in essence, a fabricated story fraught with holes and inconsistencies.
3. Joan Acocella, *Creating Hysteria—Women and Multiple Personality Disorder*, 1999. Used with permission.

4. *Creating Hysteria*, p. 87. Used with permission.
5. Gloria Steinem, *Revolution From Within*, p. 318. Steinem participated in the 1993 HBO documentary *Multiple Personalities: The Search for Deadly Memories*, part of its America Undercover series.
6. *Dialogues with Madwomen* was produced by filmmakers Allie Light and Irving Saraf and won several awards, including an Emmy for Outstanding Interview Program, a Health and Science Communications Association award, the Sundance Film Festival Freedom of Expression Award, and a Special Jury Award from National Educational Film and Video.
7. "Satanic Abuse, Horrific Tales Haunt Victims," McClatchy News Service, August 4, 1991.

chapter 15: marionette

1. Hammond's speech was delivered on June 25, 1992, at the Fourth Annual Eastern Regional Conference on Abuse and Multiple Personality in Richmond, Virginia. It is often referred to as the "Greenbaum Speech." Transcripts are easily found online, for instance at http://www.bibliotecapleyades.nct/sociopolitica/esp_sociopol_mindcon03.htm. (Accessed January 20, 2017).

   Hammond was not a new recruit to the ritual abuse/MPD phenomenon. In 1989 he participated in a taped conversation with other practitioners who promulgated belief in satanic cults. (http://www.fmsonline.org/links/braunsachshammond.html, accessed January 20, 2017.) "What we're talking about here goes beyond child abuse or beyond the brainwashing of Patty Hearst or Korean War veterans," Hammond said. "We're talking about people . . . who were raised in satanic cults from the time they were born. Often cults that have come over from Europe, that have roots in the SS, in death-camp squads in some cases.

These are children who tell us stories about being deprived of sleep all night, of being required to work at manual labor exhaustingly all day long without any food or water. When they reach point of utter fatigue they may then watch other people tortured. Perhaps a finger might be cut off and hung around their neck on a chain as a symbol to them that they had better be obedient."

2. According to the W. W. Norton website (books.wwnorton. com/books/Author.aspx?id=8867, accessed January 20, 2017), Corydon Hammond is past president and a fellow of the American Society of Clinical Hypnosis (ASCH), which honored him with a Presidential Award of Merit in 1989. He also received the ASCH Irving I. Secter Award in 1990 and the Thomas P. Wall Award for Excellence in Teaching of Clinical Hypnosis in 1994. He is Professor emeritus at the University of Utah School of Medicine's Department of Physical Medicine and Rehabilitation. He has written six books, including the *Handbook of Hypnotic Suggestions and Metaphors* and *Memory Trauma Treatment and the Law* (1998). He coordinated a national task force on hypnosis and memory and is the primary author of *Clinical Hypnosis and Memory: Guidelines for Clinicians and for Forensic Hypnosis* and of ASCH's *Standards of Training in Clinical Hypnosis.*

3. "Surviving the Unbelievable: A First-Person Account of Cult Ritual Abuse," by Elizabeth S. Rose, *Ms. Magazine*, January/ February 1993. Elizabeth Rose is a pseudonym.

4. "Surviving the Unbelievable." In a "Helpful Books" sidebar, *Ms. Magazine* listed *The Courage to Heal* and its companion book, *The Courage to Heal Workbook*. A sidebar on helpful organizations includes "Believe the Children," a group begun by parents involved in the McMartin Preschool case who continued to believe their children's stories of ritual abuse despite a consistent lack of evidence. The group set up

a speakers' bureau and created a support network for those involved in working on cases where satanic activity was alleged. When I first began my research, the group's website was active, but I have not been able to find it since. One site I found says the group's last activity was a 1995 conference held in Arlington Heights, Illinois.

5. James Glass, *Shattered Selves: Multiple Personality in a Postmodern World*, 1993, pp. 101–102. Glass examines the phenomenon of multiple personality and ritual abuse through the lens of what he terms "postmodern philosophy." He does not bring a skeptical perspective to the subject matter. In *Creating Hysteria*, Acocella notes that, after an MPD "expert" joined Sheppard Pratt's hospital staff, "the number of MPD diagnoses . . . increased 900 percent" in the next two years. (p. 54)

chapter 18: backstory

1. "The Making of a Modern Witch Trial," *The Village Voice*, September 19, 1987. After Dove's conviction was set aside in 1987, she was retried, found guilty, and sentenced to twenty years. Charges against her were dismissed in 1990. Noble was acquitted in 1988. According to the National Registry of Exonerations, at Noble's second trial "an expert witness testified that the children had been brainwashed and that the method of interviewing and interrogating the children was suggestive, coercive, and produced bizarre and false claims of abuse." The New Jersey Superior Appellate Court overturned Michaels' conviction in 1993, also citing improper methods in interviewing supposed child victims.

2. The anecdote appears in the preface of Nathan and Snedeker's *Satan's Silence*.

3. *Satan's Silence*, p. 234. Dorothy Rabinowitz won a Pulitzer Prize for Commentary in 2001 for her coverage of cultural

trends. According to the *Wall Street Journal*, she was a Pulitzer finalist in 1996 "for her columns effectively challenging key cases of alleged child abuse."

4. See Wikipedia under "McMartin Preschool Trial," and other sources.

5. "Where Was Skepticism in Media? Pack journalism and hysteria marked early coverage of the McMartin case. Few journalists stopped to question the believability of the prosecution's charges." *Los Angeles Times*, January 19, 1990.

6. "Salem Revisited," *The Economist*, August 31, 1991, Vol. 320, Issue 7722.

7. Robert Hicks, *In Pursuit of Satan: The Police and the Occult*, 1991.

8. *Satan's Silence*, pp. 129–131.

9. Kenneth Lanning, "Investigator's Guide to Allegations of 'Ritual' Child Abuse," Behavioral Science Unit, National Center for the Analysis of Violent Crime, Federal Bureau of Investigation, FBI Academy, Quantico, Virginia 22135, 1992. (http://www.religioustolerance.org/ra_rep03.htm, accessed January 20, 2017.)

10. Jeffrey Victor, "Satanic cults' ritual abuse of children: horror or hoax?" *USA Today Magazine*, November 1993, Vol. 122, Issue 2582. The article was adapted from Victor's *Satanic Panic: The Creation of a Contemporary Legend*.

11. Lawrence Wright, *Remembering Satan: A Case of Recovered Memory and the Shattering of an American Family*, p. 200.

12. *Satan's Silence*, p. 5.

13. "The Search for Satan," *Frontline*. Produced by Ofra Bikel. Aired October 24, 1995. On Burgus: http://www.chicagomag.com/Chicago-Magazine/June-1998/Dangerous-Therapy-The-Story-of-Patricia-Burgus-and-Multiple-Personality-Disorder/. (Accessed July 2, 2017.)

14. *Satan's Silence*, p. 27; p. 103. Summit created a template, "The Child Sexual Abuse Accommodation Syndrome," to explain the process children go through in responding to sexual abuse. Richard Beck provides a helpful explanation of the impact of Summit's theory in his 2015 book, *We Believe the Children—A Moral Panic in the 1980s*.
15. Ross wrote the 1989 *MPD: Diagnosis, Clinical Features, and Treatment*, and the 1995 *Satanic Ritual Abuse: Principles of Treatment*.
16. *Making Monsters*, p. 5.
17. "Recovered memory war: It began here," *The Register-Guard*, July 12, 1998, A1, A12. Jennifer Freyd outlined her theory about repressed memories of abuse in her 1996 book, *Betrayal Trauma: The Logic of Forgetting Childhood Abuse*. Freyd is a national expert in the fields of memory and institutional betrayal.
18. See above, "Recovered memory war: It began here."
19. *Satan's Silence*, p. 237
20. https://en.wikipedia.org/wiki/Wenatchee_child_abuse_ prosecutions. (Accessed 4/10/17.)
21. https://en.wikipedia.org/wiki/West_Memphis_Three. (Accessed April 23, 2017.) Richard Ofshe testified during the trial that Misskelley's confession was a "classic example" of police coercion.
22. https://www.psychologytoday.com/conditions/dissociative-identity-disorder-multiple-personality-disorder. (Accessed July 2, 2017.)
23. The releases came about with the assistance of the University of Washington's Lawyers for the Innocence Project Northwest, which was formed to investigate the Wenatchee cases. See also: "Many Injustices Call for Many Lawyers," *The National Law Journal*, December 27, 2000. (Accessed April 10, 2017.) In ensuing years, the city of Wenatchee, the state of Washington, and two counties either agreed

or were ordered to pay $10 million to plaintiffs in lawsuits claiming negligence and civil rights violations. Also: http:// www.historylink.org/File/7065.

24. Joan Acocella recounts details of Carlson's case in *Creating Hysteria*. Also: http://www.fathermag.com/news/1800-carlson. shtml. (Accessed July 2, 2017.)

25. "Memory Therapy Leads to a Lawsuit and a Big Settlement," by Pam Bullock, *New York Times,* November 6, 1997. Braun later sued his insurance company for settling the suit.

26. "Controversial Psychiatrist Suspended," Lisa Donovan, *Chicago Tribune*, October 8, 1999.

27. Press Release, R.C. Barden & Associates, June 19, 1998. (http://www.stopbadtherapy.com/experts/fredrickson/ marys.shtml, accessed July 1, 2017.)

28. Roma Hart, who was a patient of Ross's in Manitoba from 1986 to 1990, wrote in her affidavit, "My initial problem of stress became a problem of nightmares, incest, satanic ritual abuse, murder, torture, and alien abduction. I had no memories of any of those activities in my life but Dr. Ross told me that my new memories were flashbacks of real events." (https:// sites.google.com/site/memoryabuse/final-draft-affidavit.) Hart's case did not make it through the court system. On Tyo's case: https://sites.google.com/site/memoryabuse/martha-ann-tyo-vs-ross. (Accessed 4/20/17.)

Ross addressed these cases and other issues in *The Great Psychiatry Scam: One Shrink's Personal Journey,* published in 2008.

29. "Psychiatric patient tells of ordeal in treatment," *Chicago Tribune*, February 13, 2004. (Accessed April 11, 2017.)

30. Four documentaries were produced on the case. The fourth, *West of Memphis,* was released in 2012. *Devil's Knot,* a movie directed by Atom Egoyan and based on a 2002 book about the case by Mara Leveritt, premiered in 2014.

31. The allegations against the Kellers included rape and orgies involving children, sacrificed babies, serving children Kool-Aid laced with blood, and flying children to Mexico to be sexually assaulted by military officials. (http://www.states-man.com/news/local/fran-keller-freed-satanic-abuse-case/ecfBaZYcoic13YB5c4LSiP/, accessed April 23, 2017.)

chapter 19: unplugged

1. From *The Tipping Point: How Little Things Can Make a Big Difference* by Malcolm Gladwell. Copyright © 2000, 2002 by Malcolm Gladwell. Used by permission of Little, Brown and Company. All rights reserved.

2. *The Tipping Point*, p. 174.

3. Since 2006 the group has called itself the International Society for the Study of Trauma and Dissociation. Each year the society bestows the Cornelia B. Wilbur Award on an individual for outstanding clinical contributions to the treatment of dissociative disorders. Wilbur was the real-life therapist for the client in the popular book and movie, *Sybil*, purportedly about a woman with multiple personality disorder. Wilbur's veracity—including her client's MPD diagnosis—and ethics have been challenged by journalists and other practitioners. (See Debbie Nathan, *Sybil Exposed* in Chapter 11, Notes 2 and 3.) Bennett Braun received the award in 1987. Colin Ross received the award in 2016.

    The group also presents Distinguished Achievement Awards. Past recipients include Wilbur (1987), as well as Roberta Sachs (1992), Bennett Braun (1996), and Corydon Hammond (1998)—the last three were ordered to pay thousands of dollars in settlement fees to plaintiffs in court cases accusing them of malpractice. (See Chapter 18.)

    The society's journal, *Dissociation*, published thirty-nine issues between 1988 and 1997. It is now called the *Journal of*

Trauma & Dissociation and is edited by University of Oregon professor Jennifer Freyd. (From International Society for the Study of Trauma and Dissociation website, http://www.isst-d.org/default.asp?contentID=42, accessed April 13, 2017.) According to Freyd, the *Journal of Trauma & Dissociation* is published by the international academic publisher Tayor & Francis. Although the publication is the official journal of ISSTD, Freyd says it is editorially independent of oversight by ISSTD.

epilogue

1. "Castlewood eating disorder lawsuit to be dismissed," *St. Louis Post-Dispatch*, Dec. 16, 2013.
2. Rachel Aviv, "Memories of a Murder," *The New Yorker*, June 19, 2017.
3. "The Keepers." A Netflix documentary directed by Ryan White, 2017.
4. https://theintercept.com/2017/06/20/texas-couple-exonerated-25-years-after-being-convicted-of-lurid-crimes-that-never-happened/. (Accessed July 3, 2017.)

acknowledgments

I would like to thank, first and foremost, John and Mary Tallmadge, without whose assistance this memoir could not have been written. In former years, they sheltered me. During the writing of this book they tolerated interviews with me that were difficult and painful. Mary provided me letters, copies of Michelle's journals, and her medical records. John trusted me. There is no greater gift.

Thanks to Wynlee Decker and Greg Tallmadge, who shared memories of their sister, and trusted me with their care. Robert Decker was an invaluable source of online family photos. Deep thanks to Rochelle Tallmadge, an early and steady supporter of this project.

Many thanks to Tammy Young, who was generous with her words and her heart.

Thanks and appreciation to my fantastic editorial team, Angie Jabine and Ross West. Angie's fine eye, feedback, and support gave me the courage to birth my book into the world. Ross West shared his insightful and penetrating comments, and was a kind, patient sounding board throughout the publishing process. Heartfelt thanks to the visionary Brooke Warner, She Writes Press, Sparks Press and all the team members whose dedication and commitment brought this book to fruition.

Profound thanks to Debra Gwartney, who introduced me to the genre of memoir and coached me through the first unwieldy chapters. Thanks also to writer and teacher Sallie Tisdale, who said the right words at the exact right time.

I am grateful to all those who read and commented on my early drafts, especially John Daniel, whose kindness and guidance gave me the strength to keep going. Thanks also to readers Guy Maynard, Jeff Wright, Lauren Kessler, and members of my former book group—Dan Armstrong, Martha Bayless, Joe Blakely, and Bill Sullivan. Thanks to Louis Carosio for helpful counsel.

Deep thanks to all the journalists and researchers whose work guided me to a deeper understanding of the 1980s panic, and of social panics in general. They are listed in the bibliography. Special thanks to Debbie Nathan and Michael Snedeker, whose investigative work for *Satan's Silence* should have won, in my mind, a Pulitzer.

Writing this book was often draining, and I will be forever grateful to all those who extended emotional support during its long gestation. Special thanks to Cindy McCain, who would not let me quit, and to Jude Sundstrom, who was a careful listener and beacon of support. Thanks also to Yona Riel for unstinting support, and to Jill Sager, Michele Bulgatz, Anne Krutell, Sally Schoolmaster, Caroline Tallmadge, and Ellen and Barkley VanVranken.

I want to thank my parents, Edgar and Ruth Tallmadge, for their generosity, fairness, humor, and profound commitment to our family. They are responsible for my six siblings and the large extended family that showers me with continual delight, and discovery.

I also want to acknowledge the Oregon Baxter family—Geri Baxter and John Ebeling, Cecelia Baxter and Paul Heintz, Phillip Baxter, Tom Baxter and Sheri Sims, Susie Baxter, Rita Baxter, and all the junior and mini-Baxters—who for years have allowed me to share in their circle of love, not realizing how much it sustained me.

about the author

Alice Tallmadge has been a reporter, writer, and editor since receiving her master's degree from the University of Oregon's School of Journalism in 1987. She was a correspondent for *The Oregonian* newspaper from 1999 to 2005, and a reporter and assistant editor for the *Eugene Weekly* in the 1990s. Her essays and stories have appeared in *Portland Magazine, Forest Magazine, Oregon Humanities,* the *Register-Guard, Oregon Quarterly,* and *The New York Times.* Her guidebook for juvenile sex offenders, *Tell It Like It Is,* was published by Safer Society Press in 1998. She was an adjunct instructor at the University of Oregon School of Journalism and Communication from 2008 to 2014. She is currently a freelance editor.

Author photo © Yona Riel

bibliography

books cited or referenced in *now i can see the moon—A Story of a Social Panic, False Memories and a Life Cut Short.*

Acocella, Joan. *Creating Hysteria: Women and Multiple Personality Disorder.* San Francisco: Jossey-Bass Publishers, 1999.

Bass, Ellen and Davis, Laura. *The Courage to Heal—A Guide for Women Survivors of Child Sexual Abuse.* Third edition. New York: HarperCollins, 1994. (Originally published by Harper & Row, 1988.)

Beck, Richard. *We Believe the Children—A Moral Panic in the 1980s.* New York: Public Affairs (Member of Perseus Books Group), 2015.

Cleckley, Hervey and Thigpen, Corbett. *The Three Faces of Eve.* London: Secker and Warberg, 1957. (Revised edition, 1992.)

Gladwell, Malcolm. *The Tipping Point—How Little Things Can Make a Big Difference.* New York: Little, Brown and Company, 2000.

Glass, James. *Shattered Selves: Multiple Personality in a Postmodern World.* Cornell University Press, 1993.

Hicks, Robert. *In Pursuit of Satan: The Police and the Occult.* Amherst, NY: Prometheus Books, 1991.

Maran, Meredith. *My Lie: A True Story of False Memory.* San Francisco: Jossey-Bass, 2010.

Marron, Kevin. *Ritual Abuse: Canada's Most Infamous Trial on Child Abuse.* Toronto: Seal Books/McClelland-Bantam, 1988.

Nathan, Debbie and Snedeker, Michael. *Satan's Silence: Ritual Abuse and the Making of a Modern American Witch Hunt.* New York: Authors Choice Press, 1995.

Nathan, Debbie. *Sybil Exposed: The Extraordinary Story Behind the Famous Multiple Personality Case.* New York: Free Press—a division of Simon & Schuster, Inc., 2011.

Ofshe, Richard and Watters, Ethan. *Making Monsters—False Memories, Psychotherapy and Sexual Hysteria.* New York: Charles Scribner's Sons, 1994.

Pendergrast, Mark. *Victims of Memory: Sex Abuse Accusations and Shattered Lives.* Vermont: Upper Access Books, 1995.

Richardson, James; Best, Joel; and Bromley, David, eds. *The Satanic Scare.* New York: Aldine de Gruyter, 1991.

Schreiber, Flora Rheta. *Sybil—The True Story of a Woman Possessed by 16 Separate Personalities.* Washington, DC: Henry Regnery Co., 1973. (Paperback reissue, 2009.)

Smith, Michelle and Pazder, Lawrence. *Michelle Remembers.* New York: Congdon & Lattes, 1980 and New York: Pocket Books, 1981. (Now considered fraudulent.)

Steinem, Gloria. *Revolution From Within.* New York: Little, Brown and Company, 1992.

Stratford, Lauren. *Satan's Underground: The Extraordinary Story of One Woman's Escape.* Eugene, Oregon: Harvest House Publishers, 1988. (Sold to Pelican Publishing in 1990. Now considered fraudulent.)

Victor, Jeffrey. *Satanic Panic: The Creation of a Contemporary Legend.* Chicago: Open Court Publishing, 1993.

Van Til, Reinder. *Lost Daughters: Recovered Memory Therapy & The People It Hurts.* Grand Rapids: Wm. B. Eerdmans Publishing Company, 1997.

Wright, Lawrence. *Remembering Satan—A case of recovered memory and the shattering of an American family.* New York: Alfred A Knopf, 1994.

newspaper and magazine articles:

"Police keep eye on occult," *The Register-Guard*, Eugene, Oregon, August 20, 1989.

"Salem Revisited," *The Economist*, August 31, 1991, Vol. 320, Issue 7722.

"Satanic Abuse, Horrific Tales Haunt Victims," McClatchy News Service, August 4, 1991.

"Satanism in Oregon," *The Oregonian*, Portland, Oregon, August 13, 1989.

Nathan, Debbie. "The Making of a Modern Witch Trial," *The Village Voice*, September 19, 1987.

Rose, Elizabeth. "Surviving the Unbelievable: A First-Person Account of Cult Ritual Abuse," *Ms Magazine*, January/February 1993.

Shaw, David. "Where Was Skepticism in Media? Pack journalism and hysteria marked early coverage of the McMartin case. Few journalists stopped to question the believability of the prosecution's charges," *Los Angeles Times*, January 19, 1990.

Victor, Jeffrey. "Satanic cults' ritual abuse of children: horror or hoax?" *USA Today Magazine*, November 1993, Vol. 122, Issue 2582. (Article adapted from *Satanic Panic*.)

resources of note:

Loftus, Elizabeth and Ketcham, Katherine. *The Myth of Repressed Memory: False Memories and Allegations of Sexual Abuse*. New York: St. Martin's Griffin, 1994.

Rabinowitz, Dorothy. *No Crueler Tyrannies: Accusation, False Witness, and Other Terrors of Our Times*. New York: Free Press, 2003.

selected titles from she writes press

She Writes Press is an independent publishing company founded to serve women writers everywhere. Visit us at www.shewritespress.com.

Searching for Normal: The Story of a Girl Gone Too Soon by Karen Meadows. $16.95, 978-1-63152-137-9. Karen Meadows intertwines her own story with excerpts from her daughter Sadie's journals to describes their roller coaster ride through Sadie's depression and a maze of inadequate mental health treatment and services—one that ended with Sadie's suicide at age eighteen.

A Different Kind of Same: A Memoir by Kelley Clink. $16.95, 978-1-63152-999-3. Several years before Kelley Clink's brother hanged himself, she attempted suicide by overdose. In the aftermath of his death, she traces the evolution of both their illnesses, and wonders: If he couldn't make it, what hope is there for her?

All the Ghosts Dance Free: A Memoir by Terry Cameron Baldwin. $16.95, 978-1-63152-822-4. A poetic memoir that explores the legacy of alcoholism and teen suicide in one woman's life—and her efforts to create an authentic existence in the face of that legacy.

Catching Homelessness: A Nurse's Story of Falling Through the Safety Net by Josephine Ensign. $16.95, 978-1-63152-117-1. The compelling true story of a nurse's work with—and young adult passage through—homelessness.

Blinded by Hope: One Mother's Journey Through Her Son's Bipolar Illness and Addiction by Meg McGuire. $16.95, 978-1-63152-125-6. A fiercely candid memoir about one mother's roller cmoaster ride through doubt and denial as she attempts to save her son from substance abuse and bipolar illness.

Four Funerals and a Wedding: Resilience in a Time of Grief by Jill Smolowe. $16.95, 978-1-938314-72-8. When journalist Jill Smolowe lost four family members in less than two years, she turned to modern bereavement research for answers—and made some surprising discoveries.